Doggy people

Manchester University Press

For Leo, Isla, Lydia and Maisie

Doggy people

The Victorians who made the modern dog

Michael Worboys

Manchester University Press

Published by Manchester University Press
Oxford Road, Manchester M13 9PL
www.manchesteruniversitypress.co.uk

British Library Cataloguing-in-Publication Data
A catalogue record for this book is available from the British Library

ISBN 978 1 5261 6772 9 hardback

First published 2023

Typeset
by Cheshire Typesetting Ltd, Cuddington, Cheshire
Printed in Great Britain
by Bell & Bain Ltd, Glasgow

Contents

Acknowledgements   vii

Introduction   1

High society, low society
1   Queen Victoria – Family pets   17
2   Bill George – King of the Canine Castle   28
3   Jemmy Shaw – The Fancy   38
4   Duchess of Newcastle – Borzois and Fox Terriers   48

Celebrities and millionaires
5   Jack Russell – Hunting   63
6   Edwin Landseer – Canine character   74
7   Harry Panmure Gordon and J. P. Morgan – Collies   85
8   Alice Stennard Robinson – Ladies Kennel Association   96

Sportsmen and showmen
9   John Henry Walsh ('Stonehenge') – Breed and breeds   111
10   Richard Lloyd Price – Sheepdog trials   123
11   John Henry Salter – Coursing and field trials   134
12   Charles Cruft – Dog shows   145

Contents

Doctors and scientists

13 Delabere Blaine and William Youatt – Dog doctors   157
14 Charles Darwin – Evolution and emotions   170
15 Gordon Stables – Canine care and dog tales   185
16 Everett Millais – Basset Hounds and breeding   195

Campaigners and politicians

17 Mary Tealby – Dogs' homes   207
18 Frances Power Cobbe – Sentient creatures   216
19 John Cumming Macdona – St Bernards   229
20 Sewallis Shirley – The Kennel Club   240

Afterword – Pedigree chums   251

List of plates   258
List of figures   259
Notes   267
Index   294

Acknowledgements

This book has its origins in an Arts and Humanities Research Council grant supporting the project 'The Dog Fancy and Fancy Dogs', run with my colleagues Neil Pemberton and Julie-Marie Strange. The project led to the book *The Invention of the Modern Dog: Breed and Blood in Victorian Britain* in 2018. *Doggy People* is a follow-up volume, focusing on eminent and not so eminent Victorians who were the modern dog's makers. My thinking and writing on dogs continue to be influenced by Neil and Julie-Marie, so thanks again.

I am grateful to the many librarians and archivists who have helped with the research, especially Ciara Farrell and Colin Sealy at the Kennel Club, and the staff at John Rylands University Library in Manchester.

My book has over seventy illustrations and I am grateful to the following for image files and permissions: the British Library, the Kennel Club, the Royal Collection Trust, the Museum of London, Dominic Winter (Auctioneers) Limited, Blundell's School, ProQuest, the Victoria and Albert Museum, the Mary Evans Picture Library, the National Library of Ireland, the Natural History Museum of Bern, Sir Hugh Stucley, Dr Roger Bowdler and Dr Andrew King.

At Manchester University Press, I have had wonderful encouragement and support from Emma Brennan, and must

Acknowledgements

give her a special thanks for the title. Paul Clarke's expertise proved invaluable with the images and my copy-editor, Ralph Footring, greatly improved the accuracy and fluency of my writing.

As ever, 'lots and loads' of thanks to Carole for everything.

Introduction

Victorian Britain produced many inventions that created the modern world: textile factories, steam railways, iron and steel bridges, postage stamps, pedal bicycles, electric lights, photography, underground trains, and many more. To this list must be added the modern dog. Domesticated dogs have lived with humans for over 20,000 years, with different types used in work and sport, and for companionship. Function dictated form for almost all of this period until, beginning in Victorian Britain, new human–canine relationships turned this on its head: form trumped function. Then, in just six decades, dogs were reimagined and remodelled into the animal we know today. Two changes drove the transformation: first, the spread of humane attitudes and greater emotional and economic investment in dogs; and second, the creation of new roles for dogs, in homes, sports and, more importantly, shows. Dog shows led dogs' bodies to be remodelled into discrete, distinct, standardised breeds.

In twenty chapters, I explore why and how Dogdom was recreated, by whom, and with what consequences for dogs and people. My cast runs from the very pinnacle of society, Queen Victoria, to near the bottom, with Jemmy Shaw, a publican, boxer, promoter of both dogfights and rat-killing. Shaw's activities often brought him before the courts, and he was enough of a roguish celebrity to feature in Henry Mayhew's study of the London poor.

Doggy people

The remainder of the cast includes an artist, aristocrats, authors, bankers, clergymen, doctors, a dog dealer, a feminist, journalists, landowners, millionaires, philanthropists, scientists, veterinarians and a showman – Charles Cruft. Victorians had a term for these canine enthusiasts and activists – Doggy People.[1]

Victorian Doggy People

Who were the principal makers of the modern dog? There were five groupings: high and low society; celebrities and millionaires; sportsmen and showmen; doctors and scientists; and campaigners and politicians. They hailed from across Britain (and the United States) and all social classes.

The most important in high society were Queen Victoria, who made pet-keeping and emotional investment in dogs respectable; and the Duchess of Newcastle, who championed the breeding and ownership of two 'Ladies' breeds' – Borzois and Fox Terriers. The leading representatives of low society were Bill George, a Bulldog fancier and owner of London's top dog sales establishment, the Canine Castle; and Jemmy Shaw, an entrepreneur of the Fancy – the largely working-class fraternity of men involved with boxing, dog fighting and other 'rough' sports.

The celebrities were Jack Russell, now associated with a breed of Fox Terrier, but in Victorian times known as the Hunting Parson; and Edwin Landseer, the most famous artist of the age, renowned for his animal paintings, especially portraits of the dogs of royalty and the rich. The millionaires were Harry Panmure Gordon in Scotland and J. P. Morgan in the United States, both of whom used their wealth to breed and show Collies. Another was Alice Stennard Robinson (née Cornwell), a gold rush millionaire from Australia. Fancy dogs were her way into the British elite, of which she became a leading member, and it was Stennard Robinson who founded the Ladies Kennel Association.

Introduction

The most influential sportsman was the 'Great Walsh', John Henry Walsh, editor of the country's leading sporting newspaper, *The Field*, who, under the pseudonym Stonehenge, wrote the books that first set the physical standards that defined breed standards – templates of size, shape, colour, coat and so on that dogs of a specific breed had to conform to (they were and still are therefore known as conformation standards). The development of field sports was led by Richard Lloyd Price, a Welsh landowner who organised the first Sheepdog trials; and John Henry Salter, an Essex general practitioner, who tried in vain to win the National Coursing Cup and who drafted the rules for field trials with gundogs. The showmen were Walsh again, who helped with the reform of shows and field trials, and the 'British Barnum', Charles Cruft. Cruft moved from head of sales at Spratt's Dog Biscuits to being Britain's leading promoter of dog shows, transforming them into canine spectaculars.

The doctors and scientists were a very varied group of people. Delabere Blaine and William Youatt were veterinary surgeons, then called dog doctors (a pejorative label at the time). Blaine began his career in the military and Youatt in the Church. Charles Darwin cited different types of dog as examples of the power of 'artificial selection' by humans, an important analogue of 'natural selection'. He saw dogs and humans as having similar emotional states, indicating their common descent from earlier mammals. Gordon Stables began as a ship's surgeon but he switched to being a prolific author of boys' and girls' adventure books. He also wrote popular books and advice columns on canine health and disease. Everett Millais was a gentleman scientist, son of the leading Pre-Raphaelite painter John Everett Millais. He researched dog distemper, established the principles of breeding and introduced the Basset Hound into Britain.

The two leading campaigners on dog welfare were women: Mary Tealby founded Battersea Dogs' Home; and Frances Power Cobbe, though she failed to have experiments on live animals

wholly prohibited, succeeded in getting Parliament to enact a set
of regulations governing animal experiments. The two politicians
were quite minor figures in the House of Commons but both
excelled in other roles. John Cumming Macdona came late to
politics, having been a vicar and barrister, but became best known
for championing the St Bernard breed in Britain. Finally, Sewallis
Shirley owned estates in Warwickshire and Ireland and served as
Member of Parliament for South Monaghan. He took the leading
role in founding the Kennel Club, was its president for a quarter
of a century and was second only to Walsh in shaping shows and
modern dog breeds.

My cast of Doggy People is selective. Charles Lane's book *Dog
Shows and Doggy People*, published in 1902, had biographies of 114
canine experts and aficionados, all of whom had started their
careers in the Victorian period. Amongst those most unlucky
to be omitted from my book are, first, several members of the
Brailsford family. They were a line of gamekeepers and estate
managers who ran some of the country's largest estates, including during Victorian times that of the Prime Minister, the Earl
of Derby, at Knowsley. In 1859 Richard Brailsford organised the
very first modern dog shows, held in Newcastle upon Tyne and
Birmingham.[2] Second, the Reverend Thomas Pearce, who wrote
influential books and articles under the pseudonym Idstone, and
his son Frank, who edited the first Kennel Club studbook, were
valued and reliable experts.[3] Third, George Beech was a leading
member of the Birmingham Dog Show Society, whose shows were
known for their high standards and which rivalled the Kennel
Club for leadership of the elite 'dog fancy' until it reached a rapprochement in 1885.[4] Finally, Theo Marples was a respected judge
on the northern dog show circuit who founded the Manchester-
based magazine *Our Dogs*, which was the most popular canine
magazine at the end of the Victorian era.[5]

Introduction

Why and how was the modern dog made?

I. Reimagining

The first major development that led towards the making of the modern dog was the spread of more humane attitudes.[6] This change followed from greater regard being given to dogs as sentient creatures. These attitudes were reflected in celebrations of dogs' loyalty and affection, as well as empathy with their sufferings. Some Victorians went further than feelings and emotions, and suggested that dogs were intelligent, had a moral sense and perhaps were capable of some kind of spirituality. While dogs had long been man's and woman's best friend, in the Victorian period this relationship was to be reciprocated, with women and men becoming dogs' best friends.[7]

This shift was evident with Queen Victoria. The close bond she had when young with her lapdog Dash was made public only later. After her marriage to Prince Albert in 1840, portraits of the Royal Family and then photographs regularly included dogs, large and small, and they were portrayed as family members as well as pets. Her diaries show that dogs were constant companions throughout her life. Edwin Landseer painted many portraits of the Queen's dogs and in each sought to capture, not just a likeness, but character and 'personality'. Many of his paintings showed dogs' loyalty, including their unstinting devotion even after the death of their owner. Such tales were Victorian favourites, the best-known of which was that of Greyfriars Bobby, a Skye Terrier that allegedly stood for fourteen years guarding the grave of his master. Some of Landseer's paintings anticipated the Bobby cult (Figure 0.1).

New attitudes, previously private, were brought by campaigners into the public sphere in efforts to halt animal cruelty. Most notable was the creation in 1824 of the Society for the Prevention of Cruelty to Animals. In 1840, it became Royal (RSPCA), after

Figure 0.1 *The Old Shepherd's Chief Mourner*, by Edwin Landseer, 1837

receiving the endorsement of the Queen. The Society was relatively slow to take up dog welfare but it became an important supporter of Mary Tealby, who in 1860 founded the Temporary Home for Lost and Starving Dogs in Holloway, which later moved to Battersea. Tealby had been appalled at the ill-treatment of dogs (and cats) on the streets of London and, in the spirit of Victorian philanthropy, created a charitable institution to remedy the wrongs. It is revealing of Victorian society that a dogs' home was founded before the first Barnardo's home for children (1870) and the National Society for the Prevention of Cruelty to Children (1884).

While reformers stressed the human-like qualities of dogs' minds, the beast within remained. Many of the strays that Tealby pitied were aggressive and especially threatening during outbreaks of rabies, when raging mad dogs filled the popular imagination.[8] The human form of rabies, hydrophobia, was incurable and ended in the worst of all deaths, with mind and body out of control. When rabies was prevalent, regulations were introduced, including curfews, requiring the use of leads, rounding up strays and muzzling, backed by fines. There was vociferous resistance to muzzling, with campaigners arguing that restraints led to thirst and irritation, which could drive dogs mad. Many controls persisted after the eradication of rabies, which led to a steady fall in the numbers of stray and street dogs through the twentieth century, such that today there is a near-total absence of lone, roaming dogs in the street.[9] Every dog now has a home and carer.

Attempts to stop scientific experiments on live animals was another indicator of new attitudes. Frances Power Cobbe, who founded the British anti-vivisection movement, contrasted the cold, calculating cruelty of the physiologist with the kindness, respect and empathy of the dog lover. She believed dogs were very special animals, perhaps the only ones with a spiritual sense. Even scientists were intrigued that communication between dogs and humans was more readily established and more reliable than communication with apes, humans' nearest evolutionary relatives.

II. Remodelling

The second major development in making the modern dog was through new sports and entertainments, and with a move of the traditional canine sports from the private to the public sphere. Catching hares with Greyhounds had once been the preserve of those who owned large estates but in the late eighteenth century hare coursing became the first officially organised dog sport. The Coursing Club was founded in 1776 and the National Coursing Club in 1858.[10] The organisation of national events was aided by the enlargement of the railway network, as Greyhounds could be readily transported across the country to compete in the top events like the Waterloo Cup, held near Liverpool. Large attendances at the latter encouraged its organisers to promote subsidiary events, including a steeplechase that became the Grand National. To make competitions fair and achieve comparability of results, the layout of coursing grounds was standardised in terms of area, slope and vegetation. Previously, Greyhounds had been used in private hunting; those that worked in heather and rough terrain had long, protective coats and were larger than the smooth-coated, lighter hounds that ran on open grasslands or had to negotiate the fences and hedges of enclosed land. Standardised courses encouraged standardised competitors, and so the physique of Greyhounds soon converged on the same athletic form. Gundogs such as Setters and Pointers followed the same path to greater uniformity in physical form with the development of field trials under standard conditions and national rules.

Breeders had long tried to improve the abilities of working dogs through crossing, for example with Bulldogs to get more courage, or Greyhounds to produce a dog that combined speed with the ability to home in on prey. By the 1850s, sportsmen feared that this practice had gone too far, with 'true' types disappearing. The first modern dog show was held in 1859; its promoters aimed to find 'true' Pointers and Setters and to preserve these 'true' types, in part for future crossbreeding. The event was controversial because judges used physical form as an indicator of function; critics complained that anatomy was no guide to ability. Nonetheless, these events proved popular with sports people and the public. Initially they were held at agricultural shows but they later became specific dog-only events in their own right. The latter became the principal motor of change in the development of modern breeds.[11]

Promoters of shows soon included other sporting and non-sporting dogs. Events were organised on the model of livestock shows, where judging on form had been a solid guide to function, say, in cattle where muscularity and size indicated a good return in meat. But with dogs, the issues raised in 1859 persisted, with more and more evidence that form was in fact a questionable guide to function. But this concern was soon pushed aside by the success of the new shows, which led to an approved, aesthetically attractive physical form becoming an end in itself.

Dog shows boomed across the country in the 1860s, increasing in number and size. The Monster Dog Show in London in 1862 attracted over 1,000 entries and 60,000 paying visitors.[12] While shows were a popular sensation, views on them were mixed. There were accusations of sharp practices and dishonesty, ranging from bribing judges to cosmetic alterations to dogs' coats, ears, tails, and other features. Furthermore, despite the successes, some events lost money. Some sportsmen hoped that shows would disappear and with them what they saw as their baneful effect in favouring form over function. Yet, a group of enthusiasts sought to rescue shows from disrepute and make them a vehicle for improving the nation's dogs. In 1873 they formed the Kennel Club, with the aim of introducing reforms that would bring honour and integrity to the shows, and to counter bias and ignorance by ensuring judges were trustworthy, knowledgeable and of 'the right sort'. Licences to run shows would be granted only to those promoters who ensured good conduct, high standards and financial probity and who followed Club rules. The Jockey Club was the model for the Kennel Club, and the need for national rules and standards was seen in other new sports, with the adoption of a single code for association football in 1863 and for lawn tennis in 1874.

Even well-run shows had problems with the consistency of results. That is, the same dog might win in Edinburgh one week, be unplaced in Derby the next and be declared ineligible in Brighton a month later. John Henry Walsh had the answer. Through his editorship of *The Field*, he led moves to establish the ideal form to which dogs should conform – breed standards that defined as a series of 'points' the external features of a dog's body (Figure 0.2).

In 1867, under his pen name Stonehenge, Walsh published *The Dogs of the British Islands*, the first reference handbook of standards, illustrated with examples of the best in breed at recent shows.[13] Breeders and exhibitors contested many of its standards, but the

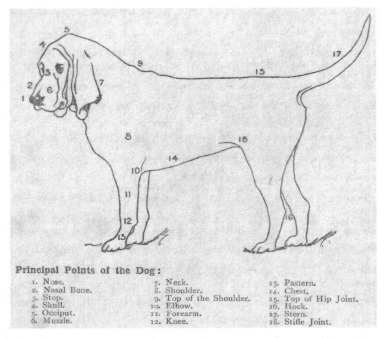

Principal Points of the Dog:

1. Nose.	7. Neck.	13. Pastern.
2. Nasal Bone.	8. Shoulder.	14. Chest.
3. Stop.	9. Top of the Shoulder.	15. Top of Hip Joint.
4. Skull.	10. Elbow.	16. Hock.
5. Occiput.	11. Forearm.	17. Stern.
6. Muzzle.	12. Knee.	18. Stifle Joint.

Figure 0.2 Principal points of the dog, 1922

principle was accepted and such standards, considerably modified over time, have continued to define dog breeds to this day. Walsh's initiative resulted in *breed* becoming the dominant term for different dogs. Previous terms, such as kinds, races, sorts, strains, types and varieties, fell away. There were profound physical consequences for dogs with the adoption of physical standards for breeds. First, within breed populations dogs took on a uniform look as breeders aimed for conformity to the ideal. Second, this uniformity was achieved by mating mainly the small number of champions, but this inbreeding led to health issues in the offspring. Third, the growth of shows led to a proliferation in the number of breeds. Dogdom was divided into an ever-greater number of constituencies. For example, disputes about the correct type of coat were often settled by 'splitting' a breed, to create new smooth and wire forms as with Fox Terriers, or colours as with Black Pugs. Fourth, Britain's leading position in global trade enabled the ready import of foreign breeds, which were modified and standardised to domestic fanciers' tastes.

More breeds meant more opportunities exhibitors to win and for breeders to earn. As both pets and as competitors in sports and shows, dogs increased in value, creating an economy in breeding, selling, buying, showing and servicing. They became akin to industrial products: designed, specified, standardised, uniform commodities, with product differentiation in elaborating fancy forms. Breeders strove to make each breed more distinct, by embellishing and beautifying, but canine health was threatened by overly exaggerated features such as larger eyes or longer coats.[14]

The extreme case of proliferation of breeds was among Terriers, the most popular type of dog in the late Victorian period. In *The Dog* in 1845, William Youatt described just two – what he called 'the' Terrier and the Scotch Terrier.[15] The catalogue for Charles Cruft's first terrier show, in 1886, featured fourteen breeds: Airedale, Bedlington, Black and Tan, Bull, Dandie Dinmont, Fox-Smooth, Fox-Wire, Hard-Wire Scotch, Irish, Skye, Smooth-Haired, Welsh, Toy, and Yorkshire. By 1901, there were seventeen.

Poodles were an example of a single breed becoming ever fancier. Youatt had described them as valuable for work and companionship:

> It was originally a water dog, as its long and curly hair, and its propensities in its domesticated state, prove; but, from its peculiar sagacity, it is capable of being trained to almost any useful purpose, and its strong individual attachment renders it more the companion of man than a mere sporting dog: indeed, its qualities as a sporting dog are seldom recognised by its owners.[16]

The illustration that accompanied this text showed a Poodle at work (Figure 0.3). The only comment about its body was that the long curly hair on its head hid its intelligence.

THE POODLE.

Figure 0.3 The Poodle, 1845

By the end of the Victorian period, the scruffy working animal had become a stylish beauty. At shows, exhibitors were allowed to coiffure their dogs by shaving and clipping coats or setting long corded braids (Figure 0.4). Leading canine authorities attacked these practices. Hugh Dalziel wrote that the breed had been made 'the buffoon of the canine race, merely to pander to a frivolous taste'.[17]

* * * * *

The biographies in this book detail the contributions of each Doggy Person to the making of the modern dog, set in the context of their life and work. Many were public figures of wide renown; others were active only within Dogdom. Some were earnest; many were eccentric. Both individually and collectively, these Doggy People

Figure 0.4 Corded Poodles, 1889

give new insights into Victorian Britain, not through dogs' eyes, though dogs would be more sensitive to what could be revealed by their nose and ears! Instead, my novelty comes from attention to changing human–dog relations amongst Victorians who were increasingly devoted to individual pet dogs and the 'improvement' of what they termed the 'canine race'.

High society – low society

1. Queen Victoria (1819–1901) Family pets
2. Bill George (1805–1884) King of the Canine Castle
3. Jemmy Shaw (1813–1886) The Fancy
4. Duchess of Newcastle (1872–1953) Borzois and Fox Terriers

Victorians at the top and bottom of society had similar attitudes towards dogs, and both used them in sport. They showed them affection, kept them as pampered pets and remembered them after death, albeit in different ways. Queen Victoria erected gravestones for dogs in the grounds of royal estates and Jemmy Shaw had a plaster model of his champion Jacko behind the bar in his pub. Members of both the gentry and the working-class canine Fancy favoured small breeds, and Bill George sold these at his Canine Castle to all classes, even, in one instance, an overseas monarch building up his royal kennel. Sport with dogs was common in the countryside and the inner city but in very different pursuits. Queen Victoria accompanied Prince Albert stalking stags at Balmoral, while the Duchess of Newcastle went fox hunting across the Dukeries in the East Midlands. Bill George had bred fighting Bulldogs but diversified into all types. Jemmy Shaw's establishments put on all kinds of entertainments but were best known for rat-killing contests that saw the upper class and underclass mix at his establishments, attracted by the spectacle and chance to gamble.

Chapter 1

Queen Victoria

➣———————— X ————————➢

Family pets

Queen Victoria's love of dogs was well known in her lifetime. It was evident in paintings and photographs, and it made pet ownership respectable and admirable. There were many reports of her love of dogs, the last and most poignant being newspaper accounts of her asking for her Pomeranian Turi to be brought to her death bed.[1] Her favourites were more than family pets: they were family members. The mutual bond of affection and devotion was an exemplar of family values. The company of pets, especially her Collie Sharp, was solace for Victoria in her long years of mourning Prince Albert (Figure 1.1). The Queen supported measures against animal cruelty, publicly as patron of the RSPCA, then privately, lobbying to control vivisection. Her diaries record that she owned 640 dogs, belonging to 32 breeds.

Princess Victoria was born in May 1819.[2] Her parents were Prince Edward, Duke of Kent and Strathearn, and Princess Victoria of Saxe-Coburg-Saalfeld. Her father died when she was a year old, leaving her to be raised by her mother, advised by a government minister, Sir John Conroy. Victoria was not expected to become the monarch. Her father had been fourth in line, but his three elder brothers died without children, so on his death she became queen, at seventeen years of age.

On Victoria's birthday the previous year, her mother had given her a portrait of her Spaniel, Dash.[3] It was painted

Figure 1.1 Queen Victoria with Sharp, 1866

by Edwin Landseer, the country's most famous artist and best known for his animal work (see Chapter 6). Victoria was brought up under the so-called Kensington system, which kept her away from other children, making Dash her best friend. One popular story about the new Queen was that on the evening of her coronation, after all the pomp, she returned to her rooms to bath 'dear Dashy'. Her favourite Prime Minister, Lord Melbourne, noted that when visiting, he thought the Queen was in danger of being smothered by dogs. Landseer painted another portrait of Dash in 1838, in a family group in a domestic setting, with the Greyhound Nero, the Deerhound Hector and the parrot Lori. The Queen wrote that the painting was 'too beautiful'.[4]

Dash died on Christmas Eve in 1840 and was buried in Windsor Great Park. The grave is marked by a marble statue with the following inscription:

> Here lies DASH, the favourite Spaniel of Her Majesty Queen Victoria, in his 10th year. His attachment was without selfishness, his playfulness without malice, his fidelity without deceit. READER, if you would be beloved and die regretted, profit by the example of DASH.

Dash's memorial was the first of many made for Victoria's dogs.

The Queen's marriage to Prince Albert of Saxe-Coburg and Gotha was widely seen as a 'love match', and the couple shared a passion for dogs. After their marriage, Albert's Greyhound Eos joined Victoria's extended family of dogs. Victoria gave Albert a small, silver statuette of Eos and a portrait of him by Landseer.[5] Eos also appeared in the family portrait *Windsor Castle in Modern Times*, again by Landseer, which included three other named dogs: Dandy Dinmont, Islay and Cairnach (Plate 1). The painting took over two years to complete. The group was carefully posed and the Queen's mother in her bathchair can be seen through the window. The painting was a family favourite. It was hung in the Green Drawing Room at Windsor Castle, but also enjoyed public circulation in exhibitions and prints.[6]

Doggy people

One feature of the painting is surprising to modern eyes: the drawing room is strewn with dead wildfowl, presumably shot by Albert. Hunting, shooting and other rural sports were daily pursuits for the British landed classes, and, in multi-species families, the boundary between home and field was blurred. There is disagreement over who is the dominant figure: Victoria, standing tall, wearing luminous white, or Albert, magisterially seated, in a black jacket, being approached by Victoria with a gift of flowers? The dogs spread their attention. One watches the young Princess, another welcomes the Queen, and two dogs look to Albert. All were like dependent children looking up at their parents. Eos was both a hunting dog and a pet, growing into the latter role with age. Another Landseer painting of Eos had him nuzzling the feet of the eight-month-old Princess Victoria, suggesting that large hunting dogs were tender carers in family settings.[7]

One celebration of the couple's love of dogs was a large, silver-gilt table centrepiece designed by Albert.[8] It was exhibited at the Great Exhibition in 1851. At an event where Britain showed its advanced manufactures to the world, the Royal Family was represented by an elaborate piece of domestic silverplate featuring family dogs. Eos had pride of place, accompanied by Islay, Cairnach and the Dachshund Waldmann. The couple embraced other new technologies, especially photography. From 1854 William Bambridge began taking pictures of the royal dogs.[9] He had a large remit, covering domestic companions, kennel residents and estate hounds. A canine album was produced in 1865, with fifty-one photographs, each accompanied by details of the dog's name, birth and, where appropriate, date of death. Pedigrees were also recorded, which showed that many had noble lineages.

The largest group of royal dogs were the Queen's Staghounds, which were kept at Ascot. There were no kills after her husband's death, perhaps due to her objections to animal cruelty. Instead, the hounds were exercised in organised chases, where a stag was released, chased and recaptured, not shot.[10] The chases often caused pandemonium when horses and dogs strayed on to the lines of the Great Western Railway. In the 1890s, there was unsuccessful pressure from the Humanitarian League to disband the pack because the stags were getting injured when they ran up against new wire fencing.

The Queen's diaries record that she visited the kennels almost every day when in residence at Windsor. It was a noisy but well-ordered establishment with its own hospital. A sitting room, with walls covered by dog paintings, was added for the Queen. She was regularly given dogs as presents, many from overseas. She led the introduction into Britain of several breeds, the best-known being the Pekinese. Her first was Looty, the name deriving from the fact that she was allegedly stolen from the Summer Palace in Beijing (Figure 1.2). She was said to be 'the smallest pet dog in the kingdom' and was featured in the national press.[11] The *Ladies Weekly Journal* sold prints. Looty was not popular in the royal household, being temperamental, snappy with strangers and fussy over food. Albert had introduced German breeds and visitors brought Eskimo dogs, Newfoundlands, Cubans, Cashmeres, Basenjis and Poodles. The Windsor kennels replicated Britain's place in the world, becoming a showcase of dogs of the Empire and beyond.

After Dash, the Queen's favoured companions were initially Pugs and Chows, but then Collies after Prince Albert's death. She spent more time at Balmoral and Osborne House and adopted companions more suited to country life. The two best-known Collies were Sharp and Noble.[12] In fact, Victoria over the course of her life had seven Sharps and five Nobles, not all were related. They were unlike modern Border Collies in look, being from working stock, valued for their character, not their coat, colours and contours. Her first Sharp, born in 1864, was bad-tempered and prone to start 'collie-shangies', a Scottish term for fights. Nonetheless, the Queen referred to him as 'good Sharp' and called him 'affectionate'.[13] Sharp I died in 1869 and was buried under

Figure 1.2 Her Majesty's pet dog 'Looty', 1863

a marble plinth that bore his likeness.[14] The inscription reads: 'Sharp, the favourite and faithful Collie of Queen Victoria from 1866 to 1879. Died now 1879 aged 15 years.'

The first Noble joined the royal household in 1872. The Queen called him 'good, dear Noble … the most biddable dog I ever saw, so affectionate and kind; if he thinks you are not pleased with him, he puts out his paws and begs in such an affectionate way'. In 1887, Eve Blantyre Simpson (daughter of the surgeon

James Young Simpson, who had given the Queen chloroform during the birth of her eighth child) wrote the following of Noble in his old age:

> Alas! His tan muzzle is now white with years, the strength has gone from his fleet limbs, the light has faded from those once keen eyes … . [The Royal Family] know, blind and deaf though the old fellow is, what a world of affection is still stowed within his true heart for them. He sets them thinking, as they stroke his time worn face, of many [that] are pleasant, many a sad hour he has past [*sic*] with them and with those who have gone 'to where beyond these voices there is peace'.[15]

Noble died at Balmoral in 1887, after unsuccessful treatment by the monarch's personal physician, Sir James Reid. The Queen was so upset that she was given a sedative and 'could not bear' to see the dog's body.[16] Noble, too, had his likeness sculpted for a memorial plinth. The inscription reads: 'Noble by name, noble by nature too. Faithful companion, sympathetic, true.' Noble's sons Sailor and Noble Junior were also favourites and were joined by another Collie, Flo, who was said to have female tact and be able to interpret the Queen's moods. Collies were an almost constant presence in royal photographs. Blantyre Simpson's verdict was that 'They are the Queen's personal friends, admitted to her rooms and society, and to be with her they love is all the boon these winning courtiers crave'.[17]

Amongst her small dogs, Pomeranians (then also called Spitz dogs) took over from Pugs as the favoured breed in the 1890s. These small creatures had long been kept as lapdogs on the Continent. The tolerance afforded to the Queen's pets was evident in Charles Burton Barber's portrait of her dog Marco, posed on a fully laid breakfast table.

The Queen had stayed aloof from dog shows until she agreed to support the People's Palace Dog Show in 1888.[18] The Palace, the brainchild of Sir Edward Hay Currie, had opened the previous year as a venue for 'improving' and respectable working-class entertainments. Its dog show was designed to be different from those licensed by the Kennel Club, as its aim was to improve the exhibitors as much as the dogs. The reporter from *The Field* approved, writing that 'shows of this kind have a tendency to promote the kind treatment of household pets'.[19]

Pride in her Pomeranians led the Queen to her first venture as an exhibitor at dog shows in February 1891. She won, albeit in unusual, some would say rigged, circumstances. The breed was usually judged in two classes – black or white. The Queen's dogs were 'fawn or sable and white in colour' and 'quite diminutive', so a special 'any colour' class was created, allowing Fluffy and Gena to take the prizes. Buoyed by success, more dogs were entered into the Crystal Palace Dog Show later that year. This time Marco, Lenda and Nino were successful in the new and exclusive 'any colour' class. They were benched apart, along with the dogs of the Prince of Wales, and were a separate visitor attraction.

The royal Pomeranians continued to be exhibited in the following years. Fluffy won again (Figure 1.3). A report on the Queen's Poms was that they were 'pretty little creatures, red or rich fawn in colour, with soft fluffy coats, nicely curled tails, and the most desirable little companions'.[20] That description was a polite way of saying they were not up to the breed standard and were best seen as strokable pets.

Until this time, the Prince of Wales had led royal involvement in dog shows. He first entered his dogs into the International Dog Show in 1863. His involvement grew. He acquired top dogs for his extensive kennels at Sandringham and made shows fashionable by opening events. In 1873 he agreed to be the first patron of the Kennel Club. The Prince was a keen sportsman, with his own pack of hounds and several gun dogs. For shows, he favoured large breeds. His kennelmen took his St Bernards, Bloodhounds and Mastiffs to local, national and international shows, including the big events in Paris.[21] With the networks and money to acquire the best in breed, his dogs won

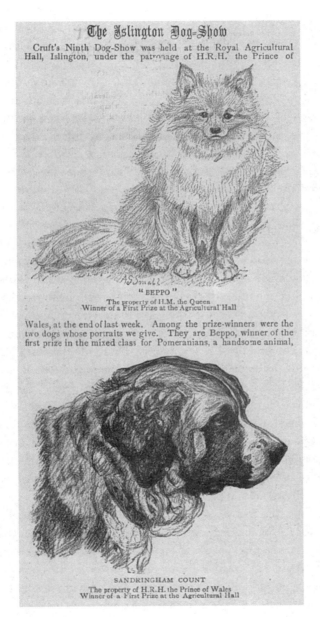

The Islington Dog-Show

Cruft's Ninth Dog-Show was held at the Royal Agricultural Hall, Islington, under the patronage of H.R.H. the Prince of

"BEPPO"
The property of H.M. the Queen
Winner of a First Prize at the Agricultural Hall

Wales, at the end of last week. Among the prize-winners were the two dogs whose portraits we give. They are Beppo, winner of the first prize in the mixed class for Pomeranians, a handsome animal,

SANDRINGHAM COUNT
The property of H.R.H. the Prince of Wales
Winner of a First Prize at the Agricultural Hall

Figure 1.3 The Islington Dog Show, 1893

regularly. In the 1890s, his wife, Princess Alexandra, showed two new imports, Borzois and Basset Hounds, and later supported the Ladies Kennel Association.[22]

The Queen was active publicly and privately in promoting animal welfare throughout her reign. She first officially demonstrated her dislike of cruelty to animals in 1837, when she agreed to be patron of what was then the Society for the Prevention of Cruelty to Animals (SPCA) but with her royal endorsement became the RSPCA.[23] In the 1870s, in opposing vivisection she lobbied ministers, and she continued to do so after the practice was regulated by the 1875 Vivisection Act. Similar concerns with welfare prompted her support of Battersea Dogs' Home. In 1885, the Queen made a £10 donation and, when approached, agreed to become its patron too. The Home had been founded in Holloway in 1860 but moved to larger premises in Battersea in 1871 (see Chapter 17). It had a high profile in the mid-1880s because of rabies.[24] Outbreaks led to the round-up and culling of strays and curs. In 1885, some 7,000 dogs were taken into 'custody' in London, most of which were sent to the Battersea Home. To deal with the overcrowding, the Home introduced Benjamin Ward Richardson's 'lethal chambers', which used coal gas to euthanise dogs.[25] Dead dogs had previously been composted, which was slow and polluting, so the Home turned to cremation. The Queen was horrified. She wrote objecting to the practice, and suggested that dogs' bodies instead be buried with quick lime. Cremation continued and the Queen, while remaining patron, cancelled her annual donation.

In 1901, the Prince of Wales took the title King Edward VII and, with Queen Alexandra, continued to be active in canine affairs. The couple had always had family pets. In 1902, *The Field* reported on 'The royal dogs', detailing the numerous breeds and successes at shows.[26] Jack, an Irish Terrier with the 'bluest of blood', was the King's constant companion. On Jack's death, Caesar, a Wire-Haired Fox Terrier acquired from the Duchess of

Newcastle, was next in line for the King's affection (see Chapter 4 on the Duchess). The royal courtiers were less favourably disposed, calling the dog Stinky.

In his will, the King stipulated that Caesar was to be in his funeral procession, positioned behind the King's charger (Figure 1.4). Caesar was ahead of Kaiser Wilhelm, who was allegedly angered by his demotion. The dog struck a poignant pose behind the coffin, with a demeanour of devotion that echoed both Landseer's painting of a Sheepdog mourning his shepherd and the story of Greyfriars Bobby. An effigy of the King lies atop his tomb at Windsor Castle, with a sculpted Caesar curled at his feet. Caesar died four years later and was buried in the pet cemetery in the garden of Marlborough House. Caesar symbolised the enduring importance of canine companionship to British monarchs and the place of pet dogs as members of the Royal Family.[27]

Figure 1.4 Funeral procession of King Edward VII, with the King's charger and Caesar, May 1910

Chapter 2

Bill George

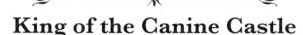

King of the Canine Castle

Bill George was a cult figure in Victorian London and his Canine Castle was a superstore for dogs of every variety. He styled himself a 'Dealer in Dogs', an occupation associated with dog stealing or napping. It is alleged that Charles Dickens visited George when writing *Oliver Twist*, to help with the characterisation of Bill Sikes's dog Bull's-Eye. George was known as the 'Father of the Fancy', a title contested by Jemmy Shaw (Chapter 3). The Fancy was the collective term for aficionados of boxing and working-class animal sports, such as cockfights, dogfights, ratting and canine beauty shows. But George cultivated respectability. He sold dogs to the upper classes and shipped them to overseas buyers. This unique spread of influence came from his expertise with two breeds: the most noble – the Mastiff – and the toughest – the Bulldog. These were dogs associated with the British nation, and George's unlikely patriotism was said by John Henry Walsh (Chapter 9) to have given 'good service to England in perpetuating the best blood'.[1]

George was born in 1806 in Buckinghamshire. He was a butcher's boy before embarking on his career in the Fancy, which began as an apprentice to London's leading dog dealer and Fancy sports promoter, Ben White. Typically for members of the Fancy, George took part in bare-knuckle boxing. He continued to be known as the 'nobby West End butcher'. The term 'nobby' was London slang for those who wore a bowler hat and had social pretensions. In the sole surviving photo, he takes the pose of a country gentleman with shotgun, but perhaps looks more like a poacher (Figure 2.1).

George was said to have witnessed a turning point in canine and social history in Britain: the fight between lions and dogs staged in Warwick. That event so outraged public sensibilities that it started the campaigns which led to the banning of dogfights in the Cruelty to Animals Act of 1835. Lion-baiting was an innovation on bull-baiting. The event was staged by the showman George Wombwell, who travelled the country with his menagerie.[2] Two contests took place in July 1825. In the first, the lion Nero was set against top dogs recruited by the London fancier Samuel Westbury. Nero showed no interest in fighting but suffered injuries when attacked by three dogs at once in the final round (Figure 2.2). The second contest was with a different lion, Wallace, and was more brutal. One of the dogs was Billy, which Westbury had bought from George. Wallace attacked each dog in turn, grabbed it and walked around with it in his mouth. Two dogs were killed, but Billy was spared. Wombwell was criticised on all sides. Spectators complained that they had not been given value for money, while animal cruelty campaigners were appalled at the butchery and the treatment of the lions.

There had been earlier moves against animal cruelty, most notably Martin's Act in 1822, which legislated over the treatment of horses and bulls, but the events in Warwick heightened calls for further reform. Progress was slow. There were no more lion-baiting spectacles, but dogfights and bull-baiting continued. Dogfights were primarily held in public houses in working-class areas, with betting on results an important feature. Middle- and upper-class men also attended. Both 'sports' were banned in 1835, though dogfighting continued out of sight, mainly in the backrooms and yards behind pubs.

After Ben White's death in 1835, George took over the business, and as the demand for fighting dogs dropped. Under the

Figure 2.1 Bill George

Bill George

Figure 2.2 Wallace (the lion), Tinker and Ball, 1827

new name of the Canine Castle, he began to create a reputable enterprise, supplying guard, working and pet dogs. He continued to breed and sell Bulldogs, as the illustration of a visit of *Punch* to his establishment in 1846 shows (Figure 2.3). One visitor described Bill's home at the Canine Castle:

> Every picture, every case of stuffed dogs, every engraving, has a history of battles and prizes won, and hecatombs of rats and other varmint destroyed. As the yard is a splendid specimen of dog life, so is the parlour of 'Old Bill George' a museum of all that pertains to dogs and their ways.[3]

An advertisement in 1855 listed the following available to buy at Canine Castle: Mastiffs, Newfoundlands, Bloodhounds, Bull Mastiffs, Pointers, Retrievers, Sussex Spaniels, Harriers, Beagles, 'vermin Terriers, rough and smooth' and 'a litter of old English Bull Puppies'.[4] One advertisement claimed it had the 'largest Collection of Dogs in the World', on some counts over 400.

One niche activity was lending dogs to artists for commissioned paintings. The novelist and sporting artist Finch Mason told a

PUNCH'S VISIT TO A VERY REMARKABLE PLACE.

Figure 2.3 *Punch*'s 'visit to a very remarkable place', 1846

story of George being found out over a stolen dog.[5] An unnamed
Royal Academician, who lived in St John's Wood and was almost
certainly Edwin Landseer (Chapter 6), loaned a Bloodhound each
day to sit for a portrait. The artist realised that the dog had been
'napped' from a fellow artist and set up a clever ruse for its return.
Finch writes that the artist was 'not only desirous of restoring the
lost dog to his rightful owner, who was nearly broken-hearted at its
loss', but 'still more anxious not to quarrel with Bill George, who
would naturally decline in future to supply him with any more
canine models, if he became aware that he had been "split" upon'.
In the plan, the true owner was to 'come across' Bill George's son
walking the dog back to Canine Castle. Finch writes:

> Young Bill, completely taken by surprise, was highly indignant at
> first and flatly declined to surrender the dog at any price. An invi-
> tation, however, to settle the matter by arbitration at the adjacent
> police station somehow did not fall in with his views, and in the end
> he reluctantly handed over his precious charge to the owner.

Bill George cultivated a public reputation for honesty, so it is
possible he was unaware the dog had been stolen. Yet his son's

willingness to give it up suggests that criminal activities continued, as in 1862 George was cautioned for refereeing an illegal prize fight.[6] George was often in court, charged with not having licences for his dogs.[7]

All social classes patronised Canine Castle. *The Field* received many letters from its 'Country Gentlemen' readers asking where to buy good sporting dogs. The editor, John Henry Walsh (Chapter 9), often directed them to Bill George. Edgar Farman, the leading authority on Bulldogs, wrote, 'Bill George stands out prominently as the most remarkable man of his time'.[8] Why? Farman goes on: 'he became noted as an honourable dealer at a time when dog dealers were looked upon as an occupation whose professors were not particularly noted for their practice of honesty'. George kept a foot in both low and high society; he bought dogs in Leadenhall Market and at Tattersall's, famous for the sale of thoroughbred horses.

Outside of the Fancy, George was best known for his Mastiffs. There was no single type, but rather different strains associated with landed estates, such as Chatsworth and Lyme Hall. He helped estates restock to avoid the effects of inbreeding. Experience and intuition meant he found good blood in the most unpromising animals and was able to choose parents that 'nicked' (were well matched) to give the best offspring.[9] Tiger was his best-ever Mastiff, valued in breeding for his noble head. But he had defects. In stud duties he had to be mated to a female with 'substance' as he had poor legs, presumed to be due to the confined conditions at the Castle. Tiger came from the Lyme Hall strain, which claimed to have a lineage continuous with a bitch, a female dog, that had accompanied her dead master home from the Battle of Agincourt. The wide geographical and societal reach of George's dealings was evident in Tiger's bloodlines. He had been born in Halifax, descended from dogs owned by: (i) leading northern industrialists Sir George Armstrong and Sir Titus Salt; (ii) the naval commander and politician Lord Waldegrave; (iii) wealthy independent gentlemen Thomas Lukey and Malcolm B. Wynn; and (iv) George's mentor, Ben White. Tiger was also the grandsire of the Prince of Wales's bitch Duchess.

The arrival of dog shows and the creation of breed standards saw disagreements over the correct 'look' of the Mastiff. One concern was the acceptability of an 'undershot' or protruding lower jaw. Many dog fanciers believed that the Mastiff and Bulldog had a common origin. There were also suspicions that breeders were crossing Mastiffs with other breeds, such as Bulldogs, to improve their look. Yet, in the heated disputes about the correct form, the nobility of Tiger's head remained the ideal for what was soon renamed the Old English Mastiff.

Bulldogs were George's other pride and joy. He bred and owned many dogs that are now said to be the foundation of the modern breed. With the demise of fighting and baiting, breeders switched from aggression to beauty. But beauty was in the eye of the beholder, and there was a demand for aggressive-looking dogs. George sold Bulldogs famed for 'the length of their fangs' to landowners to use as guard dogs to frighten away poachers.[10] The middle- and upper-class fanciers who kept Bulldogs bemoaned the new look of shrunken heads and exaggerated features. Correspondents to *The Field* complained that Bulldogs had become 'a thoroughly artificial animal', their face too short, chops too large, lower jaw too protruding, legs too crooked and too lightweight.[11] After the Islington Dog Show in 1862, one fancier observed the Bulldog freaks on display: 'Why will men persist in breeding an otherwise very symmetrical dog, with a ridiculously short nose, and great production of the underjaw. The short-faced one may win the prize, but undeniably it is a defect which wins.'[12] George's dogs were not exempt from censure. One visitor observed that a favourite at the Castle 'has a donkey's ear, a terrier's body and a pig's jaw'.[13]

Undaunted, George tried his luck at a conformation show, the first big show in London that year, in June 1862.[14] He won second prize with a dog called Dan. Reports maintained that the dog should have won first prize, and there was some amusement that the owner was listed as 'Mr. William George, Esq.' Dan seems to have been his only entry, although Bill's son, Alfred, became a regular exhibitor, specialising in Bull Terriers, and one champion was named after his father.[15] Although George kept away from shows, the 'blood' from Canine Castle continued to shape the breed. The Bulldog chosen to illustrate the standard in Walsh's *The Dogs of the British Islands* in 1867 was Romanie, a granddaughter of George's Old Madge. Leading members of the Kennel Club, including its first chairman, Sewallis Shirley (Chapter 20), kept the breed. Adoption of the breed by Britain's social elite coincided with the identification of the 'Bulldog spirit' with Englishness or Britishness. In 1855, Thomas Macaulay had written of the 'bulldog courage' of the English soldier in the siege of the Namur in his *History of England*, and by the end of the Victorian era it had become commonplace to speak of the British military as the 'Bulldog breed'.[16]

Arguments about the correct size and form of the Bulldog ran for decades. There was a particular controversy over the correct weight. One fancier, Frank Adcock, imported Toro, a dog from Spain that weighed ninety pounds, to improve the stature of the British Bulldog. Earlier, George had had the same idea, importing the appropriately named Big Headed Billy. His head was such a marvel that when he died, George had it taxidermied and displayed in a glass case.[17] In the 1870s, there was resistance to Adcock's plan and the changes made to the face, ears and tail of Bulldogs. From being condemned for breeding ugly, ill-formed animals, old-guard breeders such as George were increasingly revered for having stood out against the 'cripples and monstrosities' created by dog shows.[18] To bring order, the New Bulldog Club was established in 1875, a previous venture having failed. With the backing of *The Field*, the Club brought some order and consistency with its new breed standard and it made a strong stand against 'improvements'.[19]

Canine Castle continued to do good business. George received mail requesting advice and orders for all types of dog. Many were creatively addressed: 'To Lord George', 'King William and General George', 'K-nine Castle' and 'K.9. Castle'. In 1865, his name was mentioned in a diplomatic incident concerning invitations to ambassadors to attend a reception at Buckingham Palace. The wording was clumsy, stating that 'Her Majesty the Queen will be happy to receive the respects of the diplomatic body, male and female'.[20] Many diplomats took exception to words 'male and female', and humorous exchanges followed. An Italian minister observed that when Prince Humbert had visited Canine Castle to purchase some dogs, Bill George indicated sexes by saying, 'This is the gentleman, and this is the lady'. The minister playfully suggested that ambassadors 'could not allow themselves to be treated worse than dogs; he proposed that a petition should be presented for the appointment of Bill George as master of the ceremonies' at the Queen's reception. There was humour, too, in a court case at which George was called as an expert witness to identify, of all things, a stolen dog. There was 'great laughter' when George introduced himself as 'one of the greatest men in the world in regard to dogs', although this had some merit when his estimate of the dog's age helped win the case.[21]

George's fame became international. In 1872, he selected sixty-one dogs to be sent to the Pasha of Egypt. Many small Bulldogs from the Castle were exported to France and became foundational stock for the newly created French or Toy Bulldog. The breed was popular in Paris and northern France, and so admired by Americans on European tours that many were bought and taken home. Indeed, the first club in the world for the breed was the French Bull Dog Club of America.[22]

George died in 1884. His burial at Kensal Green Cemetery attracted a vast crowd of onlookers.[23] He left a wife paralysed by illness, who was so poor that the editor of the *Sporting Life* organised a collection.[24] Obituaries were short but laudatory. The *Kennel*

Chronicle observed that 'He was a character in his day and generation' and 'a sturdy, straightforward, honest dealing man'. He had 'maintained an honourable name in a business abounding with temptations'.[25] Such was his respectability that the Kennel Club's *Gazette* published an obituary.[26]

Chapter 3

Jemmy Shaw

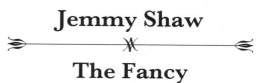

The Fancy

Jemmy Shaw was the leading impresario in the London Dog Fancy from the 1840s to the 1870s (Figure 3.1). The Fancy was a fraternity of sportsmen that had begun that bare-knuckle boxing and expanded to dogfighting, ratting and canine beauty shows. Their doggy sports took place in public houses, with mostly working-class spectators. Dogfights continued out of sight after they were made illegal in 1835, but timed rat killing by Terriers became the public face of the Fancy. The 'sport' of rat killing, in addition to the spectacle of the slaughter of vermin, extended to the breeding of top dogs and prizewinning, plus betting. In the beauty contests, the winners were the dogs with the most aggressive 'look' and athletic body. Ironically, the small size of ratting dogs meant they were the direct ancestors to many of the new Toy breeds popular with women in the late Victorian period.

Shaw was born in December 1814 in Spitalfields, London.[1] Nothing else is known of his early life. He married young and his wife died young. Their two boys, Billy and Bobby, were brought up with his second wife, Eliza.[2]

Shaw began his career in the Fancy as a boxer in 1831, when he beat Young Welsh in a bout that lasted nearly two hours. Bareknuckle boxing or pugilism was brutal, combining hitting with fists and wrestling. Its origins were in the eighteenth century, but by Shaw's entry into the fray it had an unsavoury reputation.

Figure 3.1 Jemmy Shaw and his talented ratter dog Jacko, 1865

Cheating and corruption were commonplace. It was not illegal, but promoters were often prosecuted for 'unlawful assembly, riot and tumult', not injuries or death in the ring.[3] Events were typically staged out of town, with covert announcements to avoid alerting the authorities.[4] The brawling and gambling amongst spectators brought moralising condemnation, not least because fights were frequented by the upper and middle classes, who ought to have known better. Some toffs who had boxed at public school tried their luck with the Fancy.

In the Victorian period, after a series of fighters' deaths, there were attempts to regularise boxing with the London Prize Ring Rules, set by the British Pugilists' Protective Association. Fancy boxers styled themselves 'MPR' – Member of the Prize Ring. Under the new rules, contests still had no time limit. Rounds ended when a fighter was knocked or thrown to the floor; there was then a thirty-second pause before they recommenced. Fights were typically for money put up by sponsors. Reputations like Shaw's could be built by plucky performances.

Shaw's longest bout was when he drew with Fred 'Bull Dog' Mason. It lasted two hours and twenty minutes. Shaw himself weighed only just over eight stones, and so he mostly fought heavier opponents, which meant there were good odds against him winning. In 1841, a bout was set up against Goliath Lawes, billed as 'a 14 stone piece of mortality'; this fight was promoted as 'The Dwarf and the Giant' or 'Science against Might'.[5] Lawes failed to show, allegedly having no appetite for such an uneven contest, and Shaw took the purse of £20. He lost sight in one eye in another bout, which brought a premature end to his career. He continued to seek fights, but honour among those who were MPR meant no one would agree to take on a disabled opponent.

Shaw took on other roles. He acted as a second in many fights, which involved supporting fighters between rounds and arguing with referees about rule violations. Members of the Fancy joked that it was a good job that Shaw's boxers won most bouts, as his small stature meant that he would have been unable to carry them from the ring. He also trained aspiring pugilists and participated in sparring events – show fights with gloves rather than bare knuckles. These were 'entertainments' in public houses, where those who were MPR taught their 'science' in sparring lectures.

From the mid-1840s, Shaw extended his involvement in pugilism to promoting fights. This was after he had become the publican at the Blue Anchor (now the Artillery Arms) at 102, Bunhill Row, in London, and his hostelry became a venue where contests were held and weigh-ins took place for out-of-town fights. In 1866 a boxer died after a fight at a pub run by Shaw's son Billy. The coroner's inquest heard that there was nothing irregular, yet the other fighter, two seconds and Billy were committed for trial on charges of manslaughter.[6] They were all acquitted.[7]

The Blue Anchor became best known for ratting, but illegal dog- and cockfights continued in backrooms.[8] As late as April 1865, one of Shaw's pubs was raided by the police after a tip-off from the RSPCA. Reports claimed there were around 100 specta-tors, and thirty-eight arrests were made, including some arrests of 'aristocrats'. All were fined £5.[9] The association with criminality was clear. There is no evidence that Shaw was involved in dog stealing, but there were suspicions that many in the Fancy were often involved. Also called dog lifting and dog napping, dog steal-ing was a high-profile problem in early Victorian London.[10] The well-to-do walking their dogs were targets. A variety of ruses were used to separate dogs from their owners, who were then followed home to secure an address. A day or two later, the owner would receive a ransom note and, if unpaid, the dog would be sold on, then perhaps stolen and ransomed again. The practice prompted a parliamentary enquiry and special legislation in the 1840s.

It was as a canine entrepreneur that Shaw became a London celebrity.[11] He was an expert breeder of rats and trainer of the dogs that killed them. He had two great champions, Tiny the Wonder and Jacko, whose exploits became legendary.

Tiny the Wonder was known for feats of endurance (Figure 3.2). He weighed just five and a half pounds and was said to be just 'a trifle bigger than a full-size rat'. In 1848, he destroyed 200 rats in just under fifty-seven minutes.[12] Jacko was much bigger, at four-teen pounds, and was noted for his speed: his record of 100 rats in just five minutes and twenty-eight seconds was never beaten. It was achieved on the final day of the 'Wonder Feat' of destroying 100 rats each day for ten days, in which Jacko became quicker day by day.[13] As well as appearing regularly across London, Jacko

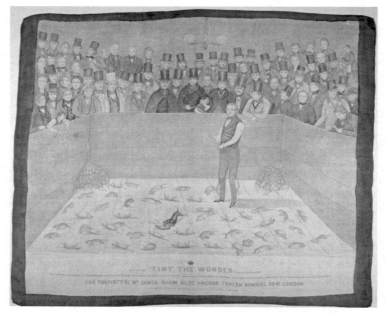

Figure 3.2 Tiny the Wonder. A souvenir handkerchief sold by Shaw, showing Tiny at work

went on a tour of the Potteries and Manchester where he took on all comers.[14] When Jacko died, Shaw was presented with a plaster model of the dog, styled as a 'Presentation Medal to Canine Fancier and M.P.R. Jemmy Shaw London 1852' (Figure 3.3). The memorial demonstrates the affection and respect that the Fancy had for individual dogs. They were pets as well as killers.

Marshall's famous painting entitled *An Early Canine Meeting* (1855) shows Shaw holding court at a beauty contest of small dogs (Plate 2). Fanciers are seated around a room; the walls are covered in paintings and drawings of ratting events, prize fights and famous fighters. The men are well dressed, with the stovepipe hats favoured by Victorians. Attempts to identify the breeds on show are misguided, as the painting was done before dog breeds were strictly defined by their physical form. There are recognisable

Figure 3.3 'In memory of Jacko, the Champion Terrier, 14 lb Weight.' The diorama was sold at auction in 2019

types, however – Bulldogs, Bull Terriers and Spaniels – but there would have been a wide variety of 'look' within each type and extensive crossbreeding. Fanciers were showing the 'beauty' of unique individuals, not exemplars of a standard form.

Henry Mayhew interviewed Shaw for his famous book *London Labour and the London Poor*, published in 1860. He misspelt his name Jimmy.[15] The rats rather than the dogs fascinated Mayhew. He was impressed by Shaw's network of rat suppliers. He mainly bought rats from the countryside, as he would not risk his champions biting diseased sewer rats. Shaw claimed, 'I should think I buy in the course of the years, on the average, 300 to 700 rats a week', which would have amounted to some 26,000 live rats a year. When business was good, he claimed to have as many as 2,000 rats in his establishment.[16] Shaw wrote *A Treatise on Rats* to share his expertise in breeding and keeping them. He had hopes of creating a unique strain of fancy white pet rats.

Ever the innovator, Shaw added variety to ratting evenings by staging contests with ferrets and an imported mongoose. The Blue Anchor eventually housed a domestic zoo, where, alongside dogs, rats, ferrets and his mongoose, visitors could see birds, a civet cat, two young kangaroos and a Tasmanian devil. There was also a miniature museum of ratting mementoes.[17]

Shaw left the Blue Anchor in the early 1850s and went on to be the publican at three more establishments, each a premier venue for the Fancy. They were said to be 'the headquarters of all old English sports'.[18] At a London pub called the Wrekin, Shaw put on entertainments seven nights a week, earning it the name the Theatrical Tavern. It was a venue for wagers on other sports, for example pedestrianism (walking and running); on Wednesdays and Sundays there were 'great harmonic meetings' with music and singing. Dog beauty contests were regular features. These were social events at which owners demonstrated their animals had the potential, in terms of their physique and character, to kill rats (and fight other dogs). As in later conformation dog shows, 'look' was taken as a proxy for ability. Contests were also opportunities to arrange stud visits, to share ideas and to exchange pedigrees. Meetings spawned clubs, such as the East End Toy Dog Club, the West London Spaniel Club, the South London United Canine Association and the Terrier, Spaniel and Small Toy Dog Club. Prince Albert was reported to be the patron of one club, and the Southampton Spaniel Club invited Queen Victoria, who regularly passed through the port on her way to Osborne House on the Isle of Wight, to be its patron.[19]

Owning and caring for domestic pets was not the preserve of the upper and middle classes. Dogs were one of many animals kept as pets in working-class homes. A picture in the *Illustrated London News* from 1874 of a pet shop in the working-class district of St Giles shows many species and, centre stage, a dog being

Figure 3.4 Pet shop, Seven Dials, London, 1874

groomed (Figure 3.4). The accompanying report states that such pet shops sold dogs, hawked by dog dealers largely to women as lapdogs. The article condemned all the parties involved:

> [Dealers] may be seen, on a fine afternoon in the fashionable season, parading their silly little beasts on the edge of the pavement in Regent-street, or at the gates of Hyde Park, in the hope that some lady in a passing carriage will open her purse to buy a canine pet. 'Only two sovereigns, Marm, for this reg'lar beauty, and nothink extra for the rosette and blue ribbin!' … The foolish creature may tomorrow have the luck to lie in a silken lap or in a nest of eiderdown, and to feed on rich cream and sweet biscuits from a silver platter. But every dog shall have his day, and his end is to die of a surfeit.[20]

Pet shops also offered veterinary services, filling the gap in the market caused by veterinarians' neglect of small-animal practice. Experienced fanciers, like Shaw, also offered their expertise in the treatment of canine diseases.

When the elite dog shows came to London in the early 1860s, there was a cross-over with those of the Fancy. At Cremorne Gardens in 1863, at a show opened by the Prince of Wales, the Fancy took many prizes and held special events to celebrate their successes the following week.[21] Cremorne's proprietor had been the guest of the Fancy before the show and had promised them fair treatment. The fraternising infuriated the show's organisers. Their disapproval was expressed in an editorial in *The Field* newspaper, which claimed Cremorne had been 'not a DOG SHOW, but a DAWG SHOW':[22]

> [T]here is as wide a distinction between a dog and a 'dawg' as there is between a sportsman and a sporting man. A dog is the faithful and intelligent animal which the sportsman makes the companion of his pursuits; a 'dawg' is the creature which the dog-dealers use to hunt money out of the pockets of cynomaniacs, pet-loving old dowagers, and other persons having more money than brains. A dog is a genuine newfoundland, retriever, a foxhound, a pointer, a setter, a terrier, a spaniel, or a mastiff; a 'dawg' may be any of these or none of these, for he may be a monstrosity or a mongrel, whose only use is to bring money to his master's pocket.[23]

Upper- and middle-class norms of masculine honour were said in the article to be under threat from the lower classes, sentimental women and 'trade'. Shaw was a particular butt of criticism, as he represented the brutality of ratting, the rough culture of the public house and disregard for the law.

Nevertheless, Shaw remained revered in the Fancy and enjoyed the title of 'The Original'.[24] He put on a dog show at a charity event in 1866 – the Annual Fete and Fancy Fair at the Crystal Palace. No doubt invited in the hope that he would amuse visitors, he did not disappoint: he put on a display of 'wonders of the canine race'. His stall was well attended and visitors could buy a 'dog-alogue', not a cat-alogue.[25] Shaw poked fun at the listings published for elite shows, inventing pedigrees such as 'the 'Epingo-Germanic Sangarian Poodle-cum-Puppy', the 'Jolly dog, by Vance out of Music Halls' and the 'Dramatic Dog, by Stage Carpenter out of Flat'.

Shaw maintained his role in the Fancy through the 1870s, though its activities shrunk as sensibilities towards animal cruelty changed and other sports gained in popularity. In the 1880s, he fell on hard times. A widower again, he was no longer fit enough to run a public house. He moved into rooms next door to his last hostelry, the Brown Bear on Grafton Street, and took up his father's old trade as a jeweller.

In February 1885, Shaw was admitted to Caterham Lunatic Asylum in Surrey. The leading dog breed expert Vero Shaw (no relation) visited him, after which he reported that Shaw could now remember faces but not events. Shaw died on 9 January 1886.[26] He was buried with some ceremony. His cortege left Cowcross Street in Farringdon at 1.30 p.m. and reached Old Brompton Cemetery an hour and a half later.[27] There was a large attendance from the surviving members of the old Fancy, who affectionately remembered him as their founder.

Chapter 4

Duchess of Newcastle

➤————————✕————————≤

Borzois and Fox Terriers

The seventh Duchess of Newcastle was the most influential woman in the late-Victorian dog show fancy (Figure 4.1). She was responsible for introducing Russian Borzois into Britain before she switched her allegiance to Fox Terriers in the twentieth century, a demonstration that women could own dogs large and small. She was the first 'chairman' of the Ladies' Branch of the Kennel Club, but a critic of the Ladies Kennel Association. Charles Lane's *Dog Shows and Doggy People* (1902) had her portrait as its frontispiece, with the following dedication: 'To her grace the Duchess of Newcastle who, by her condescension, personal patronage and support has raised the tone of dog shows and done much for the benefit of the whole doggy community'. He added that, after the Queen, she was 'the most popular of her sex in the ranks of the Doggy-People'. She remained an important member of the elite dog fancy through the first half of the twentieth century.

Kathleen Florence May Candy was born in London in May 1871. Her father was Major Henry A. Candy, and her mother, Frances, the daughter of the third Baron Rossmore of Monaghan. The couple were notable personalities in London's clubland. Kathleen grew up in Leicestershire, where she rode to hounds from the age of thirteen, including the famous Quorn. She married young, aged seventeen, after a short engagement. Her husband was the seventh Duke of Newcastle. They met at a dog

Figure 4.1 The Duchess of Newcastle and her Borzois, 1902

show, where he was competing with his Clumber Spaniels, a breed named after his estate in Nottinghamshire. Clumber Park was one of four estates in the East Midlands that together formed the Dukeries, though his title came from the West Midlands – Newcastle-under-Lyme. Large aviaries had been built on the estate during the 'poultry mania' of the 1840s, to which the new Duchess added large kennels. Both were run by John Douglas, the country's leading organiser of dog shows before he was outshone by Charles Cruft (Chapter 12).

The seventh Duke, Henry Pelham-Clinton, inherited Clumber House and Park in 1879 when he was fourteen and still at Eton. One of his wards was William Gladstone, who had gained his first parliamentary seat of Newark on the recommendation of Henry's grandfather. Henry had previously held the title of the Earl of Lincoln and kept the nickname Linny. He had poor health, due to injuries to his skull and legs after he was dropped by his nurse when he was a baby – his development was affected, leaving him with small stature and deformed legs. In any other social class, he would have been called a cripple.

The year of the Duke's accession saw parts of Clumber House destroyed by fire. His wards and trustees dealt with the repairs and remodelled the house to match earlier drawings by Charles Barry, the architect of the new Palace of Westminster, updated by his son Sir Charles Barry Jr. At the young Duke's wishes, a small church in fourteenth-century gothic style was added. A devout Anglo-Catholic and ritualist, the Duke was active in High Church organisations and spoke on Church matters in the House of Lords. Unlike former Dukes, he kept out of party politics but was involved in many charities and held many honorary public positions.

While the Duke's main interests were spiritual, his wife's were sporting. The size of Clumber Park meant she could hunt there, which led her to breed horses and dogs for hunting and other work, and then for show. She also established a prizewinning herd of Kerry cattle. But hunting was her passion, and marriage into the minor royalty opened opportunities to ride with top local hunts – the Cottesmore, Belvoir, Lord Galway's and the Rufford. She built up a pack of Harriers, a type of small foxhound (Figure 4.2). It was no small enterprise. Twenty-three couples (i.e. forty-six dogs) were drafted in from across the country and were looked after by her own master of hounds. Lady Violet Greville edited a book entitled *Ladies in the Field*, published in 1894, to which the Duchess contributed a chapter entitled 'Horses and their riders', in which

Figure 4.2 The Duchess of Newcastle, Lady Nora Hastings, and the Clumber Harriers (a type of small Foxhound), 1901

she complained about poor riding standards on hunts and called for a national proficiency test.[1]

The Duchess entered the world of dog shows at the Crystal Palace in November 1890.[2] She caused a sensation with her recently imported Russian Borzois, in the open class for foreign dogs. Her hounds were unplaced but admired as more petit and prettier versions of previous representatives of the breed. A Borzois had first appeared at shows in the 1860s, entered by the Prince of Wales, who had acquired it from his Russian relatives. These were large, rough-coated, wild-looking hunting hounds but always too few to form a separate class for judging.

The promoters of dog shows encouraged exotic specimens to provide spectacle and boost attendances. Several other types from Russia had been imported, including Spaniels, Setters, Retrievers and Poodles. They were typically seen to be coarse in 'look' and character, as might be expected of animals from what was seen to be a more backward country. Initially termed Russian Greyhounds or Wolfhounds, and sometimes Siberian Wolfhounds, they were seen as akin to British Greyhounds and Scottish Deerhounds.[3] In Russia they were used in groups of three to chase and corner wolves, and sometimes bears, until hunters arrived with guns and clubs. They did not have the size to attack their prey, as had the Irish Wolfhounds of old, nor seemingly the courage to kill. Furthermore, the dogs shown by the Duchess had been 'improved', said to be more civilised, softer-hearted, and had the milder look of 'ornamental and companion' dogs. This made them more suitable for women than sportsmen.[4]

Borzois were a sensation at Cruft's Dog Show in 1892. It was not just the large number of dogs entered but also the presence of royal dogs from Russia: four from the Tsar's kennels and others from those of Grand Duke Nicholas. The *Pall Mall Gazette* reported on the spectacle and the leading British owner:

> The Duchess of Newcastle, who owns fifty of the hounds, had sent a fair lady representative, on whose green hat the violets were in bloom, to lead her pets into the ring. Close to her were two men in Russian attire, not the would-be Russian costume as worn on the Parisian boulevards, but the genuine dress of the middle-class Russian when he turns out in his short shubka (fur coat) and round fur cap after the coldest days are over.[5]

After the show, the Duchess bought one of the Tsar's hounds, Oudar, for 200 guineas and another, Milkha, from the Grand Duke. Her Borzois began to win prizes at dog shows around the country, and at the prestigious Birmingham dog show at the end of the year her dogs won every Borzois class.[6] These dogs brought wider fame to the Clumber kennels. Endorsements by their kennel man featured in advertisements for Spratt's dog biscuits.

A small group of aristocratic owners saw their Borzois take over the Kennel Club studbook. Pedigrees in the following years demonstrate that the Duchess's dogs Oudar and Milkha, along with Ooslad, Kaissack and Golub, were foundational for the breed in Britain. They defined the conformation standard and provided true-blue, Russian blood.[7] They also set fashion standards and contributed to the wave of interest in Russian culture in Britain in the late 1890s. The Duchess had a photograph published of her dressed as Princess Ekaterina Dashkova from the court of Catherine the Great.

British breeders did not just reproduce foreign breeds – they made improvements. Borzois were no exception. Indeed, their so-called 'acclimatisation' was so swift that they were soon adopted as British. Breeders no longer looked to import coarse Russian hunting hounds, and sought instead the best stud dogs and bitches from kennels like those at Clumber. The Duchess nevertheless continued to import a better class of Borzois, taking advantage of her royal connections.

Befitting a newly refined breed, the requirements for prize-winning Borzois were exacting and quite fancy. The head was all important. The ideal was that: 'The skull should be flat and narrow ... the muzzle long and tapering', and 'The head from fore-head to nose should be so fine that the direction of the bones and principal veins can be seen clearly, and in profile should appear rather Roman-nosed'.[8] A significant change was in the coat, which was made longer and silkier; 'profuse frill' was needed on the neck, and the legs had to be 'well feathered' with long, soft hair.

In 1893 the Duke embarked on a year-long world tour. He was accompanied not by the Duchess but by Gambier Bolton, known as 'the Landseer of photography' and a leading spiritual-ist who published books on ghosts and psychic forces. Such a long separation fuelled gossip about the couple that went back to their marriage. There had been talk about the Duchess's Oriental-style honeymoon undergarments made of Kashmir wool and her unladylike devotion to rural sports. The couple had long spent much time apart. The Duchess preferred country life at Clumber, while the Duke favoured prayer in London and his continued an association with Eton.

The Duke's reputation suffered from failed business ventures and the bankruptcy of his younger brother Francis. On the recommendation of his close friend Carlos Blacker, the Duke had invested in the Alabama Land Development Company, which went bankrupt in 1895, leaving the Duke with significant losses. Possibly for revenge, the Duke accused Blacker of cheating at cards, then a particularly damaging slur. Blacker left the country, but not before his friend Oscar Wilde offered to help him sue the Duke for defamation. The three men were acquaintances, and Wilde, although he said he had never liked the Duke, had attended his wedding. Wilde had his own troubles with the courts and the proposed action was dropped.

The Duke's correspondence with Blacker suggests that he and the Duchess were not a well-matched couple. Only a month after the marriage, Blacker wrote, replying to a letter from the Duke: 'It is not wonderful that there is no unmixed joy in this world, since your lady is suffering from objective aggressions. ... Remember me to your lady, for the riddance of whose ills I will offer up a prayer.'[9] The marriage was the inspiration for the main characters in Howard Overing Sturgis's novel *Belchamber*, published in 1904.[10] Belchamber was a country estate, and its lord had been disabled by a fall and had poor health. He was unlike his forebearers, being timid, honest and religious; while he enjoyed embroidery, he hated sports. He was known as Sainty. His wife Cissy found him physically repugnant; the marriage was unconsummated and they led separate lives. But there were differences between the fictional couple and Duke and Duchess. Cissy had no interest in dogs and had a child after an affair with Sainty's cousin Claude. The book has recently drawn interest over whether Sturgis was portraying Sainty as homosexual.

The success of her Borzois gave the Duchess prominence amongst elite Doggy People. It was no surprise, then, that, in 1898, she was made the first 'chairman' of the Ladies Branch of the Kennel Club (LBKC). Women were not admitted as full members of the Club until as recently as 1979. The role of the LBKC was ill-defined, but its political purpose was clear: it was to challenge the position of the Ladies Kennel Association (LKA).[11]

Since 1894, the LKA had provided special shows for women and their dogs, most of which were high-profile London society events. Initially, relations with the Kennel Club were amicable, but tensions soon developed and escalated into a major fallout. At issue were administrative matters but underlying these was a cultural clash. The LKA was led in an autocratic manner by Mrs Alice Stennard Robinson, an Australian millionaire (Chapter 8). She wanted changes to be made to the Club rules such that they would better suit women and give equal status for LKA shows in the Club's studbook. Echoing the broader struggle for suffrage, the LKA's leadership wanted representation for women in canine affairs. The leaders of the men-only Kennel Club had no time for such nonsense.

The Club enjoyed the support of the Duchess, who wrote that could she 'see no good in a Show held entirely by ladies, for as a rule their dogs are the worst in the class, and seldom get more than vhc [very highly commended]'.[12] There no place either for the award of special ladies' prizes at other shows. In a letter to the *Stock Keeper and Fancier's Chronicle* she criticised the LKA directly:

> Dog shows, I imagined, were started to improve the breed of dogs – this association seems to me started for the sole object of giving prizes and specials to dogs mostly not worth their entry fees. I consider a show held only for ladies' dogs is very liable to set the wrong value on dogs shown.[13]

The LBKC soon proved not to her liking either, and in 1901 she resigned. Why? She had never been keen on a Ladies Branch and had joined only as a favour; also, the Club had refused it even meagre support. By this time, the LKA was in financial trouble and was wound up. Perhaps chastened by the Kennel Club's attitude to its Ladies' Branch, the Duchess had changed her mind about the need for a separate organisation for women. In 1904, she accepted the post of vice-president in a new LKA. Lady Aberdeen was president, indicating that it was now catering for the right sort of lady. The reformed Association flourished and the Duchess remained active in it until her death.

Through the 1890s, the newly introduced requirement for quarantine to stop the spread of rabies made it difficult to import Borzois, which led the Duchess to switch to breeding and showing Fox Terriers. As with Borzois, she is credited with foundational work for the breed, defining the modern Wire-Haired Fox Terrier with her 'of Notts' strain. Today, breeders claim that every Wire-Haired Fox Terrier in the world can be traced back to one of her dogs – Cackler of Notts.[14]

Fox Terriers became popular as pets and at shows. Many clubs for breeders and exhibitors ran their own single-breed events, and published books and their own newspaper – the *Fox Terrier Chronicle*. There was acceptance that the breed had been changed by shows, having been remodelled for beauty, with the loss of some ability in hunting. Fox Terriers were amongst the largest and most competitive breed classes. Pressure from exhibitors led to the separation of the rough-coated, renamed Wire-Haired Fox Terriers, and the Smooth. Indeed, the only difference between the two was said to be the coat, or 'hair' as it was unusually termed. The specification of the type of hair for the former was detailed: '[It] should be hard and crisp, not too long, neither too short, but of a tough, coarse texture … . There must not be the slightest sign of silkiness anywhere, not even on the head.'[15]

In 1908 the Duke bought Forest Farm in the Windsor Forest in Berkshire, near his beloved Eton. It was not a 'farm' but rather a large mansion with lands that required six estate workers. It was the Duke's preferred residence, while the Duchess still favoured Clumber, even though the south wing had been destroyed by fire. Both were involved in good works. The Duke kept up his support of schools, hospitals and church charities in north

Nottinghamshire and the Home Counties. The Duchess also supported Nottinghamshire charities, but in addition animal welfare initiatives, nationally. The most famous dog to come from her kennels was Caesar of Notts, the constant companion of King Edward VII (see Chapter 1).

The Duchess had long been associated with the Fox Terrier Association (FTA). She supported its standard that stipulated that 'Smooths' and 'Wires' differed only in their 'hair'. This changed with the requirement for Wires to have longer side-hairs (whiskers) on the muzzle, a longer head and shorter backs. As a judge, she was adamant that show champions should have 'expression and character' and perfection in 'look'.

After the Great War, the Duchess continued to be active in the FTA and with charities. With clearly no sense of irony, she organised a fancy dress party at the Savoy for the children of the wealthy to raise money for the Peace of Thanksgiving Fund for Waifs and Strays Society.[16] She also supported the People's Dispensary for Sick Animals and the Nottingham Hospital for Women and was active in the Conservative and Unionist Association. Her sporting interests extended to horse racing, both as an owner and as a regular attender at Ascot, in the Royal Enclosure.

The Duke died in 1928. His title passed to his brother, the unreliable Francis, but Clumber was left to Francis's son, Henry, who became the ninth Duke. After her husband's death, the now Dowager Duchess and her dogs moved to Forest Farm. The house at Clumber fell into disrepair, which the family blamed on high taxation. Pictures, sculptures and other treasures were given to Nottingham galleries and the house was demolished in 1938.

The Duchess continued to judge Fox Terriers and Borzois, bringing expertise and eminence to dog shows (Figure 4.3). Fox Terriers were 'the ruling force' at shows in the inter-war years.[17] Their classes had the largest numbers of entries, and they also had the largest numbers registered in the Kennel Club studbook.

Figure 4.3 The Duchess of Newcastle with a Borzois and Smooth-Haired Fox Terrier, 1935

The Duchess had switched to breeding and showing Smooth-Haired Fox Terriers, with which she also proved a great success. Borzois seem to have been kept by the Duchess for photographic portraits, and these reveal how the breed had continued to be altered, as they now had longer, finer and whiter coats.

During the Second World War, the Duchess set up and ran a medical supply depot on the Forest Farm Estate, for which she was awarded an OBE. She continued to judge and show her dogs after the war. She died in 1955 at Forest Farm, leaving an estate valued at £79,000 (£2 million in 2020 value), gifts of paintings to the Kennel Club and generous legacies for her staff. Her work in the doggy world spanned the Victorian and New Elizabethan eras, with her influence apparent in the physical and cultural reshaping of both Borzois and Fox Terriers.

Celebrities and millionaires

5. Jack Russell (1795–1883)   Hunting
6. Edwin Landseer (1802–73)   Canine Characters
7. Harry Panmure Gordon   Collies
   (1837–1902) and J.P. Morgan
   (1837–1913)
8. Alice Stennard Robinson   Ladies Kennel Association
   (1852–1932)

In Victorian Britain the press grew in terms of number of
titles, types of publication and readership numbers. Always
seeking to attract readers, editors sought colourful stories
with flamboyant individuals and in doing so created celebrities. Victorians did not know Parson Jack Russell for a
breed of terrier, but rather for his devotion to hunting and
for his friendship with royalty. Edwin Landseer enjoyed
fame due to his prizewinning paintings, royal patrons
and reports of his turbulent lifestyle, not to mention the
many homes that had a Landseer print on the wall. The
great wealth of Harry Panmure Gordon and J. P. Morgan
brought public attention, not only to their stock dealings
but to their hobbies. Their competitiveness in business was
carried over into their dog dealings and the not always successful pursuit of winning prizes with their Collies. Alice
Stennard Robinson was an Australian goldrush millionaire who bought the London *Sunday Times* and, controversially, installed her lover as editor. The paper became a
leading vehicle for the promotion of Alice's pet project, the
Ladies Kennel Association, the money troubles of which
led her to become a notorious celebrity.

Chapter 5

Jack Russell

➤⸻ ⋇ ⸻⸺

Hunting

Jack Russell is now identified with a breed of Fox Terrier, but he was best known as a parson sportsman in the Victorian era. His obituary notice in the *Illustrated London News* in 1883 portrayed him as 'the well-known North Devon clergyman, or rather country gentlemen in clerical orders, as he was better known for his performances in the hunting-field and his social popularity'.[1] His fame was international. He had obituary notices in American newspapers. In the *Washington Post*, for example, he was said to have been 'The last of the old school of reverend English sportsmen', while the *New York Times* observed that he was known as 'a mighty hunter throughout the West'.[2] Only one of his many obituaries mentioned his Terriers, not as a breed as such, but as one of many types of Fox Terrier. It was many years after his death that his name was linked to a specific type of dog: a mainly white, rough-coated Fox Terrier.[3] Yet, despite its great popularity, the Jack Russell Terrier (JRT) was accepted as a breed by the Kennel Club only in 2016.[4]

John (Jack) Russell was born in Dartmouth in 1795. His father was a rector, and the family had lived in the county since the sixteenth century. He was initially educated at his father's church school, and then boarded at Plympton Grammar School and Blundell's School in Tiverton, known for its strict regime and corporal punishment. Hunting was a popular pastime of clergymen and the Russells were no exception. At school, Jack kept ferrets to hunt rabbits and rats, and maintained a 'scratch pack' of dogs with a local blacksmith to hunt hares and other small game.[5]

Russell went to Oxford to read theology at Exeter College, but he spent more time on sports than studying. He boxed, which was then bare-knuckle, and, like a true West Countryman, enjoyed wrestling. His enthusiasm and ability in fox hunting won him rides with famous hunts, including those of the Duke of Beaufort and Sir Thomas Mostyn. He graduated in December 1818 with a pass degree.

While at Oxford, Russell acquired a Fox Terrier, Trump, the dog now taken to define the breed. Amongst JRT aficionados, how Russell found Trump has become legendary:

> It was on a glorious afternoon towards the end of May, when strolling round Magdalen meadow … . But before he had reached Marston a milkman met him with a terrier – such an animal as Russell had as yet only seen in his dreams; he halted, as Actæon might have done when he caught sight of Diana disporting in her bath; but, unlike that ill-fated hunter, he never budged from the spot till he had won the prize and secured it for his own.[6]

There is a paradox. Russell always maintained that he valued dogs for their ability, not their beauty. Yet here, at the alleged foundation of the breed, he took 'look' as a marker of ability.

Russell was ordained as a deacon in 1820 and as a priest the following year. His first posting was at George Nympton, near South Molton, before he became curate at his father's parish at Iddesleigh. He stayed until 1832, when he moved to Swimbridge, near Barnstable, as perpetual curate of Swimbridge and Landkey. A modest salary was no hindrance to his pursuit of his passion for hunting, as he used his charm and position to secure invitations to local hunts. In 1825 he had married Penelope Incledon Bury, the youngest daughter of Admiral Bury. Russell was something of a catch. He was tall, handsome and athletic, and the clergy was a respected profession. The Bury family were relatively wealthy, and Penelope's dowry enabled Russell to have his own horses and a share in a pack of foxhounds. Perhaps out of sentiment, but also showing good Christian thrift, when his horses died, their hides were used to cover armchairs in his home.

Russell hunted wherever, whenever and whatever he could. He shot otters, stags and hares and chased down foxes. There were many local hunts to join, but he became famous for the miles he would travel to find sport. Regardless of the distance, he was usually there and back in a day. He was out hunting three or four days most weeks, and he would take Sunday services wearing his hunting gear under his robes, ready to dash off at the end of the service. But he did not neglect his flock. Parishioners loved him and aided his sport by refraining from killing the local foxes to conserve them for Russell. His sermons were popular and he supported local charities, welfare institutions and agricultural improvement. Although his politics were never overtly expressed, he was understood to be Liberal, which stood him apart from other local worthies, who were mainly Tories and who had opposed parliamentary reform.

Russell's hunting was greatly facilitated by his friendship with a local landowner, George Templer of the Stover Estate at Teigngrace.[7] He, too, was a character. He lived openly with a mistress and their six children. He built the Haytor Granite Tramway, which brought the granite down from the tor that was used to construct the new London Bridge in 1831. By then, he had sold the estate to repay his debts. The friends continued to hunt together and earned a national reputation for their prowess. They pioneered the new, faster hunting, which required good horse skills, as riders followed hounds at speed, jumping over hedges and ditches. Russell featured in a book on British sporting men published in 1835, which noted that 'he stands high amongst the Devonshire bruisers. This gentleman finds hunting so conducive to his health that with stag-hounds, fox-hounds, harriers, and otter-hounds, he contrives to enjoy it all the year round'.[8] Templer was killed in a hunting accident in December 1843.

Politics may have been behind a minor scandal in 1840. John Nott was a landowner in Russell's parish, a Tory who had been targeted in the Swing Riots a decade earlier. Nott wrote to the Bishop of Exeter accusing Russell of excessive hunting, neglecting his parish and following horse racing, then associated with gambling. There were rumours that the Bishop might be sympathetic to Nott. He had previously expressed concern about the sporting activities of the Reverend John Froude of Knowstone, Russell's long-time friend and neighbour. A meeting between the Bishop, Nott and Russell ended in a stalemate. But Nott was unwilling to let the matter drop. He wrote a letter repeating his accusations, which found its way into Russell's hands, who sued for libel. The case was heard in March 1841 and became a local sensation. Russell won and was awarded costs of £200. His ride back to Swimbridge was a triumphal procession: 'The Reverend gentleman was greeted on all hands by the warm congratulations of his friends and on his return through South Molton the bells were ringing merrily, and numbers of the most respectable inhabitants crowded round him to express their gratification at the successful termination of the suit'.[9]

Russell's profile as a huntsman continued to grow, but increasingly he was seen as old fashioned. In his biography, Charles Noon suggests he became 'a Jorrocks of real life'. John Jorrocks was the creation of Robert Smith Surtees, whose comic adventure stories were first serialised in sporting magazines.[10] Jorrocks was a successful Cockney grocer and Master of Fox Hounds, who spent as much time as he could hunting, but his days in the field were always full of humorous misadventures. Russell represented a particular type of clergy – muscular Christianity.[11] The creed, in the context of the rise of Anglo-Catholicism, was against piety as such, and for physical endeavour, as it built character. The author of a report in the *Sporting Magazine* in 1854 explaining the creed probably had Russell in mind.

I fancy that there are more sporting parsons – a good old English title, almost obsolete in these days of priests and Puseyites garments … if so be they are really 'sportsmen', as I would desire the honourable appellation to be understood? which would in no manner prevent their being noble-hearted Christian gentleman and benevolent parish clergyman – doing infinitely less harm in occasionally riding after a pack of fox-hounds, and living in peace and charity with all men, than walking about dressed up like Jesuits, taking tea and talking balderdash with silly old women outwardly declaring themselves orthodox divines and pocketing tithes, inwardly fiddling as Roman priests and spending those tithes, paid by protestants, in teaching error and promoting auricular confession.[12]

Russell was reserved on religious questions, preferring charitable work to theological doctrine. He was a Freemason and supporter of temperance, though never that active with either, no doubt too busy hunting. Popular socially, he was a regular at hunt balls, society dinners and local festivities. He was a personality in the modern sense of celebrity, whose presence gave prestige to an event.

His public profile as a huntsman stressed endurance and frequency in the field; within hunting circles his reputation rested on other skills. He was known for 'the acute intelligence that he displays in everything appertaining to the habits of a fox, his mode of finding, and his quickness in getting to him in strong coverts'.[13] Moreover, it was said that 'he is equally good in the kennel as in the field', achieving discipline in his hounds by kindness rather than by using the whip. It was common to deny dogs meat the day before a hunt to keep them hungry and their scenting keen. Russell did the opposite, indulging their appetites to excite their senses.

The 1902 biography of Russell by E. W. L. Davies only briefly discusses his views on dogs. He is said to have favoured what was termed 'the modern foxhound', one bred for speed and that had 'power, symmetry, and grandeur of form'.[14] Without the money to draft in good blood, he made up for the poor form of the dogs he did have for breeding with his acute understanding of his individual hounds. Davies wrote: 'the constitution of each hound being so well known to him; he could tell to a scruple the proportion of broth or flesh which should be given to one and not the other'.[15] Davies quoted Russell as saying in the mid-1870s that 'True [Fox] terriers [differ] as much from the present show dogs as the wild eglantine differs from a garden rose'.[16] This statement has led many writers to claim that Russell was hostile to conformation dog shows. Such a view is mistaken. Russell was a founder member of the Kennel Club and was a judge at the Club's Crystal Palace show in 1874, where he adjudicated on Harriers and Fox Terriers.[17] Even at that time he was not new to shows, as he had entered his dogs in the Barnstaple Dog Show in 1871. He went on to judge all breeds at the Tiverton Dog Show from 1874 to 1877.[18] His profession made him an ideal judge: dependably fair, being accountable to God and above the Mammon of dog dealing. Russell was also an expert on breeding, having kept a kennel for over forty years, and having been active in local networks where dogs and bitches were traded, stud duties negotiated and puppies sold. He had kept rough-coated Fox Terriers, whereas smooth-coats were most favoured at shows. His dogs were already being styled as 'Jack Russells', referring to his personal strain, not a breed. His dogs were said to be 'rough and ready' and a 'hard bitten … varmint'.[19]

When it came to physical form, the defining features of Russell's strain were an all-white coat and short legs, with no preference for smooth or rough coats – what mattered was ability. Russell speculated that the smooth-coated Fox Terriers taking the prizes at shows were new 'composite animals', produced by crosses with Italian Greyhounds for a finer coat, beagles for their ears and bulldogs for courage, but it was the wrong sort of courage. It made them likely to fasten on a fox and kill, rather than drive it out of hiding to renew the chase. Over time, Russell favoured rough-coated or wire-haired dogs, but his strain were one strain amongst many particularly suited to north Devon and its style of hunting.

At the Crystal Palace Dog Show in 1874, Russell may have bumped into an old friend, the Prince of Wales, who attended the event as president of the Kennel Club. They had first met at a dinner held at the Royal Agricultural Show in Plymouth in August 1865. Eight years later Russell was invited at Christmas to Marham House, the home of Henry Villebois, the master of the West Norfolk Hounds and great-grandson of Sir Benjamin Truman, founder of the great brewing dynasty. The estate was near Sandringham and Russell mixed with the royal neighbours. He was invited to a royal ball and stayed to deliver the New Year sermon at Sandringham.[20] Russell and the Prince met again in July 1879 in Dartmouth and the following summer at Dunster Castle.[21] The Prince's stay at the Castle was to enjoy a day's sport with the Devon and Somerset Staghounds. Russell, by then an octogenarian, did not join the hunt but provided good company. Russell made his final visit to Sandringham in February 1882.[22]

His association with royalty made Russell a national celebrity (Figure 5.1). He was sought after to officiate at marriages. He died in April 1883, aged eighty-seven.[23] Over 1,000 people attended his funeral, to which the Prince of Wales sent a wreath. He was initially remembered for his sporting prowess and his social popularity rather than for his Fox Terriers, which, if mentioned at all, were referred to only in the past tense. For instance, in his volume on terriers in his *Modern Dogs*, Rawdon Lee wrote:

[The terriers] owned by the Rev. John Russell acquired a world-wide reputation, yet we look in vain for many remnants of the strain in the Stud Books ... . But, although the generous clerical sportsman occasionally consented to judge terriers at some of the local shows in the West, he was not much of a believer in such exhibitions. So far as dogs, and horses too, were concerned, with him it was 'handsome is that handsome does', and so long as it did its work properly, one short leg and three long ones was no eye-sore in any terrier owned by the late Rev. John Russell.[24]

Figure 5.1 Jack Russell in later years

Although Russell's strain was extinct, Lee believed that 'Russell blood' must be present in many Fox Terrier strains in the West of England. It was challenging to find a Russell Terrier, let alone substantiate its origins, because of the absence of pedigree records.[25] Some terrier breeders claimed to spot characteristics of the strain in the 'look', coat and weight of specific dogs, but there had been so many strains and so much time had passed that such speculation counted for little. And anyway, the Fox Terrier breed overall was said to have been modernised by the improvements driven by competition in dog shows. Nonetheless, Russell began to enjoy posthumous standing among breeders, and his portrait appeared as the frontispiece in Rawdon Lee's 1889 book on Fox Terriers.

JRTs were revived and promoted as a breed in the 1910s. The leading breeder then was Arthur Heinemann, who claimed to have four dogs given to him by Jack Russell. There is, though, no evidence that he ever met the parson; in fact, even if he had, given their respective ages, there would have been no dogs to pass on. Nonetheless, in 1914 Heinemann founded the Parson Jack Russell Terrier Club. Tellingly, it was a name change from the Devon and Somerset Badger Digging Club. Heinemann bred dogs to go to earth for badgers, rather than to follow a hunt and flush out foxes like Russell's dogs, and, worse, he was said to be a 'dog dealer' who was merely using 'Jack Russell' as a brand name to promote his business. The First World War ended this initiative. In the 1920s and 1930s, Fox Terriers bred for the show ring were divided into smooth- and wire-haired; the latter championed by the Duchess of Newcastle (Chapter 4), looked quite different from those shown in the Victorian era. No one sought to have the Kennel Club recognise JRTs as a breed. On the other hand, small primarily white dogs but of variable shape and size were bred and owned by a few sportsmen. This fraternity kept the name JRT alive, emphasising that their dogs were for work and sport, not show.

In the 1950s and 1960s, JRTs continued to be bred as working dogs while growing in popularity as pets. Stanley Dangerfield, the canine correspondent of the *Daily Express*, regularly wrote on them and why they were not a breed. He was a critic of the Kennel Club and had a soft spot for JRTs.[26] He observed they had 'charm but not papers', and that they were 'classless', the 'non-conformists' of the dog world. Indeed, they had become a 'reverse status symbol'. A Jack Russell Terrier Club of Great Britain (JRTC-GB) was formed in 1974, with a policy that Dangerfield would have welcomed. It aimed to maintain the dog's working abilities and to counter attempts at Kennel Club recognition.[27] A challenge to the JRTC-GB came in 1983 with the foundation of the Parson Jack Russell Terrier Club (PJRTC), which wanted breed status for the dog.[28] Its founders had chosen to add 'Parson' to the Club's name to distinguish it from other clubs and to indicate it was more committed to heritage. The Parson Jack Russell was eventually accepted as a breed in 1997, but the decision was controversial as the 'look' was taller and more square-bodied than the working types.

By the end of the twentieth century, JRTs had become popular in many countries as a show dog. The American Kennel Association recognised a version called the Russell Terrier in 2004 and an Australian breed variant was accepted in 2007. The Kennel Club and the JRTC-GB resisted similar moves in Britain, albeit for different reasons. The pressure told and in 2015 the JRT was accepted by the Kennel Club as a distinct breed. Many breeders and owners were unhappy. Robert Killick, a canine columnist, speculated satirically that JRTs' temperament would be calmed to suit life as a pet and that its name might be changed again to, say, the 'Priestly Jack Russell'.[29] But then a new name and standard would be needed for the 'old type' JRT, which he facetiously called the 'Fred Russell'. The imaginary breed standard began:

> He should be a cunning, loving dog who will bite your visitors and then sit dotingly on their laps. He will catch any living creature including the postman. And he is under the impression that he is as big as Great Dane.[30]

Killick suggested that JRTs were unsuited to exhibitions and would not follow instructions, and so might cause mayhem in show rings with their anarchic behaviour. He ended by saying, if your Fred Russell Terrier had these attributes of character and activity, rather than specific conformation points, 'the very Reverend Gentleman who invented the breed, would be very pleased'.

Chapter 6

Edwin Landseer

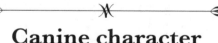

Canine character

Edwin Landseer was the most famous painter of the Victorian era and dogs were his forte. His paintings were popular across society. The Queen was a patron and commissioned many portraits of her pets. He had friends in the underclass of dog stealers and dealers, from whom he acquired many of his models. Engravings of his paintings circulated widely as prints, making 'a Landseer' a common sight in parlours across Britain. His paintings were admired for revealing dogs' human-like feelings, emotions and even thoughts. Such depictions reflected and helped shift attitudes towards dogs. Landseer was sympathetic to campaigns against cruelty to animals although he was never an activist. Nonetheless, he would have been pleased that his pictures were used in campaigns by animal protection societies.

Edwin Landseer was born in London in 1802, the youngest of three brothers, all of whom had successful artistic careers. Their father was an engraver who ensured they had the best training, first with Benjamin Robert Haydon and then at the Royal Academy Schools. The eldest, Thomas, was an engraver and printmaker. The middle brother, Charles, was a painter who specialised in historical subjects and became keeper of the Royal Academy. Edwin was a child prodigy. At the age of twelve years, he won a prize from the Society of Arts for his drawing of a Spaniel.

He showed his first painting at the Royal Academy two years later, a Pointer bitch with her puppy.

Landseer's work gained wider public attention when he was sixteen. *Fighting Dogs Getting Wind* was praised for its realism and capturing the dogs' passions. One enthusiast wrote:

> Did we see only the dog's collar, we should know that it was produced by no common hand, so good is it, and palpably true. But the gasping, and cavernous, and redly stained mouths, the flaming eyes, the prostrate dog, and his antagonist standing exultingly over him, the inveterate rage that superior strength inflames but cannot subdue, with the broad and bright relief of the objects, give a wonder-producing vitality to the canvas.[1]

Landseer bridged class divides. The subject showed his familiarity with the infamous and largely working-class world of dogfighting, yet was bought by the Duke of Beaumont.

Two dog breed standards were based on portrayals in Landseer paintings: the Dandie Dinmont Terrier and the Newfoundland. Landseer began to make regular summer tours of the Highlands of Scotland, which became the inspiration for many famous paintings depicting noble stags and mountain glens. He was usually accompanied by Georgiana, Duchess of Richmond, his lover for over thirty years.[2] On his way north, he often visited Walter Scott in the Borders (or Lowlands). He painted Scott's portrait on his first visit and made sketches of his Terriers. At this time, there were no distinct Terrier breeds but in Scotland geographical separation had produced three regional variants: Highland, Skye and Lowland, with further variations within each region.

From the 1860s, dog shows saw the creation and proliferation of distinct Terrier breeds, with fourteen classes at Cruft's first Terrier show, in 1886. Soon after, there were six native to Scotland alone: Border, Dandie Dinmont, Cairn, Scottish, Skye and West Highland. Border and Dandie Dinmont were both Lowland Terriers, the latter named after a farmer in Walter Scott's 1815 novel *Guy Mannering*. In the book, the farmer's Terriers are described as pepper and mustard in colour, and it was to the book that fanciers initially turned for the ideal. They found that Scott wrote more about character than physique, and what he said on the latter was insufficient for a breed standard. So, they looked to Landseer, but he had made only sketches and consequently was no help on colour. Also, his sketches looked nothing like the Dandie Dinmonts already winning prizes at shows! Was it possible such a fine artist's drawings were wrong? No. Instead, fanciers concluded that these Terriers had 'improved' since Scott's time.

Landseer produced two famous paintings of Newfoundlands: *Lion* in 1824 and *A Distinguished Member of the Humane Society* in 1838, prints of which circulated widely (Figure 6.1). *Lion* was commissioned by the dog's owner, and *A Distinguished Member of the Humane Society* was a homage to Bob, who had reportedly saved over twenty people from drowning in the Thames. The painting was a homage rather than a portrait, because Bob proved too scruffy and weather-beaten to appear 'distinguished', so Landseer painted a dog called Peter Pry. The Royal Humane Society was a charity that promoted artificial respiration and tobacco smoke enemas to revive people near death from drowning. Landseer's painting became its trademark. It remains one of Landseer's most recognisable works. In the early dog shows of the 1860s, fanciers had decided that the Newfoundland's coat should be entirely black. White and black dogs, like Bob, were said to be inferior. One authority wrote that these dogs were 'open in their frames, weaker in their middles, and generally displaying a more shambling and ungraceful gait in walking'.[3] They were said to have a bad coat that 'often resembles the wool on the back of a Shropshire sheep', while in stature 'they generally fall off in their hindquarters, being tucked up in the loin and leggy, and lack quality and type'.[4] Landseer's standing meant that white and black dogs continued to be popular and were entered in dog shows, despite having no chance of success. However, show promoters keen to accommodate fanciers' tastes created competition classes specifically for white and black

Figure 6.1 *A Distinguished Member of the Humane Society*, by Edwin Landseer, 1838

Newfoundlands. In time, they were accepted as a distinct breed, appropriately named the Landseer Newfoundland.

In 1839 Landseer produced another popular study, a paired portrait of Grafton, a large Bloodhound, and Scratch, a tiny Terrier. It was titled *Dignity and Impudence* to indicate the dogs' different temperaments (Figure 6.2). The painting had a feature always present in his animal portraits, what Victorians termed humanism – now termed anthropomorphism – that is, giving human qualities to animals. Landseer said that when painting dogs he invented stories about his subjects to help capture their thoughts and feelings.

Another technique, as seen in *Dignity and Impudence*, was to pair animals. He did this first in 1829, in separate paintings conceived as a pair, *High Life* and *Low Life*, which had the 'aristocratic' Deerhound intended for display next to a 'working class' Crop-Eared Terrier. The Deerhound sits in a well-appointed room, next

Figure 6.2 *Dignity and Impudence*, by Edwin Landseer, 1839

to 'hawking gloves, two rapiers, a sixteenth century-style helmet and breastplate, a standing cup, old leather-bound books, a partially unrolled document, a quill pen, a candlestick made from an eagle's talon and a bellpull'.[5] The Terrier sits at the entrance to a butcher's shop, next to a beer tankard, clay pipe, whip, keys, knife, bottle and old boots.[6] As well as the dogs' personalities, the painting also spoke of the social class of the dogs' owners and perhaps their character too.

Landseer's paintings appealed to contemporary sentimental taste and earned wide acclaim. He was close enough to the Royal Family to give drawing lessons to Victoria and Albert and helped to produce frescos in the summer house at Buckingham Palace.[7] Walter Scott and Charles Dickens were amongst his friends. There were many stories of Landseer recovering valuable stolen pets from dog stealers and dealers – the men who provided him with good-looking dogs to paint.[8]

Those who knew Landseer felt he had special powers with dogs, with insights into their hearts and souls, and even a 'mesmeric' influence over them. He was considered an authority on all aspects of the dog, including training, feeding and treating diseases, and consequently he often acted as a canine consultant. Another friend, the painter John Everett Millais (father of Everett Millais, discussed in Chapter 16), told a story of one of Landseer's less successful cures that nonetheless illustrates his methods: 'Edwin approached on all fours a notoriously savage dog tied up in a yard and smiled so convincingly that the terrified animal snapped his chain, jumped the wall, ran off howling and was never seen again'.[9]

In 1837, Landseer had painted *The Old Shepherd's Chief Mourner* (Figure 0.1), in which a Collie has his head resting on the coffin of his master. Reactions were mixed. A review in the *New Sporting Magazine* read 'This bit of sentimental claptrap is scarcely worthy of Edwin Landseer', while one in *Blackwood's Edinburgh Magazine* said it was 'a tale of bygone familiarity, duty, and mutual affection ... a very touching picture'.[10] Nonetheless, the latter review concluded that while most of his paintings had 'charming, fabulous power', with good composition and fine execution, many were now losing feeling, even becoming flashy.

Landseer got into personal and professional difficulties in 1840. His mother, who was close to him, died in January. He had new duties at the Royal Academy and became overwhelmed by commissions. He was unreliable in completing pictures and became involved in disputes. There was also continual gossip about his relationship with the Duchess of Bedford, who was twenty years his senior. His health broke in May and, typical of the wealthy, he sought recovery by taking a continental tour. That period of convalescence worked, and he was soon back in London. He remained popular. An article in the *Ladies' Treasury* of 1857 explained his appeal:

> He is the *Raffaelle des Chiens*. Other painters have painted dogs, but none ever painted such as Landseer's. He bestows upon them not only new graces of form and colour, but occasionally imparts an intelligence calculated to involve the question of instinct and reason in still further perplexity than ever.[11]

High-profile commissions continued. Engravings of his paintings sold in their thousands and adorned the rooms of all classes. Wealth and status enabled him to control the quality of the prints, and he would frustrate printers with his demands for changes and excellent-quality etchings.

Images of Landseer dogs were commonplace across the press and in advertising, where they were used to support moral as well as marketing messages. Dog portraits filled the front page of the temperance newspapers the *British Workman* and the *Band of Hope Review*, with reproductions of paintings such as *Suspense*, where the worried dog is waiting for the return of his injured master, who is being treated behind a closed door (Figure 6.3). There was an accompanying poem by George Crabbe that could have gone with many of Landseer's dog paintings:

> With eye upraised, his master's look to scan,
> The joy, the solace, and the aid of men;
> The rich man's guardian, and the poor man's friend,
> The only creature faithful to the end.[12]

Although Landseer amassed a considerable fortune, happiness eluded him. He struggled with chronic mental and physical

Figure 6.3 *Suspense*, 1862

ailments, drank heavily and took drugs to manage his symptoms. Undaunted, he continued to work, but his painting style changed. There was less realism, a broader brushed technique, and he moved to serious topics. He continued to paint dogs but in more contrived scenes. In 1845 he produced a canine version of

Alexander meeting the philosopher Diogenes, with the former as a white Bull Terrier and the latter a shaggy Terrier.

In 1851, Landseer exhibited *The Monarch of the Glen*, which came to define the Scottish Highlands for Victorians. His many images of individual stags were often said to capture something transcendental. *The Sanctuary* (1842) showed an exhausted but elated stag that had escaped the day's hunt, while in *Stag at Bay* (1846), 'red in tooth and claw', a terrified stag is being attacked by two hounds. While those who bought these scenes enjoyed the spectacle of sport and the excitement of the kill, Landseer had different sentiments. He opposed cruelty to animals and supported the Royal Society for the Prevention of Cruelty to Animals (RSPCA). There was no contradiction between love of hunting and opposition to cruelty. In Victorian times, the RSPCA mainly campaigned against working-class sports and the effects of cruelty on the perpetrators as much as the animals. In contrast, deer stalking, fox hunting and game shooting went unchallenged, and indeed the spirits of upper-class hunters were said to be lifted, not corrupted, by their sport.

In the 1860s, Landseer took part in the new dog shows. At the Monster Dog Show in Islington in June 1862, he exhibited his black and tan Retriever. It was not entered into the competition as Landseer had been invited to be a judge.[13] The promoters of dog shows sought celebrities to give kudos to their events. Landseer had very different ideas from breed aficionados about what made a good dog and whether cropped ears and docked tails were acceptable. After the show, a letter to *The Times* revealed that 'Sir Edwin Landseer … tried to establish the principle that all mutilated dogs should be excluded from the competition'.[14] He failed, and his views were ridiculed in an editorial in *The Field*.[15] Landseer hit back by writing to *The Times*, 'to set the ear-croppers right on a few points'.[16] He argued that rounding the ears of working and sporting dogs to prevent injury was acceptable, but cropping for purely aesthetic reasons was a 'barbarous custom'. Revealing his long-held 'humanism', he concluded: 'If the article in the *Field* represents the views of the dog fancy, it is quite clear they are in vulgar ignorance of the outward beauties of the various breeds of dogs, and unable to appreciate the ways and higher qualities of the noble animal'. Anti-cruelty campaigners drew upon Landseer's art to illustrate their conviction that animals were sentient creatures.[17]

Landseer continued to enjoy royal patronage, as in his now-famous painting of Queen Victoria on a horse held by John Brown. There were also elaborate, imagined scenes of people and animals in Scotland: *A Highland Flood* (1864) and *Rent-Day in the Wilderness* (1868), plus paintings of deer, wild cattle, Arab horses, polar bears and a lion. The lion study was integral to the commission to design lions for the base of Nelson's Column in Trafalgar Square, London. Ten years passed before the four bronze statues were unveiled in 1867. These were his last major work.

Landseer's mental and physical health deteriorated again. In 1872 he was certified insane. Like other wealthy patients, he was nursed at home, and it was there that he died, on 1 October 1873. Queen Victoria wrote in her journal that it was 'a merciful release ... as for the past three years he had been in a most distressing state, half out of his mind, yet not entirely so'.[18] His standing and celebrity made his funeral a national event. The service was in St Paul's Cathedral. The funeral cortège took nearly two hours to cross from St John's Wood to Ludgate Hill. There were twelve carriages and, on the route, shops shut or drew their blinds, flags stood at half-mast and thousands of people stood in silence. The eulogy celebrated Landseer as a principled painter:

> His morality ... preached a gospel of kindness to dumb creatures and it showed that, limited as were the capacities of that order of beings, they had traits of character such as fidelity, memory of gentle treatment, and even a deep affection for their masters, which ought to call forth from those masters at least the recollection of that maxim – 'The righteous man regardeth the life of his beast'.[19]

Landseer was interred in the crypt beside Joshua Reynolds and J. M. W. Turner. The monument had a profile of his head and a relief of *The Old Shepherd's Chief Mourner*. The obituaries in newspapers and journals were all laudatory. In the sporting weekly *Bell's Life*, it was suggested that his influence on attitudes towards dogs might be more enduring than his influence on art.

> But LANDSEER, whatever be his rank as an artist, had the gift of controlling, directing, and even forming the popular thought, the popular imagination, and the popular affection. How did he do it? He fostered the English love of dogs into a passion, and nearly into a worship.[20]

Two of his paintings, the Newfoundland rescue dog and mourning Sheepdog, were used by the British anti-vivisection movement in its publicity to illustrate that dogs were noble and feeling creatures (see Figure 18.2). One version had the Newfoundland in the pose of the *Distinguished Member of the Humane Society*, with the message, 'Save me! I would save you.' A wider change in attitudes to nature more generally was also attributed to the painter. The *Bell's Life* obituary went on:

> Nowadays, we cannot take up a book, a review, a newspaper, without feeling that the whole attitude of man towards brutes is completely changed. If there is one man who by the force of his native genius is the cause of this extraordinary change it is SIR EDWIN LANDSEER.[21]

Indeed, the writer suggested that Landseer's dog paintings had influenced the debates on evolution:

> Mr Darwin and his opponents appeal to the judgment at all classes because LANDSEER had taught the humblest ignoramus that ever gazed into the window of a print shop to look with new eyesight at his familiar cur.

Chapter 7

Harry Panmure Gordon and
J. P. Morgan

Collies

By the end of the Victorian era, the Scot Harry Panmure Gordon (Figure 7.1) and the American John Pierpont Morgan (Figure 7.2) were amongst the richest people in their respective countries. They were friends who shared not only business interests but also a passion for Collies. Gordon had a long association with dogs, serving for many years as president of the Scottish Kennel Club, which promoted native breeds. Morgan acquired many of his Collies from Britain, often bought on Gordon's recommendation. What contemporaries termed the 'Gordon–Morgan Confederacy' came to dominate the breed's competitions at shows on both sides of the Atlantic.

Harry Panmure Gordon

Harry Panmure Gordon was born in 1837 in Bombay (Mumbai), India. His father was a merchant and the family was distantly related to Lord Byron. He inherited a collection of the poet's memorabilia, which he bequeathed to his old school, Harrow. His education continued at university in Oxford and Bonn. In 1856 he was commissioned into the Tenth Hussars, which he left in 1860 on his father's bankruptcy, which some alleged was due, in part, to his son's excessive spending.

Gordon then went to Shanghai to work for a banking and shipping company. During the Taiping Rebellion, his military training

Doggy people

Figure 7.1 Harry Panmure Gordon with his Bearded Collie

Figure 7.2 John Pierpont Morgan, 1892

proved helpful during his service with the Shanghai Mounted Rifles. He returned to London in 1865, when he joined the Stock Exchange as a junior partner and within a decade had his stock-brokerage, Gordon and Co., later Panmure Gordon and Co. The company specialised in Chinese and Japanese loans, drawing on Gordon's networks in the Far East. Over time its interests became global, and the company benefited greatly from the growth of the American economy. Gordon visited the East Coast of the United States and published a book on his experiences, in which he marvelled at the new technologies. He wrote that the electric train promised riches 'beyond the dreams of avarice' and that Thomas Edison had 'genius stamped in every line of that mobile countenance'.[1]

Gordon's association with Collies began at the Brighton Dog Show in 1876, but this proved to be an ill-fated start.[2] He lived

nearby, in Hove. It is not without irony that someone who championed all things Scottish, to the extent of having bagpipes played
during evening meals, lived on the south coast of England.[3] He had
been invited to judge at that show a class then called Sheepdogs,
but his award was questioned in the canine press. In a letter to
The Field, he wrote that 'Few men have had better opportunities of
noting their [Sheepdogs'] respective points and working capabili-
ties on sheep amidst my native hills, than I have; further, I have
bred many a score'.[4] The editor commented wryly that 'residence
in Scotland among Collies does not necessarily make a man a
judge of that breed, the writer's powers in that capacity must be
estimated by their results'. Gordon hit back, promising to publish
his views on the breed, but never did.

Gordon was the City banker most in the public eye, principally due to his eccentricities.[5] He was described as 'the extrovert par excellence of an extrovert community'.[6] He moved from
Hove to London, first to Carlton House Terrace and then Charles
Street in Mayfair. He lived like a prince. He leased his estates in
Scotland for hunting and fishing, drove four-in-hand carriages
around London and turned out in all manner of fancy clothes.
His house parties were grand affairs, attended by a *Who's Who*
of late-Victorian worthies. He owned 1,000 neckties, had a suit
for every day of the year and regularly appeared in full Highland
dress. Garrulous and generous, he had many powerful friends and
acquaintances, including the Prince of Wales. His wife, Carrie,
who was twenty years younger, enjoyed the same partying lifestyle.
In the late 1890s, she was a fashion setter in the style-conscious
Ladies Kennel Association (see Chapter 8).

When business allowed, Gordon withdrew to his country estate,
Loudwater House, near Rickmansworth in Hertfordshire. In typical Victorian fashion, he filled the house with objects, many of
which he acquired from the East, and his wealth meant he never
stopped accumulating. His specialty was carriages, from Egyptian
chariots to motor cars, along with rickshaws, phaetons, buggies,

Figure 7.3 Mrs Panmure Gordon and her sister in one of her husband's carriages – a Jinrickshaws – with two ornamental birds and two staff in mock oriental dress, 1902

American charabancs and tricycles (Figure 7.3). It was alleged to be the most extensive collection in the world and required eight staff to maintain it. Always keen on new technologies, he designed vehicles that became boats when the wheels were removed, and a caravan, then described as 'a travelling carriage with home comforts'. Another leading dog fancier, Gordon Stables, shared his enthusiasm for caravanning (Chapter 15), but, unlike Stables who drove his caravan around the country, Gordon had his transported by train to Scotland. At his the Loudwater kennel, Gordon kept many breeds, with prize winners bought in rather than bred. He paid high prices for top Collies, although he never matched those paid by Morgan.[7]

Gordon's primary involvement with dog shows was through the Scottish Kennel Club (SKC), of which he was president from 1888 to 1900, as well as its principal benefactor, balancing the accounts each year with generous donations. The Club had been founded in 1882 and, like its counterpart in London, was mainly concerned with regulating shows. It had no formal role in promoting or protecting Scottish breeds, although many members felt this was their patriotic duty. The SKC's activities were fully integrated into the Kennel Club in London but subordinate. Dogs from England were allowed in its shows and vice versa. The SKC's main annual show alternated between Glasgow and Edinburgh, grew in size and attracted more and more entries from England, Wales and Ireland.[8] Nonetheless, the overall geographical balance of dog shows, with many more staged in England, meant the standards for Scottish breeds were set south of the border.

When Gordon became president of the SKC, just four Scottish breeds were recognised by the London-based Kennel Club: the Collie and three Terriers – Scotch, Skye and Dandie Dinmont.[9] Collies were the most popular. Queen Victoria had made them fashionable, with features and photos of her favourites in the press (Chapter 1). But what was a Collie? Just another name for a Sheepdog or a specific physical type? Was the breed uniquely Scottish? Favoured dogs were from the Borders, but many farms crossed into England. There were claims for a smooth-coated Welsh breed, with a 'peculiar sort of greyish hue, to which the terms harlequin, plum-pudding, [and] tortoise shell' were given.[10] The main issue was the change from working dog to pet. On farms they had been bred and valued for their abilities on hills and mountains. There was not *a* Collie, but rather *many* Collies. They were found in a variety of shapes, sizes and colours, suited to particular locations, types of work and owners' preferences. Regions and even individual farms had unique 'strains', which were a resource for crossbreeding to produce variants to suit different tastes and needs.

As a show breed, Collies had to be remodelled to meet a physical standard, and over time the population of Collies had an increasingly uniform look. Critics complained of 'dog show evils', with intelligence and condition sacrificed for beauty.[11] The creation of the template for Collies, as with most breeds, was started by John Henry Walsh, who claimed the best and most elegant dogs came from the Borders (Chapter 9). His standard was strict on most points, but quite loose in connection with the coat, allowing both smooth and rough, and three colours: black-and-tan, red-tawny and marbled. At shows, judges favoured smooth-coated black-and-tans, with 'an intelligent face' and with fine, long, flowing white hair ('feather') on their front, legs and tail. Gordon began with both smooth- and rough-coated dogs, but changed his allegiance to a supposedly older and more truly Scottish type from the Highlands, the Bearded Collie. His new favourites were kept as pets, not for shows, and accompanied him on his caravan holidays and sat at his feet in photographic portraits.

In his stockbroking business, Gordon regularly used the courts to settle differences with clients and creditors. His wealth and ability to hire the best lawyers often led adversaries to withdraw. In 1898 he took this approach to the dog show business. He sued two breeders for fraud, claiming to have been mis-sold a Collie by the name of Southfield Rightaway. He complained that its ears had been 'altered' and that this had not been disclosed.[12] Altering dogs' appearance was known as 'faking'. Faking ran from excessive grooming – for example, over-trimming or dying hair – to reshaping features by surgery. A key breed point with Collies was the shape of the ears. The standard was for 'semi-erect' or 'tip-eared', specifically for pricked ears to have their tips bent over. This shape was an ideal that few dogs fully met. Some modernisers favoured a 'new style' of 'simple prick' ears, but Gordon was against this. To achieve the accepted standard, some fanciers thought it legitimate to use artificial means, the most common of which was to weight the tips of ears to 'train' them to flop over. Gordon claimed that Southfield Rightaway's ears had been so manipulated, and this was the basis for his suit.

The trial, held at the Edinburgh Court of Sessions, was reported under headlines such as 'The Great Collie Ear Trial'.[13] The defendants were working class, a baker and a power loom tuner, but they were not intimidated and defended the action. Gordon had paid £100 for the dog, equivalent to a year's wages for both men. He said that 'he would not have bought the dog had he known that artificial means had been used'. Testimonies revealed that he had acquired the dog without seeing it in person, instead relying on an agent. The defendants admitted to applying weights to the ears, but they maintained that this was usual practice and not 'faking'. They had had no intention to deceive. The judge found against Gordon. And there was a further censure: he suggested that Gordon should seek to have the Kennel Club change its rules to ban ear tampering, rather than bring such matters to the courts.

The defeat rankled. Gordon complained about ear tampering again at the SKC's Edinburgh show in 1901. He claimed that a Collie named Parbold Pagoda, which had won several classes, had had its ears altered. The show committee rejected the complaint, so he took it to the Kennel Club in London. He expected to win. By then, he was a senior member of its governing committee and it was he who had proposed the main toast at the Club's annual dinner that year. As in the court case, at the Club's hearing veterinarians and Collie fanciers testified for both sides. Gordon was able to call upon the Queen's veterinarian, Charles Rotherham, and Parbold Pagoda was brought for examination. But Gordon lost again. The committee upheld the SKC's dismissal of the complaint on the grounds of 'not sufficient evidence'.[14] Gordon immediately resigned from the SKC and the Kennel Club's committee, affronted by the verdict and the Club's unwillingness to stiffen its rules.

Panmure Gordon's health was failing, and in the summer of 1902 he travelled to the spa town of Nauheim in Germany to take the waters. It was there that he died, on 1 September. His obituaries all stressed the same attributes: his wealth, flamboyant character, eccentric collecting and love of Collies.[15] After Gordon's death, his kennel master moved to the United States to look after J. P. Morgan's Collies.

J. P. Morgan

John Pierpont Morgan was in his fifties when he took up competing with his dogs at shows. He was born in 1837, in Hartford, Connecticut, into a wealthy family. His first job in banking was in London but he soon moved back to New York, where he worked with many partners across many ventures to build a considerable fortune. His millions came principally from investments and dealings in railroads and steel. His wealth became so large it afforded him political influence on US government economic policy. It also enabled the accumulation of large collections of art and artefacts and gave him a high profile on the East Coast social scene.

Morgan owned many dogs, and his celebrity made them newsworthy even before he started entering them in dog shows, as when a Bull Terrier, His Nibs, lost a fight with a cat and allegedly died of shame. He took up showing Collies in the early 1890s,[16] after seeing the breed on a visit to Britain. To get started, he paid top prices for two champions, Bendigo and his dam Bertha. They were kept on his estate at Cragston, in kennels with electric lights, central heating and bathrooms (Figure 7.4), as were more prize-winners imported from Britain. The Cragston Collies made their debut at the grand Westminster Show in New York in 1893.[17] Morgan's domination of prizes began the following year, with Sefton Hero, Charlton Phyllis and Ruffield Ormonde. Sefton Hero became a pet, sleeping under Morgan's bed, and was mentioned in obituaries. Success continued year after year until Morgan temporarily withdrew from dog shows in 1900. His main sporting interest had become the Americas Cup, the international yachting competition, which he won in 1899 and 1901.

Figure 7.4 Cragston Kennels, 1896

Cragston Collies returned to the show ring in 1904 with two new stars from England, Wishaw Clinker and Ormskirk Olympia. Successes followed until Morgan's dominance was challenged by dogs from the Greystone kennels of Samuel Untermyer, a wealthy corporate lawyer. He had been a political and economic conservative when amassing his fortune, but in the 1900s he took up liberal causes, such as anti-Semitism, human rights and anti-trust actions. The last brought him into conflict with Morgan, when, in 1912, the Pujo Committee, with Untermyer as lead attorney, held its hearings into the 'money trust', a term used for the Wall Street bankers and financiers said to have too great an influence over the country's economy.

Even before then, Morgan and Untermeyer had been bitter rivals, but at dog shows rather than in business. At the East Coast dog shows this was styled the 'Collie feud'. A verdict on the impact of their rivalry on Collies was given by Homer Davenport, a leading American breeder. He wrote: '[Y]ear after year they demanded longer and flatter heads for the Collie dog, with less above the eye and more below. That kind brought big prices, and the Morgan's and the Untermyer's paid as much for one of these stupid Collies as a home would be worth on Manhattan Island'.[18] It was understood that 'less above the eye' would mean less brain. The 'feud' ended in 1907, when Untermyer's dogs swept the board in a show at Brighton Beach, winning ten prizes to Morgan's one.[19] Morgan never entered Collies in shows again. The difference seems to have been with the kennel masters: Joe Burrell at Greystone made more astute purchases, albeit paying record prices.[20]

The feud at the Pujo Committee was called the 'clash of titans'. Untermyer cross-examined Morgan over two days. They were gruelling sessions. Morgan was in poor health and was exhausted by the ordeal. The critical final report damaged his standing and his business empire. To escape and recover he travelled to Europe, but died in his sleep in March 1913, in Rome. Morgan's family and associates blamed the death on Untermeyer's interrogation the previous year, but this claim found little sympathy.

Despite the view of Homer Davenport, the kennels of Morgan and Untermyer, along with that of Gordon, had little impact on shaping the modern Collie in the longer term. Their main interest was in winning. They bought rather than bred. Their dogs reflected the standards favoured by the breed aficionados who judged at shows, although by making Collies fashionable and popular, they encouraged the trend for pets to outnumber working dogs.

Chapter 8

Alice Stennard Robinson

Ladies Kennel Association

Alice Stennard Robinson, née Cornwell, challenged the authority of the male-only Kennel Club in canine affairs and helped develop a women's alternative (Figure 8.1). Her initiative was orchestrated through the Ladies Kennel Association (LKA), founded in 1894, which gave women a greater, though still subordinate, role in the British doggy world. Her influence came from her drive and wealth. Her brusque manner and unconventional personal life meant she attracted controversy. Scandal was never far away. Her millions came from the Australian goldrush, earning her the name Princess Midas, and she was said to be 'one of the most remarkable women of her time'.[1] Pugs were her chosen breed, and while she had only moderate success in shows, she helped establish the black variety.

Alice Cornwell was born in the East End of London in January 1852. When she was a year old, the family moved to Australia following the goldrush that began after discoveries at Ballarat. The family settled in Melbourne and her father became a leading railway contractor. George Cornwell and Co. built bridges and stations on the Melbourne and Suburban Railway. In 1861, the family moved to Dunedin in New Zealand, and her father again took on large projects, including the Bank of New Zealand building. Having moved back to Melbourne in 1869, her father's company was awarded contracts for major civil and private buildings,

MISS ALICE CORNWELL.
(Princess Midas.)

Figure 8.1 Miss Alice Cornwell, later Mrs Stennard Robinson, 1889

including Melbourne Grammar School, the Model School and the iconic Jack's Magazine, a gunpowder store.

Alice was a good marriage prospect, given her father's social position and the colony's scarcity of eligible young women. One contemporary described her as 'a handsome woman ... tall, fair and massive'. At twenty-three, seemingly against her parents' wishes, she became the second wife of John Whiteman. He was thirty years older. Whiteman had also come from London, working variously as a blacksmith, veterinary assistant, sometime gold prospector, hotelier and eventually a Member of Parliament in Australia. The couple settled at the Clarence Hotel in Melbourne and had one child, named after Alice's father.

The marriage was unhappy and the couple separated after six years. Whiteman resisted the split and harassed his wife. To escape, Alice left for London and, as wives had few rights, had to leave their child with his father. Mother and son were reunited in London only in 1892, after Whiteman died. George Whiteman changed his name to Sydney Carroll, became a theatre manager and impresario, and helped found the Open Air Theatre in Regent's Park. He was also a renowned theatre critic, writing for the *Sunday Times* and *Sunday Telegraph*.[2]

Back in London, Alice readopted her maiden name, studied literature and took classes at the Royal Academy of Music. She played the piano to a good level and had some of her compositions published.

In 1883, a telegram announcing her mother's death prompted her return to Australia to help with her father's businesses, which had expanded into gold mining. He had invested £40,000 in mines in Dowling Forest near Ballarat and had seen no return. Alice took over, taught herself geology and mineralogy, and proved a far better manager than her father and, for that matter, most of her male contemporaries. Her newly founded Midas Mining Company struck gold and made millions.[3] She was styled 'a heaven-born genius of mining, [who] has generally contrived to find ore where everybody else has failed'.[4] International fame came from the find in 1887 of a nugget weighing 617 ounces, measuring 1 foot by 8 inches, making it then the seventh-largest ever found. It was named Lady Loch, after the wife of the governor of Victoria.[5]

A millionaire in her mid-thirties, and presenting herself as a spinster, Alice was given titles such as 'Australia's Gold Queen', 'the astute Amazon', 'the Lady of the Nuggets', 'the Queen of Finance', 'the Australian lady financier', 'the Midas Queen',

'Princess Midas' and, most frequently, 'Madame Midas'. Alice poignantly referred to the Midas mine as her 'baby'.

In Melbourne, Alice's wealth brought her into contact with the city's rich and famous. She was drawn to writers and befriended Fergus Hume, whose bestselling novel *The Mystery of a Hansom Cab* had been published in 1886, and Henry Lawson, who had an esteemed career as a poet.[6] Lawson's aunt claimed that Alice offered Henry 'three years [of] university education, a trip to England and probably marriage later'.[7] It was her friendship with Hume that brought Alice real fame and some infamy. His third book, *Madame Midas*, was based on Alice's life, with no attempt at disguise. There were suggestions that it was a 'massive collusion' between Hume and Alice for revenge on John Whiteman. Like Alice, its heroine, Kitty, had enjoyed considerable wealth as a child due to her father's success in business. She marries Randolph Villiers, an Englishman whose gambling and drinking force estrangement and acrimonious separation. But then Mrs Villiers's company strikes gold and she becomes incredibly wealthy. The story then departs from Alice's and develops around escapades with two escaped French convicts and a stockbroker. Whiteman was outraged by the character of Randolph Villiers and threatened to sue. In the event, he took no action but threatened again when a stage version of the book appeared.

In July 1887, Alice met another author, the journalist, war correspondent and writer on natural history Phil Robinson, who was lecturing in Melbourne. She invited him to visit Ballarat to write about her mine and a romance blossomed. Robinson was born in India, educated in England and had a short academic career at Allahabad College in India. He returned to England and was the war correspondent for the *Daily Telegraph*, reporting on the Afghan and Zulu Wars, then for the *Daily Chronicle* in Egypt and Sudan. He also worked as a book editor and penned twenty-three books, 'mostly whimsically humorous essays on Indian natural history'.

Within months of meeting, the couple sailed together to Britain. Alice took the 'Monster Nugget', intending to use it to attract investors to new ventures. She established offices in the City and planned flotations on the Stock Exchange. The newspaper *The World* reported her success:

> The sensation of the hour in the City is the doings and sayings of the 'lady of the nuggets'. Miss Alice 'Cornwell' in a few weeks has achieved wonders. She has softened the heart of the Secretary of the Stock Exchange; she has exhibited the latest 'finds' to admiring Archbishops and Bishops at the Mansion House; she has convinced Mr Bryant that gold searching is more profitable than match-making; she has held her own with speculators and financiers; and she has successfully floated a company which rejoices in the familiar name of 'Midas'.[8]

Another report observed that she was attracting 'A large share of the interest hitherto bestowed on lady-doctors, lady-astronomers, and lady-bonnet makers'.[9] Her new Midas Gold Fields Company Limited was five times oversubscribed. The world was her oyster and, seemingly on a whim, she bought the *Sunday Times* newspaper and made Phil Robinson its editor.

Early in 1888, the couple returned to Australia. Alice used the capital raised in London to settle land leases and then embarked on a tour to explore new opportunities.[10] She bought estates in Queensland, invested in a new type of silver smelter and light battery, and considered speculating on Adelaide's proposed new outer harbour.[11]

In the spring of 1889 and back in London, she launched the British-Australia Mining Investment Company to support new projects. Alice was featured in the publication *Men and Women of the Day* where she was described as 'singularly earnest and sincere ... a woman who has adopted a role unprecedented among her sex'.[12] Phil resumed editorship of the *Sunday Times* and boasted of having increased sales by 40,000. Apart from wheeling and dealing in the City, Alice became a lady about town. She lived in Kensington and had a country house, Frog Hall (sometimes called Mortivals), in Tarporley, Essex. The couple was often referred to as the 'Swish' Family Robinson.

Alice was not shy to use her position to promote herself. In June 1889, the *Sunday Times* reported on a soirée at her London home:

> Miss Alice Cornwell gave a particularly pleasant 'At-home' on Wednesday, when a very large number of people distinguished in art, literature, music, and finance, foregathered at 31 Roland Gardens. The drawing room is a veritable museum of beautiful and valuable things from China, Japan, and Morocco, and it was as much as many amateurs present could do to avoid envying the kindly and hospitable hostess the possession of so much taste, and so many treasures upon which to exercise it. Plaques, cabinets, and hangings of great rarity, and beauty, dragons that might give pause even to a Japanese imagination, make the rooms a storehouse of delight.[13]

But Alice had a secret; two, in fact. She was five months' pregnant and unmarried, 'living in sin' with Phil Robinson. Three months later, she left the capital, reportedly seriously ill with typhoid fever.[14] A daughter was born on 26 October at Frog Hall and registered as Myrtle Dorothy Wentworth Robinson. Her parents were recorded as Alice Robinson and Frederick [Phil] Stennard Robinson.

Alice returned unabashed to the London scene in the new year, attending the marriage of her sister Kathleen to the music critic Herman Klein.[15] Kathleen wrote several novels, for which she adopted a new publishing name with each new husband. She was known, in turn, as Clarice Klein, then Kit Dealtry and finally C. Groom or Mrs Sydney Groom or K. C. Groom. Her daughter, Denise Robins, was the author of over 150 popular romance novels and a rival of Barbara Cartland.[16]

Alice was soon back in business but had lost her Midas touch. The battery company failed and the Adelaide harbour scheme was abandoned.[17] In October 1891, she sold the *Sunday Times* and decided to try her luck on Wall Street. New Yorkers were primed for arrival with a pen portrait:

She became a millionairess at 30, and is now 34, and if not pre-possessing is not unhandsome. She is inclined to be stout, but has a symmetrical figure and somewhat irregular features. Her chief charm is in her eyes which her admirers say command instant confidence. She has a soft, earnest, womanly voice, a kindly disposition and is charitable to a degree.[18]

A New York office never opened.

Alice Cornwell then disappeared, to be born again as Mrs Alice Stennard Robinson, though there is no record of a marriage to Phil (or Frederick). It was a bizarre re-entry and came at a dog show. She entered her Pugs as Miss M. D. Mortivals – one name of her Essex home, with the double bluff that Miss Mortivals was in fact her four-year-old daughter Myrtle (Figure 8.2).[19] The canine press was aware of the ruse, and placed Mortivals in inverted commas. The Pug breed was so novel that in many shows Miss Mortivals, together with her one rival, Mrs Fifield, monopolised both the entries and the prizes.[20] Entirely black dogs were particularly valued, as they were said to be hardier and less trouble than their more popular fawn cousins.[21]

NAP II.   NIGGER SAM.   PAPOOSE.   LITTLE NAP.   LITTLE MISS.

Figure 8.2 Miss Mortivals aged five years, with three Black Pugs, 1894

Alice Stennard Robinson

After winning some prizes at the Toy Dog Show in May 1894, Mrs Stennard Robinson chaired a meeting to discuss establishing a ladies' dog club. The venture won support and Alice agreed to be honorary secretary, the effective leader.[22] She took up the role with her usual enthusiasm and entrepreneurship.

The name Ladies Kennel Association (LKA) was adopted after the Kennel Club disallowed the name Ladies Kennel Club, seemingly fearing its brand being damaged by association with women. The LKA campaigned principally for better facilities for women at shows and special classes for what were seen as ladies' dogs. Initially, the Kennel Club had been sympathetic, as too was the *Stock Keeper and Fancier's Chronicle*, which made available offices and rooms for officials. The LKA announced itself at the Kennel Club show in October 1894, where it offered forty-eight silver medals as prizes for female exhibitors.[23]

The honeymoon was short-lived. The Kennel Club turned against the LKA ahead of the Association's first show in June 1895, which was limited to female exhibitors. The change in attitude was led by a woman, the Duchess of Newcastle, a formidable opponent (Chapter 4). The LKA show went ahead anyway and, according to one report, proved 'a brilliant social function'.[24] In 1901, the drawings in the *Illustrated London News* accompanying the report of the LKA show at Earl's Court had comments which suggested that it was less than serious affair (Figure 8.3).

LKA shows attracted large crowds and visits from the Prince and Princess of Wales. Some events had novel features, including an art show and, to some consternation, whippet racing, a northern working-class sport.[25] If anything, the LKA was too successful, as overcrowding led to charges of chaotic organisation. Unsurprisingly, the *Sunday Times* praised Mrs Stennard Robinson as 'a brilliant organiser and untiring worker'.[26] Reaction in the doggy press was divided. Those against the LKA, like the Duchess of Newcastle, typically fused denigration of the show with prejudices about a certain type of 'Lady'. Only the *British*

103

Figure 8.3 'The Championship Open Class of the Ladies Kennel Association at Earl's Court', 1901

Fancier, which had a weekly 'Ladies Page', came to the LKA's defence.[27]

In subsequent months and years, Mrs Stennard Robinson bore the brunt of attacks on the LKA and suffered many personal insults.[28] Reports in the *Ladies Kennel Journal*, the Association's magazine, unsurprisingly, were supportive. One observed that at shows she was 'like Ariel sailing majestically across the meadow … laden with a whole silversmith's shop in the way of prizes'.[29] As in business, Mrs Stennard Robinson was unafraid of confrontation and led from the front, which often put her at odds with the LKA membership, prompting comments that she was autocratic and operated a 'reign of terror'.[30] On several occasions she resigned from her position as honorary secretary, but was always invited back.

The LKA had a major fall-out with the Kennel Club in 1898. The LKA's Committee objected to the publication of women's private addresses in exhibition catalogues and to the fact that the Club gave no recognition to the winning of LKA championships. Underlying these differences was hostility on the grounds of sex and social class.[31] Stennard Robinson was cast as 'a new woman', with 'new money', and with working-class and colonial roots. There was also the tittle-tattle over her relationship with Phil Robinson. But she gave as good as she got, once calling the Kennel Club committee baboons.[32] When a report in *Our Dogs* complained about her 'use of the lowest slang expressions', she threatened to sue; the magazine published an apology.[33]

The LKA continued to hold annual shows in London and then around the country. Its events were successful socially and became a regular part of the summer season. Organisers were innovative in what could be in a dog show. Confirming the worst fears of critics, celebrity and glamour were important. There were competitions exclusively for the dogs of actresses, named 'Sarah Siddons Classes', judged by the socialite Lady Colin Campbell.[34] These entertainments were treated with sarcasm in the doggy press, as in December 1897, when it was suggested that a cloud hung over the LKA's show due to the recent death of 'Fussy', Sir Henry Irving's Fox Terrier, which had been given to him by Ellen Terry.[35] The *Daily Mail* reported seeing classes offered at a show for low-comedy dogs, professional beauty dogs, general utility dogs and paying amateur dogs.[36] When the LKA introduced a prize for the Champion of Champions in 1899, the idea was laughed at by elite fanciers, who claimed it was meaningless to compare breeds.[37] But in 1928, Cruft's awarded its first Best in Show, a prize which continues to this day.

An increasingly prominent feature at LKA shows, which distinguished them from those of the Kennel Club, was that profits went to good causes, such as the RSPCA and the Great Ormond Street Hospital for Sick Children. And shows were not wholly about breeds. There were special prizes for life-saving and charity-collecting dogs, the latter a common sight on railway stations with boxes strapped to their backs. Such innovations reaffirmed the moral status of women breeders, who generally considered themselves the real dog lovers, above Kennel Club members' pecuniary and competitive motives.

In 1897, the Kennel Club announced a challenger to the LKA, its own Ladies Branch (KCLB).[38] The Branch was slow to get going, and this allowed the LKA to continue to infuriate the Kennel Club. Matters came to a head when the Club banned the LKA from holding shows under its rules, on the grounds that prize money was unpaid. Dog shows had always struggled to cover costs and LKA events were no exception. Of the sixteen shows it held between 1894 and 1902, only two made money.[39] The financial model operated by Stennard Robinson was to use entry fees from the upcoming show to cover the prize money given at the last event. Her way of managing finances led to repeated complaints about delays in paying prize money and accumulating losses.

To avoid the ban Stennard Robinson borrowed money from her sister and brother-in-law, Clarice, and Berkeley Dealtry. The funds were used to sponsor new LKA shows in October and December 1902. The hope was that these would produce enough profit to break the cycle of losses. Another aim was to stop the Kennel Club's attempts to crush the LKA. The gamble failed, leaving the Dealtrys to meet the £1,080 owed in prize money. They did not have the sum, were declared bankrupt and sued the LKA to cover their debt.

The case went to trial in 1905 and was relished by the popular press, with headlines such as 'Doggy Cause Celebre', 'Ladies and the Dogs', 'Society Ladies Sued', 'Dog-Loving Ladies at War' and 'Duchesses and Dogs' (Figure 8.4). The action was against the LKA Guarantor Committee, of which Stennard Robinson was not a member. Nonetheless, it was her administration that was on trial. She gave evidence over two days, dressed in black with a veil, still mourning her Phil, who had died in January 1902.

In her evidence, Stennard Robinson, no longer an LKA official, supported her sister, maintaining that she had acted in all good faith on behalf of the LKA. Her financial dealings over many years were examined in forensic detail. It was hard going. The judge became infuriated, declaring, 'I do not believe that any jury in the world will ever arrive at an understanding of these accounts … . It is perfectly clear that every precaution which could have been taken to make these accounts incomprehensible had been taken.'[40] One complication was that Stennard Robinson had moved monies

SEQUEL·TO A DOG SHOW : The Case against the Ladies' Kennel Association. Special "P.I.P." sketches.

Figure 8.4 Mrs Stennard Robinson, was the Secretary of the Ladies Kennel Association, Mrs Dealtry – The Plaintiff, 1905

between the LKA and other ventures: the National Cat Club, the International Kennel Club and a mysterious '"Mortivals" account'.[41] The LKA's defence was that it had no liability because the shows in question were not its events. The jury agreed and the Dealtrys lost. They were soon back in court, but their appeal was dismissed, although the judges were sympathetic and said the couple had 'suffered an undeserved wrong'.[42] It was suggested that the plaintiffs had sued the wrong party – they should have acted against Stennard Robinson. There were other appeals, and the case dragged on into 1906, but no changes in the verdict. The Dealtrys left the country and settled in the United States.

The LKA was reformed under new leadership and found a niche in the doggy world.[43] The support of the Countess of Aberdeen and, once again, the Duchess of Newcastle gave it higher social standing and led to a rapprochement with the Kennel Club. Stennard Robinson withdrew from the worlds of dog and cat shows and returned to mining speculation, though with little success. She retired to Hove on the south coast of England, where she lived out of the public limelight until she died in February 1932, predeceased by her daughter. She is now celebrated on a walking tour entitled the Notorious Women of Brighton, Hove and Kempton. Alice Stennard Robinson's legacy to the doggy world was in establishing both a role for women, albeit rich ones, in elite dog shows and alternative competitions to those established by the Kennel Club.[44]

Sportsmen and showmen

9. John Henry Walsh (1810–88)   Breed and breeds
10. Richard Lloyd Price (1843–1923) Sheepdog trials
11. John Henry Salter (1841–1932)   Coursing and field trials
12. Charles Cruft (1852–1938)   Dog shows

Dog shows had their origins in agricultural shows and the rural sports of hunting, coursing and shooting. John Henry Walsh was Britain's leading authority on all sports; he held the influential position of editor of *The Field* newspaper and was author of many sporting manuals. When dog shows were changed to include non-sporting breeds, it was Walsh who first developed physical standards against which each breed could be judged. An unintended consequence was the remodelling of Dogdom into the proliferation of distinct, discrete, standardised forms that we know today as breeds. Many sportsmen worried that the emphasis on physical form would lead to a loss of ability in working dogs, and to counter this set up trials for sheepdogs and gundogs. The standardisation of these competitions was led by Richard Lloyd Price and John Henry Salter, both of whom shot game on a prodigious scale. While trials kept up gundog numbers, these were small compared with those of show dogs, which also became preferred family pets. No one did more to boost shows and non-sporting breeds than Charles Cruft, whose success can be measured by his journey from dog biscuit salesman to international canine entrepreneur.

Chapter 9

John Henry Walsh

>————————— X ————————<

Breed and breeds

John Henry Walsh made the greatest individual contribution
to the creation of the modern dog (Figure 9.1). He is included
here under 'Sportsmen and showmen', but he wore many hats.
His position as the editor of Britain's leading sporting newspaper, *The Field*, allowed him to influence canine affairs nationally
for over thirty years. Individual dog owners used his self-help
books on dog health and disease. He published under the pseudonym Stonehenge, chosen because the ancient stone circle
was a favourite haunt of Greyhound coursers. Walsh led the
reform of Dogdom into distinct and discrete breeds, defined
by their physical form. This was not his intention. Personally,
he favoured sporting dogs, for which function mattered
more than form. In the sporting world, he was known as 'the
Great Walsh' due to his energy, expertise and activism. He also
enjoyed the title of the 'Godfather of Guns' for his efforts to
improve the design, safety and accuracy of shotguns. Beyond
dogs and guns, he promoted national rules and standards in
many sports.

Walsh was born in Hackney in 1810, educated privately and
qualified in surgery in 1832. Whilst a student, he gained some
fame when he made a wax model of the Siamese twins Chang and
Eng when they visited London. He worked at the Ophthalmic
Institution in London and then became a general practitioner

Figure 9.1 John Henry Walsh, 1858

in Worcester, in partnership with his brother Thomas. Tragedy struck. Walsh lost two wives, each within a year of marriage: Margaret (née Stephenson) and Susan (née Maldon). He married for a third time in 1851, to Louisa Parker, the daughter of the vicar of Little Comberton, a village six miles from Worcester. By this time, he had had his first taste of publishing, when he coedited the *Provincial Medical and Surgical Journal*, the forerunner of the *British Medical Journal*.[1]

Successful medical practitioners had the time and money to indulge their enthusiasms, and Walsh had many. He rode to hounds, went coursing with his Greyhounds, shot game with his Pointers and Setters, trained hawks and coached the local rowing club.[2] He applied his medical knowledge to treat his own horses and dogs. He was a keen shot until he lost his thumb and forefinger when a gun barrel exploded. The injury forced him to abandon his medical career but set him on a lifelong mission to improve the safety of firearms.

In 1852, he moved to London and became 'a public writer', a modest term he coined for his editing, journalism, and authorship. His first book was *The Greyhound*, which had begun as a series of articles in *Bell's Life in London and Sporting Chronicle* and was expanded to a 400-page volume. He also wrote for the rival, upmarket sporting newspaper *The Field*, becoming its editor in 1857. The paper had an exhaustive remit, covering angling, archery, cards, chess, the country house, coursing, cricket, falconry, farming, gardening, golf, hunting, natural history, poultry, recipes, rowing, shooting, the turf, veterinary science and yachting.[3] Its proprietors claimed it was the largest newspaper in Europe, probably because of the many pages of advertisements.[4] Its reports, news, gossip, articles, letters and advertisements reflected the interests of its upper- and middle-class readership. Other sports and games were added to its coverage, including the new spectator sports of rugby and association football. In his editorials, Walsh also commented on current affairs and encouraged technological innovation in farming, shooting and transport.

In his early years as 'a public writer', Walsh proved to be a polymath. He published in the home-making genre, eventually dominated by Mrs Beeton, where his titles included *A Manual of Domestic Economy* (1856, 1857), *The Economical Housekeeper* (1857), *A Manual of Domestic Medicine and Surgery* (1858) and *The English Cookery Book* (1858). Two landmark sporting publications appeared in 1856: *The Coursing Calendar and Review of the Season*, which became an annual publication, and the mammoth *Manual of British Rural Sport*. The latter's popularity was such that it reached its fifth edition in five years and seventeenth by 1888. In over 600 pages, Walsh detailed the history, character and rules of twenty-seven rural sports and nine games (cricket was in the first edition, rugby and association football were added later). There were also chapters on the diseases of the horse and dog. Other sporting titles followed: *The Shot Gun and Sporting Rifle* (1859), *The Horse in the Stable and the Field* (1861) and *Riding and Driving* (1863).

One of Walsh's first initiatives at *The Field* was to organise trials of different types of shotgun. He came up with tests to settle a dispute about the merits of the new breech-loading guns over the older muzzle-loaders. Walsh designed innovative tests to measure the pattern and penetrating power of pellets at different distances. The result was that, while muzzle-loaders were slightly more accurate, the speed of repeat firing gave breach-loaders the overall advantage. *The Field*'s trials became regular events for comparing different guns (e.g. large- versus small-bore) and mixtures of shotpowders. Walsh endeavoured to make the events more scientific by using inventions such as a standard rest and gauges that measured the recoil and force of guns. Ever the innovator, he patented his own blend of gunpowder.[5]

Safety was also a concern. The number of injuries and deaths caused by faulty firearms had led to the opening in 1813 of a national test and certification centre – the Birmingham Gun Barrel Proof House.[6] It did not enjoy a good reputation. *The Field* monitored its work, not just with sporting guns but also with national security in mind, as army weapons were tested there. In 1885, the Proof House Guardians brought a case for libel against Walsh following allegations in *The Field* that understrength gun powder was often used in its tests. This meant dangerous guns could be certified. Walsh had relied on information from an unnamed but reportedly reliable source. Unwilling to disclose his source and with no other witness, Walsh lost the case. He was fined just forty shillings,

John Henry Walsh

however, and the judge even stated that Walsh left with his reputation unblemished. After the trial, Walsh and the Guardians met and agreed to work together 'to prevent sportsmen in the future from being maimed as he had in the past'.[7]

Walsh was enthusiastic about new sports, such as pedestrianism (walking and running) and cycling, and team games such as rugby and football. With J. G. Wood, a popular writer of natural history and science books, he published *Archery, Fencing and Broadsword* (1863 and 1865) and *Athletic Sports and Manly Exercises* (1864). Both extolled the value of exercise and competition to improve mind, body and soul, as part of wider movement that is now termed 'muscular Christianity'.[8]

Walsh was a devotee of croquet, which had social value as men and women could play on equal terms (Figure 9.2).[9] The game had grown in popularity due to two innovations: the mechanical lawnmower, which could produce grass of an even height, and the suburban railway, which allowed players to travel easily to tournaments away from their local club. But as with football, there were different rules in different towns.[10] Lewis Carroll picked up on this in *Alice's Adventures in Wonderland*, when Alice commented during a game that 'they don't seem to have any rules in particular; at least, if there are, nobody attends to them'. Walsh took the issue in hand.[11] He became *The Field*'s croquet correspondent and used this position to bring order. A group was formed in 1866 to agree national rules, which were published as *The Field Rules for Croquet*. Then, there were calls for a supervisory body analogous to the Marylebone Cricket Club (MCC). With Walsh's support, things moved quickly. In July 1868, the All-England Croquet Club (AECC) was founded, and was given space in *The Field*'s offices. Walsh soon fell out with his rival for leadership, Jones Whitmore. Civil war followed. In 1869 both groups staged national tournaments, one at the Crystal Palace and the other at Highgate School. Walsh's event at the Crystal Palace was the more successful and prompted moves to establish a permanent home for the AECC.

Figure 9.2 John Henry Walsh with his wife and daughter at the
All-England Croquet Club, 1870

The Club bought land at Wimbledon, which became the national
centre for croquet and later lawn tennis.

The croquet craze began to run out of steam in the mid-1870s,
and Walsh argued for badminton and lawn tennis to be added
to the AECC's activities.[12] As honorary secretary, he proposed a
name change to the All-England Croquet and Lawn Tennis Club
(AEC&LTC).[13] To enter its first lawn tennis championship, held in
1877, players had to send their entry form and fee to Walsh at his
home address – The Cedars, Putney (Figure 9.3).[14] The winner of
the tournament won *The Field* Cup.[15]

Unsurprisingly, *The Field*'s journalists were conservatives,
though not necessarily Tory in their politics. Walsh's editorials

Figure 9.3 All England Lawn Tennis Championship at Wimbledon, 1877

were pragmatic, dealing with questions issue by issue. He championed many technical innovations, in housing, sanitation, farming and transport. For example, all aspects of carriage design were covered, including special vehicles for transporting birds and dogs. In the cycling craze of the 1870s, *The Field* reported on bicycle racing, but for everyday cycling advocated the tricycle. Walsh found existing models unsatisfactory, so he designed something better – the *Field* tricycle.[16] Arrangements were made for its manufacture and sale for eighteen guineas.

Walsh's most important books on dogs were *The Dog in Health and Disease* (1859, 1872, 1879, 1887) and *The Dogs of the British Islands* (1867, 1872, 1878, 1882, 1886). The former took over from William Youatt's *The Dog* as the standard work on types, breeding, sports and self-help veterinary care (Chapter 13). Walsh's reputation, as much with guns as with dogs, saw him invited to be a judge at the show of Pointers and Setters in Newcastle upon Tyne in

September 1859, now widely cited as the first modern dog show (Chapter 11). The event was organised by gun merchants to identify the best example of each type of dog. It was not a beauty contest, rather one to identify 'true' Setters or Pointers, as these were being lost because of extensive crossbreeding. Critics questioned the wisdom of choosing winners by their shape and proportions, as there was no evidence of a link between physical form and ability in the field.

Dog shows grew in number and size over the next five years, becoming divorced from their sporting roots. Organisers added competitions for non-sporting and toy dogs. Good physical form no longer mattered as an indicator of ability; instead, it was an end in itself. The events became popular social attractions, appealing to all social classes, though these were kept apart by different entry fees on different days. Soon there were shows in towns and cities across the country. The 'Monster Dog Show' in London in 1862 drew over 1,000 entries.[17] Reports of shows and lists of winners were regular features in *The Field* and other sporting papers, often followed by lengthy correspondence. Top dogs became celebrities, with their deaths mourned in obituaries.

While a social success, the competitions were riven with rancour. There were complaints, sometimes backed up by legal actions, of bias, favouritism, bribery, corruption and sharp practice. Walsh was concerned about how dog shows had developed. His ideal was that they were 'to represent the interests of sportsmen and to illustrate the science of dog breeding to the country' and 'to improve the condition of the canine race'.[18] But critics, especially elite sports people, bemoaned that they had become commercial ventures for individual profit and had been infiltrated by 'dog dealers'. Walsh stated that if shows departed further from the values of 'genuine sport', his paper would have nothing to do with them. In the eyes of some sportsmen, they were already beyond the pale. While *The Field* continued reporting, it campaigned for reform and control by gentlemen.

The promoters of dog shows had to negotiate contradictory Victorian values. Their shows had to make a profit and encourage competition, but avoid association with 'trade' and 'speculation'. Exhibitors were heavily invested in their dogs and took results personally, so there were self-satisfied winners and bad losers. Spectators at shows sought entertainment at what were described as zoo-like exhibitions of canine Natural, or to some un-Natural, History. Even at shows run and judged by gentlemen, who claimed to be impartial, there were still complaints about unfair results. Why? Walsh had the answer. Even gentleman judges might be ignorant or biased, and in fact the principal problem was the absence of agreed physical standards of each breed. He argued that dog shows should adopt national rules and standards in the same way that cricket, rugby and football had. He campaigned for this in editorials and show reports and started a series of articles in *The Field* that set out physical standards for each dog breed, which would serve as a benchmark for judging.

Walsh wrote the first essay on the Pointer, centred on a dog named Major (Figure 9.4). The description and enumeration of Major's 'points' were presented as an ideal. Standards for other breeds followed and in 1867 these were published together in *The Dogs of the British Islands*, which Walsh intended to be the show judge's handbook. The standards were not fixed. Indeed, they were expected to alter as breeds were 'improved' by competition. In the first edition thirty-four breeds were described; by the fourth the total had risen to fifty-six. This initiative to regularise competition at dogs shows had an unintended and momentous outcome – the invention of modern dog breeds and *breed* as the principal way dogs were seen, not just at shows but everywhere. This way of understanding dogs spread from Britain to an international network of dog shows. In time, it brought about the demise so-called mongrels and mutts, many of which were later rebranded as crossbreeds. Walsh's hopes that his book would become a reference guide were met. His way of describing breed standards was

FRONT VIEW OF "MAJOR'S" HEAD.

MR. SMITH'S POINTER "MAJOR."

Figure 9.4 Mr Smith's Pointer, Major

followed, as was, for a while, his scheme of awarding a numerical score for each physical 'breed point'. More and more dogs were bred to the new standards, both for success at shows and as good-looking pets. Owners were assured that not only were their dogs perfect externally but internally had pure pedigree blood.

In the late 1860s, dog shows suffered financial and operational problems. There were calls for reform. Four 'national' bodies were founded in Birmingham, Nottingham, Durham and London to bring order.[19] The London-based Kennel Club, formed in 1873, saw off its rivals to gain the dominant position in canine affairs that it still holds today. In its early years, the Club only regulated the organisation of shows by accrediting events. It neither set nor policed breed standards; these were left to experts like Walsh and the collective decision-making of show judges. The Club's assumptions were typically Victorian: competitions would select the best and ensure the improvement of breeds, and in turn the nation's dogs.

Walsh stood aloof from the Kennel Club.[20] He complained that they were autocratic and failed to set standards. As the number of non-sporting breeds grew and with them specialist clubs, Walsh worried that less favoured, mostly sporting breeds, were being neglected. He called for the Kennel Club to support 'club-less breeds' and to check the negative effect of 'trade' on dogs. The final edition of *The Dog in Health and Disease* appeared in 1887, a year before Walsh's death. It was a substantial revision, with the inclusion of the new standards developed by breed clubs, despite Walsh's disapproval. In addition, he added 'several breeds which have come out of obscurity, as with the case of the Basset Hound, Welsh and Scotch Terriers, &c. or manufactured, as in that of the Irish Wolf-Hound'.[21] The latter had disappeared with the extinction of the wolf in Ireland but had been resurrected by crosses between four breeds: Scottish Deerhound, Tibetan Mastiff, Great Dane and Borzois.[22]

In an editorial published the month before his death, Walsh reflected on changes in dogs and shows since 1859.[23] His verdict was that there had been progress, but he was concerned that shows and the Kennel Club had lost sight of 'improving the nation's dogs'. There were fewer 'bad dogs' and mongrels at shows, and there had been improvements in non-sporting breeds. On the other hand, sporting dogs had suffered. He wrote, 'their "outward appearance" had been improved, though their working quality [was] quite another matter'. Setters and Spaniels were both under threat. Too few were being bred for sport, with degeneration following from inevitable inbreeding and the dilution of ability from mating with show dogs.

Walsh 'died in harness' in February 1888. Obituarists celebrated his virtues as a 'gentleman sportsman'. The *County Gentleman* commented that he had 'many old-fashioned ideas', but these were well grounded and meant he was 'always sticking up for the truth'.[24] One letter in *The Field* captured his unique way with dogs and sport:

> It is one thing to ride the hounds, to shoot your game, to watch the excitement of a course, to play a fair game of cricket, and to be fond of dogs, &c.; but accurately to know how a horse should be ridden, how hounds and other dogs should be managed in and out of their kennels, the ways and manners of the birds you shoot and the beasts you chase or kill – all this is not given to everyone.[25]

Time allows a wider appreciation. Walsh invented the idea of conformation dog breeds and their standardisation. Initially designed to ensure fairness and consistency at dog shows, the breed standards created were adopted across British society and the world. That said, there can be no doubt that Walsh would be horrified by the number of breeds at shows today, and especially with their 'fancy-fication'.

Chapter 10

Richard Lloyd Price

➣————X————➢

Sheepdog trials

The first Sheepdog trial was held on the estate of Richard Lloyd Price in 1873. Ironically, he was more committed to field trials, where gundogs competed against each other to find and retrieve shot gamebirds. As a founding member of the newly formed Kennel Club, he willingly helped with its newest venture, which was to test shepherds and their Collies. He had been just twenty-one years old when he first entered dogs into shows and remained active in canine affairs for fifty years.

Richard Lloyd Price was born into a landed family in April 1843; his father had died eight months previously. This meant he was born heir to the 64,000-acre estate of his grandfather, Rhiwlas near Bala, which had been built up from lands first granted after the Battle of Bosworth Field. His grandfather died when he was seventeen, leaving Lloyd Price one of the wealthiest young men in the country. He was educated at Eton and Christ Church, Oxford, where he kept a Bulldog called Taff. One day Taff escaped to Balliol College, where he bit the leg of the Master, the influential theologian and classicist Professor Benjamin Jowett. The incident led the university to ban students from keeping dogs.

Lloyd Price graduated in 1864, the same year as his coming-of-age, which was celebrated with a week of festivities in and around Bala to honour 'the young squire'.[1] The scale of events demonstrated the family's wealth and power. There was a 'monster procession' through the town, with a military band and six meat wagons for 'the poor, tenants, ... friendly societies, scholars and other inhabitants'.[2] Houses, shops and public houses were decorated, and there were stalls and street amusements. The next day, the main event was 'cutting the first sod of the railway' at Pen-y-bony Hill in Bala, where the projected lines from Corwen to Bala and Bala to Dolgelly would meet.[3] Like other landowners in North Wales, he helped promote economic development by supporting road and rail projects.

Lloyd Price found immediate success in his canine career. His first winner at a dog show, in 1865, was Bruce, a Clumber Spaniel, which he bought for £20 and which won him £220 in prize money. He wrote in old age that this experience 'laid the seeds of that insidious disease the dog show mania, from which I have only just only of late years recovered'.[4]

Lloyd Price was a regular exhibitor and judge at shows in North Wales and the north-west of England. He first specialised in Bulldogs but gave them up after Romanie, a dog that cost him 150 guineas, died on its way to a show in Manchester. He was so upset that he had him taxidermied and kept him on display at home. Switching to Pointers, he enjoyed success with Wagg, but fate struck again when the dog's show career ended when he was accidentally shot in the eye. Lloyd Price built up a large kennel and started to exhibit his dogs in the big national shows in Birmingham and London. He joined the committee that organised the Crystal Palace dog show in 1870, which became the group that founded the Kennel Club.

Like other sportsmen, Lloyd Price worried about the effects of dog shows on sporting breeds. Rewarding anatomy rather than ability was likely to weaken gundogs' scenting, stalking and retrieving powers. An attempt to meet the criticism was made in 1865 by the promoters of the Islington Dog Show. They organised an event on the Southill Estate of the brewer Samuel Whitbread to test the ability of Pointers and Setters entered in their upcoming show.

Dogs were set against each other in pairs to find and flush out gamebirds, which were then shot, and the dogs then had to find and retrieve the shot birds. It was a knock-out competition, with the winners in each round going through to the final. The dog that first found birds did not necessarily win, as this may have been chance. There were marks for pace and ranging in the search, plus obedience, style of hunting and 'staunchness', that is, keeping steady and calm on finding a bird and not reacting to the shotgun. Over a day's sport, birds became harder to find, and the dogs tired. At the Islington Show, little or no notice was taken of the field trial results in the judging, which pointed to the future, where dog shows and field trials became entirely separate.

The number of knock-out rounds meant that field trials were most successful on large estates, well stocked with game birds. Rhiwlas had the necessary resources and became a favourite venue. Lloyd Price organised the first Bala field trial in September 1867.[5] It was a small affair with just five dogs and Lloyd Price did not enter any of his own. He did 'handle the gun' and bagged thirty-six partridges on the first day. The Bala trials became annual events, with the August 1873 event the first under Kennel Club rules. It enjoyed aristocratic patronage and the participation of the elite of the new dog shows – the leaders of the Club and John Henry Walsh (Chapter 9). A good crowd of spectators attended. The trial was of sufficient note for the London-based *Graphic* to publish a report with an illustration. Lloyd Price ran his dogs every day, winning with his Setter Ginxs Baby and his Pointer Belle.

The success of the Bala field trials set up Lloyd Price to become a field sports entrepreneur. He was the obvious person to promote the first Sheepdog trials in Britain. Such events had been first organised in New Zealand and Australia in the late 1860s and were anticipated to be popular additions to the British rural calendar. They were said to be democratic, as the participants were humble shepherds, though typically tenants on large estates. Lloyd Price organised the first Bala trial with T. T. Ellis, the

Chief Constable of Merionethshire. It was held over two days at Garth Goch on the Rhiwlas Estate in October 1873 (Figure 10.1). There were two tests: driving three sheep in a controlled manner for over half a mile; and collecting and penning three sheep in a small enclosure. Welsh shepherds dominated the entries and were expected to win. The victor was local but a Scot, and his dog's name was Tweed. Over 300 spectators attended, and this encouraged other trials to be held across the country. The majority were in Wales, but shepherds in the Lake District, Pennines and Scottish Lowlands took up the challenge. The following year, a second trial was held at Garth Goch, before the event moved to Vivod, near Llangollen, a site at which it was easier to charge spectators.

The popularity of these events prompted Lloyd Price to organise a trial in London in June 1876, staged in the parkland surrounding Alexandra Palace in North London. There were three aims. First, on the model of gundog trials, it was hoped to help promote working abilities in Collies over fancy looks. So, owners of the

Figure 10.1 National sheepdog trials at Bala, 1874

winning dogs at the big Crystal Palace show that same month were invited to enter their dogs. None did. Surprisingly, the trial Collies were judged for 'appearance', by Lloyd Price and Sewallis Shirley no less (Chapter 20). Seemingly, they used conformation standards and, unsurprisingly, winners were described as 'imperfect' and 'ordinary-looking'.

The second aim was to allow Scottish and English shepherds the chance to challenge their Welsh peers on neutral ground. Having founded the sport, the Welsh claimed innate national supremacy for their men and their dogs, and, in the event, Mr J. Thomas and Maddie did win the day for Wales.

The third aim was to bring the new sport to the capital, building upon the popularity of dog shows. Spectator numbers were low and the trial was disappointing as a spectacle. But there was comedy. On the first day, three sheep ran off into the crowd and were not seen again.[6] Lloyd Price remarked that he had 'treated the cockneys to a wild, woolly Welsh show' and supplied spectators with free mutton.[7] Once underway, the progress of driving was slow, while the half-mile course meant that any action was often distant. Matters were not helped when the committee and competitors adjourned for a long lunch. Many spectators left before trialling recommenced. Trial aficionados complained that the terrain and conditions of the parkland were 'unusual', with features such as shelters and fountains not found on moorland. The dogs, they said, had no opportunity to show their 'sagacity'.

Lloyd Price answered the criticisms in two letters to *The Field* in which he blamed 'southerners' for the event's problems.[8] The parkland was not prepared correctly; much more could have been done to naturalise the runs by restricting the use of guiding flag posts. And Londoners were ignorant and dishonest – sheep stealers. They had not appreciated the skills of the shepherds nor the intelligence of the dogs; they needed to be better educated in country ways and sports. Overall, the trial was seen as a failure. Six years passed before another was staged at Alexandra Palace.

Figure 10.2 Sheepdog trials at Alexandra Palace, 1882

In that time, the number of trials across the country had grown, as had attendances. That second London trial, in 1882, organised by the newly formed Collie Club, of which Lloyd Price was a member, drew a good crowd (Figure 10.2).[9]

The annual Bala Sheepdog trial remained a major event in the sporting calendar, but Lloyd Price withdrew from national canine events. He was still in demand to judge Collies, Pointers and Setters at shows, but his views were often challenged as being old fashioned, favouring a sporting look. He stayed local, spending time on his estate and with his neighbours angling, hare coursing, fox hunting and shooting. He readily shared his experiences and advice in letters to *The Field* and in several books. Conditions for fly fishing on the Rivers Dee (Afon Dyfrdwy) and Dovey (Afon Dyfi) were a constant preoccupation. He bred his own pack of Harriers, and his favourite sporting dogs were kept as house pets, such as his black Spaniel Funny Fanny Fat Paws. Dog breeding was also a business. He regularly offered dogs for auction at Aldridge's, where they could fetch up to 1,000 guineas and attract overseas buyers.

Rhiwlas was one of the largest estates in the country, regularly hosting hunting parties for the great and good. The quantity of game needed for these sports led Lloyd Price to breed rabbits, pheasants and partridges on an industrial scale, on what he called his Game Farm. The scale of the slaughter could be enormous. The record number of kills at Rhiwlas for a single day was set by eight guns on 16 October 1884, when 3,646 rabbits were shot at a rate of eight and a half per minute.[10] This occurred on the second day of a four-day shooting party, at which the two-day kill was 6,102, made up of 36 grouse, 142 partridges, 349 pheasants, 228 hares, 5,332 rabbits, 3 woodcocks, 1 wild duck, 6 snipe and 5 others.

Lloyd Price's attitudes to animal cruelty were typical of his social class. It was appropriate and fair for gentlemen to kill for sport but questionable whether scientists should be permitted to perform vivisection. When the incidence of rabies increased in the 1880s, Lloyd Price supported the adoption and vigorous enforcement of dog licences, hoping that it would encourage responsible dog ownership, with the poor priced out. In rural areas, the threat was from potentially rabid, 'mad' marauding Collies.[11] He blamed irresponsible shepherds for keeping too many dogs and allowing them to roam at night. Lloyd Price advocated night-time curfews, with any strays out after dark being shot. He opposed the use of Pasteur's vaccine and muzzling, which, if imposed in rural areas, would prevent hunting and shooting, leading to an increase in vermin.

There were elements of xenophobia in his attitudes towards vaccination to treat potential rabies (hydrophobia) in humans. Louis Pasteur's vaccine had been developed from experiments on dogs, but Lloyd Price sided with those anti-vivisectionists who believed that his work was the cause, not the cure. In their view, Pasteur had manufactured more virulent rabies in his laboratory, and it had spread from there. Lloyd Price's sympathies were no doubt influenced by connections. The leader of the anti-vivisection movement was Frances Power Cobbe, the lifelong companion of Lloyd Price's aunt Mary Lloyd (Chapter 18). In the late 1880s, the couple retired to North Wales and were regular visitors to Rhiwlas. Lloyd Price became more open about his views, signing up as a founder member of the British Union for the Abolition of Vivisection (BUAV).

Lloyd Price published two books in 1888: *Practical Pheasant Rearing: With an Appendix on Grouse Driving*; and *Rabbits for Profit and Rabbits for Powder*. The demand for alliteration in the second title seems to have required 'powder' to be used as a synonym for shooting – gunpowder. Three further books followed: *Dogs Ancient and Modern, and Walks in Wales* (1893), *The History of Rulacc, or Rhiwlas* (1899) and *Dogs' Tales, Canina Facundia* (1901).[12] These volumes combined Lloyd Price's passions for both dogs and his Welsh surroundings. His writing showed knowledge and some wit.

In the *Saturday Review*, his style in *Dogs Ancient and Modern* was said to be 'chatty, discursive, [and] confidential'.[13] Price addressed the question: 'Are dogs ... better now than they were of old?' He was clear that his favourite breed, Pointers, had been improved; others he was unsure about. Never missing an opportunity, he warned that all dogs were threatened by the measures adopted to control rabies and by the indoor life of a pampered pet and plaything. He had also taken against dog shows, arguing that they were driven by profit and had damaged the nation's dogs. Writing about the 1892 Birmingham show, he highlighted that there had been 262 competitions for different types, with 'many of them being specimens of newly-created breeds of entirely modern invention'.[14] The walks mentioned in the title of the 1893 book were not intended for tourists, whom he dubbed 'Goths and

Vampires', but to tell anglers where to find the best spots on the Dovey and Mawddach estuary.

Lloyd Price was inspired to write *The History of Rulacc, or Rhiwlas* when he found mention of his estate in a 1610 encyclopaedia, which called it Rulacc, and Lloyd Price proposed restoring the original name. The reviewer in the *Athenaeum* said this was 'fantastical'.[15] Rather than being clever, he had made an elementary mistake: Rulacc was only a typographical error: Rulace was the English phonetic version of Rhiwlas! Another reviewer tired of the author's 'would-be facetiousness' and complained that an illustration of the house 'smacks of [a] hotel advertisement'.[16]

Dogs' Tales had the subtitle *Wagged by R. J. L. Price: A Book for Middle-Aged Children*, indicating that it was 'a funny dog book'. Reviewers were not amused. They found the book's style 'distinctly unconventional' and the stories full of dreadful puns.[17]

Although more than comfortably wealthy from rents, farming and sports, Lloyd Price fancied himself as an entrepreneur. In part, this was to increase his own wealth but it was also a continuation of his grandfather's efforts to boost the local economy. Most ventures were centred in Bala and were small-scale and short-lived, as with Rhiwlas bottled sparkling water and a brush-making factory. The largest business was the Welsh Whisky Distillery Company, set up in 1889 with planned capital of £100,000 – £10 million today. Only £38,000 was raised, just enough to build and equip a distillery at Frognoch near Bala. The Welshness of the whisky was signalled by the label, which featured a woman in traditional dress, based on a photograph of Lloyd Price's wife Evelyn, though an experienced Scottish distiller was hired to ensure the product's quality.

Lloyd Price was typically optimistic and penned a doggerel poem in praise of the venture:

And England and Scotia will both cease to boast,
When Welsh 'white eye' has got them both simply on toast,
And this still-born idea will not perish still-born,
When Fame sounds Welsh Whisky's praise loud on her horn.[18]

The spirit was also marketed as 'The Dew of Frognoch', with the easily ridiculed strapline 'Once drunk, Always drunk.'

Initially, the enterprise did well. Dividends were paid to shareholders and the whisky was given a royal warrant in 1895. It only ever received mixed reviews for its taste. Bottles were sold within a year, meaning the whisky had little time in barrels to age and colour. One review in *Harper's Manual* stated that 'The whisky was not maturing properly; it remained rawish, crude and practically flavourless for a pure malt product'.[19] Poor sales led to heavy discounting and damaged hopes of building the brand. In 1900, the company was put into liquidation.[20] Though solvent, there were only funds to pay creditors and reimburse shareholders for part of their capital.[21] The distillery closed in 1903. The building was used to house German prisoners during the Great War and in the early 1920s to hold Irish Nationalist prisoners, including Michael Collins.

Like many North Wales landowners, Lloyd Price had interests in mining and quarrying, which extended to investments in Tasmania in Australia.[22] One ambitious local venture was the North Wales Development Syndicate, where his partner was Arthur Crawshaw Bailey. The venture included allowing Bailey to take over parts of the Rhiwlas Estate for quarrying. Bailey made several investments in North Wales and had extensive Australian interests. He overreached himself with the Western Australian Development Corporation and its subsidiaries, to the extent of issuing misleading statements and submitting false accounts. In 1900, Bailey appeared at the Old Bailey charged with fraud, found guilty and given a five-year sentence. The North Wales Development Syndicate was wound up the following year. Lloyd Price escaped lightly. He kept his land as, perhaps unsurprisingly, the paperwork for the deals had never been filed.[23]

At this time, Lloyd Price withdrew into what he loved best: running his dogs in trials and coursing events, breeding dogs and game, and shooting the latter. As president of the Bala Golf

Club he oversaw the development of its course in the 1900s. His book on rabbit breeding found a new audience in the Great War, when shortages led families to rear rabbits for food. He also continued squire-like duties, serving as a Justice of the Peace in Merionethshire.

Lloyd Price died on 9 January 1923.[24] His obituaries were few and short; he was remembered chiefly only for his Pointers and his founding of sheepdog trials. He had been one of the dying breed of minor Victorian worthies who had lived on into an era when the Victorian activities and values that had given them eminence had not.

Chapter 11

John Henry Salter

⋙━━━━━━━━━━━━━━ ※ ━━━━━━━━━━━━━━⋘

Coursing and field trials

John Henry Salter was influential in two Victorian rural sports: hare coursing with Greyhounds, and field trials, where game-birds were stalked by Pointers and Setters (Figure 11.1). He kept a diary for over eighty years, in which he meticulously recorded his achievements: 2,123 dogs bred; 2,696 dogs owned; 44 breeds kept; 611 prizes at dog shows, including 199 firsts and 30 silver cups.[1] He was a general practitioner in the Essex village of Tolleshunt D'Arcy for sixty-five years, and he similarly meticulously recorded the number of babies he delivered – over 7,000. He was a larger-than-life figure, with what one obituarist called 'a titanic personality'.[2] Needing just five hours' sleep, on a typical day, when not away competing, he would shoot wildfowl at dawn, minister to his patients in the morning, tend his dogs and garden in the afternoon, serve on committees in the evening and, of course, complete his diary.

John Henry Salter was born in July 1841 at Arundel in Sussex. He attended Grix's School in Littlehampton and King's College School in London before studying medicine at King's College Hospital, graduating in 1863. He enjoyed a raucous student life, attending pubs to watch boxing and, in the back rooms, cockfighting and dogfighting. He lost the sight in his right eye in a brawl on Derby Day at Epsom in 1862. The injury prevented him from pursuing his hoped-for career as a surgeon. Instead, in 1864

Figure 11.1 John Henry Salter, 1875

with his new wife Laura, he moved to Essex and became a general practitioner. The couple enjoyed family wealth and bought a sizeable Georgian property, D'Arcy House. They were soon pillars of the local community.

His practice was typical for an English country village. He dealt with everyone and every illness, from birth to death. Salter boasted about delivering several generations of babies to the same family. Smallpox vaccination, pulling teeth and operating on kitchen tables were amongst routine procedures. His manner was stern yet compassionate, and this won him fierce loyalty from his patients.

Salter played many sports, including cricket, rowing, swimming, pedestrianism (long-distance running and walking) and archery, and was a keen follower of boxing. His diaries record that he was unafraid to use his fists, especially with local 'ruffians'. Soon, dogs became his passion. In his diary, he described how he took to coursing:

> I was working in my practise [sic], and all the farmers around kept greyhounds and had meetings every week in the winter at one or other of their farms, finishing off with a dinner, pork, and cards in the evening in the old-fashioned yeoman's style. I was at once smitten! – the orderly beating, the fair play displayed to both hare and dogs – the friendly attitude of the contestants and pleasant revelry at the finish were all to my liking.[3]

Ambition soon took over. He moved on to the top national coursing events, and began to breed dogs, both to compete and to sell.

Greyhounds had been kept for centuries, principally to spot, chase and kill rabbits and hares.[4] A possible origin of the name is a corruption of gazehound – hounds that hunted by sight, not scent or sound. The control of rabbits and hares as vermin changed with the adoption of accurate and powerful rifles. Hunting hares was made into a sport (Figure 11.2). Greyhounds competed against each other to chase a hare, with prizes for winners and betting

Figure 11.2 Stages of a coursing event, 1883

on the result. Typically, events were organised with around six-teen entrants. In successive rounds of heats, dogs were eliminated until two competed in the final. Coursing took place on open ground. A hare was released and two Greyhounds were 'slipped' (released) together to compete in chasing it down. The winner was not necessarily the one that caught the hare; indeed, there was always a chance that the hare might escape. Instead, the winner was the dog that, in the opinion of the judges, who watched on horseback, kept up and followed the twists and turns of the hare most accurately and elegantly.

The railway helped coursing become a national sport, which meant that dogs, handlers and spectators often had to travel long distances. Past performances, betting odds and results appeared in national newspapers. Coursing grounds became standardised and so too did Greyhounds. Previously, their size, colour and coat varied by region to suit different geographies. The new coursing Greyhounds, however, began to have the same look. Convergence in physical form, as with thoroughbred horses, was aided by selective breeding from champions, which led to a degree of inbreeding.

On the national scene, Salter was initially best known as a breeder. He had established a large kennel and put each season's puppies, called 'saplings', up for auction at Aldridge's Sporting Dog Sales, the top London agents. In February 1877, he sold thirty-five dogs for 319 guineas, the most expensive going for fifty guineas. Salter had significant influence over the breed's development; indeed, one of his stud Greyhounds, Glenavon, was chosen as an exemplar in Dalziel's influential book *British Dogs* in 1879. Yet, Glenavon was a sporting rather than a show type. Dalziel wrote that Glenavon was 'reddish fawn, with splendid back and loin, good shoulders, and muscular quarters, with good legs and feet, and altogether a thoroughly well-shaped dog'. There was a full-page illustration and, like the aristocrat that he was, his family tree was added.[5]

The premier event in the coursing calendar was the Waterloo Cup, run every February on the Earl of Sefton's Altcar Estate near Liverpool. Held first in 1836, it was so successful that the organisers added a steeplechase for horses, which became the famous Grand National. The Waterloo Cup operated as an exclusive club, with entries restricted to subscribers. Salter first made it on to the list in 1872, with Siesta, which was eliminated in the early heats. His best result came in 1876, when Squatter made it through to the semi-finals. Salter kept his place on the list of subscribers for thirty-one years, and would enter the dogs of friends and associates when he himself had no potential winner. Ever popular in the coursing world, Salter served on the committee of the sport's governing body – the National Coursing Club.

As well as taking part in coursing events across the country, Salter also competed with his poultry and dogs in shows. The early Victorian period had seen 'poultry mania'.[6] Amongst the middle and upper classes, there was a vogue to own and breed poultry and to compete with their birds at shows, a fashion said to have been started by the building of a vast aviary at Windsor Castle by Prince Albert.[7] Salter first showed poultry at the Birmingham show in 1870, which had 2,578 entries. His speciality was game-fowl, popular birds formerly used in cockfighting because of their aggression.[8] Poultry shows had turned game-fowl into 'friendly beauties', with longer legs, shorter necks, strikingly coloured feathers and a larger, fanned tail. Chickens kept as domestic animals differed, being valued instead for egg-laying and Christmas dinner.

Salter's first ventures into dog shows were at Crystal Palace in 1871. He won prizes with his Greyhound Fair Rosa and Sussex Spaniel Chance. Judging sporting dogs on their physical form at shows remained controversial. What was being assessed with Greyhounds? Was physical form a sure indicator of speed and ability, or an ideal of elegance and beauty? There were fears that two types of hound would be developed – 'coursers' and 'beauties'. In time, courser blood would be diluted by the growing number of beauties kept as pets, and the breed would degenerate.

As in coursing, Salter's energy, enthusiasm and wealth led to a rapid rise in his standing amongst leading Doggy People. He was elected to the committee of the Kennel Club in 1875, although he had criticised shows for favouring 'drawing room' dogs over good workers.[9] He specialised in sporting breeds and, as with Greyhounds, worried that breed standards were wholly defined by beauty. Damage would follow: 'I think it a prostitution of dog breeding, and antagonistic to the propagation of genuine sport for any man to breed pointers, setters, spaniels, and the like simply to win prizes at dog shows'.[10]

Such fears had been aired a decade earlier and led to the creation of trials to test the ability of gundogs to find game birds. In 1865, before the International Dog Show in London, 'field trials' had been organised to test and rank the ability of dogs ahead of judging on the show bench (see Chapters 10 and 11).[11] As in coursing, there was a series of knockout heats, where two dogs were put to ground to flush out game birds and were judged on their performance both in sweeping an area and in their 'staunchness' in approaching the bird.[12] But not everyone was impressed with such trials. Some objected that these competitions involved such contrivance that they would be no guide to ability at dawn on a moor or in a marsh.[13] Also, trials told of ability only on one day, when all sports people knew the number of birds and the conditions for scenting varied from hour to hour. Despite such complaints, field trials continued, separate from dog shows, and became regular events in the sporting calendar.

Salter devoted more of his time to field trials and became a leading judge as well as competitor (Figure 11.3). It was no surprise that he joined the Kennel Club's sub-committee tasked with revising trial rules. The main issue was the unfairness of the elimination heats.[14] Good dogs could be out of the competition in the early rounds if they were matched against, say, the eventual winner. After an enquiry, new rules were drafted by Salter. The heat system was retained, but judges were given discretionary powers to intervene and ensure fairness.[15] They had the authority to reinstate 'good dogs' beaten in early rounds and

Figure 11.3 John Henry Salter stalking game birds with his favourite dogs

eliminate dogs with 'no merit'. At the same time, Salter campaigned successfully for the results of field trials to be recorded in
the Kennel Club studbook. This signalled, at least formally, that
dogs that won at trials had equal status with those successful at
shows.

Salter continued to send his dogs to field trials and his kennels produced valuable gundogs, many sold to overseas buyers.[16]
Two of his Pointers, Mike and Romp, became the foundation
of gundogs in the United States. He was an occasional judge at
shows, including overseas, first in France and then regularly in
Russia. On these visits, he took the opportunity to go hunting and
returned with ever-larger game trophies. His house, already filled
with stuffed birds, was further furnished with a polar bear, two
wolves, an elk and a lynx. Salter donated a huge stuffed bear to the
Kennel Club, where it stood in the entrance hall for many years.
In 1899 he was elected vice-president of the Kennel Club in what
was a medical takeover, as the new chairman, Sidney Turner, was
also a general practitioner.

Alongside all his efforts in canine sport and politics, Salter built up his standing in the Essex elite. He hunted and dined with landowners and served on voluntary and state bodies. He was appointed a Justice of the Peace in 1888 and regularly sat at the local assizes. In the Freemasons, he accumulated offices, finally reaching the rank of Grand Deacon (Figure 11.4). In the new century, Salter maintained his busy daily schedule, first on the marshes, then in his surgery, followed by the garden and public service. Unsurprisingly, he was competitive with his plants, winning 1,400 prizes. In 1902, he produced a new blood-red alstroemeria (named after his wife), which won an award of merit from the Royal Horticultural Society. He registered his own variety of dessert apple, the D'Arcy Spice. In local affairs, he served as a Tory councillor, Poor Law Guardian, and on school boards. He was chairman of the Tolleshunt and Mersea Oyster Fishery, set up to restore the local beds. He lobbied to have swimming taught in schools to prepare boys for a life at sea.

In the Great War, he held the positions of major in the Essex Volunteer Force and Chief Special Constable for the north side of the Blackwater Estuary. He was responsible for evacuation in the event of a German invasion but had a plan to repulse 'the Hun'. He had acquired a Mauser gun from the Boer War and said he would use it to 'exact a severe penalty' on any invader. After the war, his many roles, and perhaps eccentricity, saw his local celebrity status hit new heights. He regularly featured in the local newspapers, advising on many topics. When interviewed about his prescription for a long and happy life, he recommended just two meals a day, breakfast and dinner, along with 'Hard work, and plenty of it'. Salter's judging was now confined to horticultural shows and the local assizes. He finally retired as a Justice of the Peace in his eighty-ninth year.

Salter died in April 1932, just short of his ninety-first birthday. There was a funeral service in the village church. Local dignitaries and Freemasons attended, and the local lanes were packed with

Figure 11.4 John Henry Salter in his Masonic robes

onlookers, many fourth-generation patients. One of his friends wrote as follows of his wake:

> I saw him lying in his coffin ... with two huge, gaunt, grey wolves sitting gazing glassily at the old hunter who had slain them more than thirty years before. So passed a man who epitomised all that is most admirable in the character of the English country gentleman.[17]

Salter had written a lengthy will and distributed his wealth widely. His estate was valued at £24,785 (£1.6 million in 2020). He was generous to his staff, leaving £3,500 (£238,000 in 2020) to his housekeeper and £1,000 (£68,000 in 2020) to his gardener; other members of staff, associates and local institutions all received monies.

In 1935 Margery Allingham, a crime writer and contemporary rival of Dorothy L. Sayers, moved into Salter's house. Her family had lived at Layer Breton, three miles from Tolleshunt D'Arcy, and Allingham's mother Emily (Em) was a friend of Salter. Indeed, she was said to have been besotted with him and, indicating how friendly they might have been, hoped he would leave his house to her. The house eventually came into the family when bought by Margery and her husband. D'Arcy House is one of the few in Britain with two blue plaques (honouring Salter and Allingham). In 1937, Allingham published her novel *Dancers in Mourning*, in which the character Dr Bouverie, an aged, 'eminent Victorian' and keen gardener, was based on Salter. In the story, the first impression of the doctor was that: 'His whole manner was truculent and highhanded to an extent which would have been ridiculous or merely rude had it not so obviously sprung from a lifetime of authority. As it was, he was frankly awe-inspiring, with a "God voice".'[18] Those who had dealings with Salter, from Essex villagers to sportsmen across Britain and Europe, would have recognised the character.

Chapter 12

Charles Cruft

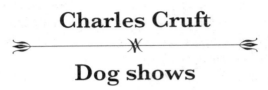

Dog shows

Charles Cruft transformed dog shows into mass entertainment and raised the public profile of conformation dog breeds. His promotional skills earned him the title of 'the British Barnum'. He was not a top hat, red coat, breeches, black-boot, whip-cracking ringmaster, but instead an innovative entrepreneur who produced spectacular and profitable events year after year. His motto was 'the show's the thing'. His Terrier shows were the first to be known by the promoter's name, and their enduring success led the Kennel Club to purchase the right to use the name. Cruft's entry into the doggy world was as the sales manager of Spratt's Patent, which he helped make the largest manufacturer of dog food in the world. Spratt's changed what and how all dogs were fed. Its Fibrine Dog Biscuit was a ready-made, all-in-one food, an alternative to feeding scraps and leftovers. Cruft peddled convenience foods for dogs well before they became a feature of the human diet in the modern Western world.

Charles Cruft was born in June 1852. His father was a gold-smith, wealthy enough to send his son to public school. Charles left Ardingly College, Sussex, at fourteen, to work for his father, but continued his education by taking an evening class at Birkbeck College, London. One day while walking through Holborn, he saw an advertisement for an office boy at Spratt's Patent. He fancied a change and went in. He was interviewed by James Spratt and was taken on immediately. A second office boy soon joined, releasing Cruft to become a travelling salesman. He targeted large kennels on country estates, hawking sacks of free samples around, enticing Masters of Hounds and stewards to bulk buy the company's products. After ten years and still only twenty-six years of age, he was appointed head of the business.[1]

James Spratt was an inventor-entrepreneur from Cincinnati, Ohio, who had travelled to England to sell his patent lightning conductors.[2] These were made of woven copper and zinc, and while effective in protecting buildings, they corroded readily in the British climate. Ever resourceful, Spratt came up with a new product – dog biscuits. The story told is that the idea had been with him since his arrival at Liverpool. He had seen sailors throw their unwanted hardtack on to the quayside to waiting dogs. Agricultural suppliers had long supplied cereal-based foods to estates with large kennels, but these had to be supplemented with stews and bones. Spratt's innovation was to add meat, creating an all-in-one biscuit for the omnivorous dog.

Spratt's biscuits had three unique selling points. First was the addition of meat, called 'fibrine'. They were marketed as 'Not Bread Alone, But Bread and Meat'. Fibrine, imported from the cattle yards of Chicago, was made from 'the dried, unsalted gelatinous parts' of carcases, rendered into fibres, dried and shipped in bales. Second, combining the meat with cereal gave the mixed diet that physiological science had shown to be essential for dogs. This 'health food' feature was underlined by the claim that the product was 'Patent', like popular medicines. To protect the 'Patent', Spratt's was regularly in court suing 'unprincipled tradesmen' who copied its product. Third, the biscuits were sold as convenience food: easy to handle, with a long shelf-life, that could be fed directly or made up with water, milk, stewed vegetables, fruits (dates were recommended) or meat broth. Every biscuit's trademark 'X' came from Cruft's marking of valued customers in his ledger, while another brand motif was a St Bernard, Cruft's preferred breed.

Initially, Spratt had contracted the manufacture of the product to a company that made sailors' biscuits. In time he built his own factory, with the capacity to create a range of other dried foods – for cats, poultry, horses and, unsurprisingly, hardtack for sailors. The growth of Spratt's Patent was phenomenal, but a more remarkable achievement was the creation of an entirely new industry. In its early years, Spratt's business model was that of an agricultural merchant who sold foodstuffs to farmers and large estates. This orientation was evident with the addition of game and poultry feed to its range, with products sold by the hundredweight (fifty kilograms). A second phase of growth saw the company's association with field sports and dog shows. It was with gundogs that Spratt's had its first success. In 1871, Britain's leading sporting newspaper, *The Field*, tested the biscuits with sporting dogs.[3] The investigation was prompted by letters from readers, perhaps encouraged by Cruft, recommending the brand. *The Field*'s editor, John Henry Walsh (Chapter 9), was sceptical but, ever committed to scientific trials, he agreed to experiments. He had been a doctor and author of a best-selling book on dog health and disease. Spratt's supplied biscuits with different amounts of fibrine (7, 10, 20 and 40 per cent) which were fed to dogs and their reaction assessed. The results showed value in the lower percentages: 10 per cent for Foxhounds and Greyhounds, which needed stamina, but just 7 per cent for gundogs, to avoid 'heated noses', which would affect their scenting. The higher meat content was not recommended for sporting dogs because it would be 'over-stimulating' and heat the blood.

Many sportsmen, like Walsh, were also supporters of the new conformation dog shows, and Cruft found another opening – feeding dogs at events. Ready-to-serve biscuits, available in bulk, were ideal for feeding hundreds of dogs that were being kept indoors for days. By providing complimentary samples, Spratt's gave exhibitors a free trial and provided Cruft with the opportunity to make contacts with the elite of the doggy world and other pet owners. The company also offered prize money and trophies. With a good record of supplying the big shows in London and Birmingham, Spratt's branched out to events far and wide. It added other services, notably the provision of exhibition benches and stalls. Cruft went further, taking over all aspects of the housekeeping, which was a challenge. Shows were an assault on the senses of smell and hearing, and were chaotic, with dogs fighting and escaping, and dangerous with dogs bitten or catching distemper. Almost every report in the sporting and canine press spoke highly of the order brought by Cruft.[4]

Spratt's exploited its work at shows. Marketing changed from using the small ads that covered the front pages of Victorian newspapers to whole-page presentations. The results of *The Field*'s feeding trials were prominently displayed, along with endorsements from leading figures in the canine world. By the mid-1870s, advertisements included recommendations from Charles Rotherham, the Queen's veterinary surgeon, C. H. Jackson, keeper of the royal kennels, Richard Lloyd Price (Chapter 10), a pioneer of gundog trials, and Sewallis Shirley (Chapter 20), the chairman of the Kennel Club. The company moved to a greater variety of products, with ingredients matched to different ages and breeds. Its puppy food had to be mixed with milk, while there were special mixtures for Toy dogs with delicate constitutions. The latter were promoted as healthy alternatives to pets being indulged with rich, fattening diets. Foods for different breeds were created, appropriate for their physiology and lifestyle. Non-food products followed. Spratt's Dog Soap promised to remove vermin in fur, while its pet medicine chests offered the opportunity for home dog-doctoring, guided by Spratt's do-it-yourself veterinary manuals, written by Gordon Stables (Chapter 15).

In 1878, Cruft took Spratt's services to France. He organised the feeding for the dog section of the Paris Universal Exhibition, at which the company's biscuits won medals. A factory in New York opened in 1885, five years after Spratt's death, and other overseas businesses followed. Having promoted the idea that the company could supply a special biscuit for every animal, it received unusual requests. For example, the Long Island Fishing Club asked if Spratt's made a biscuit for trout and salmon. The company did not, but soon invented one and added it to its range.[5]

Under new ownership after Spratt's death, the company continued with Cruft as general manager.[6] He had become a member of breed clubs and his profile amongst elite Doggy People led him to organise an event for Terriers only in March 1886. 'The First Great Show of All Kinds of Terriers' was successful (Figure 12.1). In all, 1,466 dogs from fourteen Terrier breeds were judged in fifty-seven classes. This event was a decisive moment for Terriers; it endorsed the proliferation in the number of breeds that had occurred since the arrival of dog shows.

The show's success encouraged Cruft to become an independent promoter. The Terrier show became an annual event, with ever more entries and additions to the competition classes judged.[7] In 1891, it was first promoted as 'Cruft's Dog Show'. No longer a terrier-only affair, it was for all breeds and was described as the 'most extraordinary show of dogs ever held'. Although the first under the Cruft's brand, it was promoted as his seventh by back-counting all the terrier shows.[8] A record 3,050 entries were judged in 500 classes that year, ensuring many winners.[9] The Queen, the Prince of Wales and other notables exhibited their dogs.[10] The report in *The Field* was sniffy: 'It is doubtful ... whether an exhibition of this kind is for the actual improvement of the dog, partaking as it does more of the public "showman" business than otherwise'.[11] At this time, the big shows were organised by the Kennel Club, allegedly for 'the improvement of the nation's dogs', or were local and breed club events. Cruft's was a private venture for profit, disparagingly termed 'a speculation'. The new owners of Spratt's Patent, worried about reputational damage, made it clear that Cruft was acting independently.

Figure 12.1 Winners at Cruft's First Great Show of All Kinds of Terriers, 1886

In the final decade of the nineteenth century, Cruft branched out into other shows.[12] He tried cat shows, but these attracted few entries and lost money. The organisers of agricultural and poultry shows employed Cruft to bring his brand of publicity and profit to their events. These excursions were short-lived, and Cruft concentrated on his dog shows. Income from just three days every February allowed him to leave Spratt's and enjoy a wealthy lifestyle for the rest of the year. In 1891, he lived with one servant and a lodger on Holloway Road in London; a decade later, he moved to Ashurst Lodge in Islington and had more staff.

Cruft's shows were known for their innovations. Every year, there seemed to be a new attraction at what was sometimes unfavourably called Cruft's Canine Carnival. He seemed to find a new exotic breed every year. In 1892 the show featured the biggest and smallest dogs in the world: a Tibetan Sheepdog and a two-and-a-half pound Yorkshire Terrier. The dogs of the British and foreign royalty were sought after as exhibits. Queen Victoria showed some of her Pomeranians, with mixed success. Still, the elegant Borzois of the Russian aristocracy were initially a draw for their elegant beauty but later they were accused of having spread distemper. Always looking to expand, Cruft multiplied further the number of classes to accommodate new breeds and put ever more silverware on offer. Sometimes he tried to bend Kennel Club rules, for example by introducing paid Club memberships that bought entry into exclusive classes and a greater chance of winning. Cruft usually gave in to Kennel Club objections but such wrangles did nothing for his reputation or that of his shows amongst leading fanciers.

It did not help either that he was unashamedly creative with entry counts. His inflation of the numbers at each show became a joke. He tallied the dogs entered rather than those that turned up, and when a competition for the best-stuffed dog was added, they too were counted. Frank Jackson sums up the position at the turn of the twentieth century:

Charles Cruft, while establishing a show which was, when measured by the test used by an unrepentant show and businessman, a success ... had failed to produce a show which commanded universal respect among exhibitors, or which could be regarded as a top-class exhibition of good quality dogs.[13]

After 1900 matters improved. When the annual January show in Liverpool was abandoned, Cruft's became the first big show of the year and attracted exhibitors who wanted an early test for their dogs. While relations with the leaders of the Kennel Club were never easy, the parties needed each other and always settled their differences. Cruft continued to cultivate aristocratic patronage, enjoying continued support from the Duchess of Newcastle (Chapter 4) and the Dukes of Beaufort and Portland and Sir Humphrey de Trafford. He remained a master of publicity. In 1905, appealing to nationalist sentiment, the show's staff dressed as 'Jack Tars' in sailor uniforms. Royalty still entered their dogs, and in 1905 Queen Mary's Borzoi Sandringham Moscow won first prize.[14] The following year, Cruft came up with an innovation that was meaningless to breed aficionados but won public attention – 'Best Champion'. It was unclear how justice could be done in comparing a large Mastiff with a tiny Terrier, but it made a brilliant climax to the event overall. The events continued to enjoy royal support, and in 1914 Queen Alexandra won with her Basset Hounds (Figure 12.2).

Cruft's shows continued through the First World War, with predictably declining entries, until halted by the threat of Zeppelin raids in 1918. They did not resume until 1921, when they struggled with restrictions on travel, as rabies had been reported in London. A major attraction was Earl Haig classes, reserved for the dogs of ex-service personnel. Anti-German feelings remained strong, and so Dachshunds were banned and the German Shepherd Dog was renamed the Alsatian Wolf Dog. In subsequent years the number of entries grew, and reached over 8,000 in 1925 and 9,777 in the following year, but the Depression meant that 10,000 was not

Plate 1 *Windsor Castle in Modern Times*, by Edwin Landseer, 1841–43. Queen Victoria, Prince Albert, Victoria, Princess Royal, pet dogs and shot game

Plate 2 An early dog show, Queen's Head Tavern, 1855. Jemmy Shaw is the standing figure

Plate 3 *The Hunting Parson*, by J. Loder, 1841

Plate 4 *The Connoisseurs: Portrait of the Artist with Two Dogs,* by Edwin Landseer, 1865

Plate 5 Richard Lloyd Price, 'Pointers', 1885

WITH **4** EXTRA PAGES.

THE

CANINE WORLD
AND

SPORTS AND SPORTSMEN.

Vol. II.—No. 39.   FRIDAY, FEB. 13, 1891.   REGISTERED AS A NEWSPAPER AND FOR TRANSMISSION ABROAD.   [PRICE TWOPENCE.

The Canine World and Sports & Sportsmen.

Mr. CHARLES CRUFT.

Plate 6 Charles Cruft, *Canine World and Sportsmen*, 13 February 1891

Plate 7 *The Boyhood of Raleigh*, by John Everett Millais, 1870. The young Everett, as Raleigh, is on the left, with his brother George on the right

Plate 8 Sewallis Evelyn Shirley

Figure 12.2 Queen Alexandra greeting her prizewinning Basset hounds at Cruft's, 1914. Dog biscuits were prominently advertised

reached until 1936. The Crash and the Great Depression affected numbers and quality in the intervening years. Cruft moved from royal to celebrity endorsement to maintain public interest, with personalities such as Amy Johnson hired to attract the press. Now innovations were fewer and there was a sense that shows had aged with their promoter.

Cruft reached eighty years of age in 1932 and increasingly delegated the show's running to his secretary, Miss Hardingham, and his wife, Emma. Their efforts ensured it continued to be run efficiently and receive favourable reviews. Cruft enjoyed his wealth and status. He divided his time between his large house in Islington and his country home, Windmill Farm at Coulsdon in Surrey.

Cruft died in September 1938. He left an estate of over £26,000, worth over £1.5 million in 2020. Confounding those who doubted that the show could go on, Emma Cruft organised one the following year, but nevertheless her age and the start of the Second World War raised questions about the show's future. Its profile and profitability meant that Emma Cruft was not without offers to buy the business, even in wartime. In 1942 she sold it to the Kennel Club, whose main show has been branded as Crufts ever since (the grammatically correct apostrophe was dropped in 1974).

Cruft's obituaries were complimentary, celebrating above all his showmanship and his understanding of dog fanciers and their needs. There was no mention of his knowledge of dogs. Cruft sometimes remarked that he preferred cats and, perhaps to provoke, claimed there had been no family dogs. In fact, he had kept St Bernards. His shows had changed the public profile of dogs in Britain. Their competition classes established distinct and discrete dog breeds, with competitions based on physical form deciding the top dog in each breed. It is appropriate, then, that one of Cruft's legacies is 'Best in Show', a spectacle that plays to the public rather than the true fancier.

Doctors and scientists

13. Delabere Blaine (1770–1845)   Dog doctors
    and William Youatt (1776–1847)
14. Charles Darwin (1809–1882)   Evolution and emotions
15. Gordon Stables (1837–1910)   Canine care and dog tales
16. Everett Millais (1856–1897)   Basset Hounds and breeding

The authors of the most popular books on dog health and disease in Victorian Britain were not veterinarians. Rather, they were doctors – Delabere Blaine, John Henry Walsh and Gordon Stables – and a clergyman – William Youatt. Veterinarians earned their living and status from treating horses, and those who treated pets were demeaned as 'dog doctors'. However, there was some basis for the transfer of knowledge from human to veterinary medicine. Before the adoption of guinea pigs and lab rats, dogs were widely used in medical training and research. They shared with humans the same mammalian physiology and their size made them easy to work with. Everett Millais took physiological methods from the laboratory to his kennel, experimenting with artificial insemination to show how the evils of inbreeding in pedigree dogs could be avoided. In psychology, too, it was common to work with dogs. Charles Darwin pointed to seemingly common emotional states and behaviours in dogs and humans as evidence of evolution from a common ancestor. Gordon Stables also wrote fiction, including dog-narrated stories, which told that dogs had the same feelings and thoughts as humans.

Chapter 13

Delabere Blaine and William Youatt

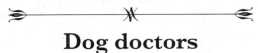

Dog doctors

Delabere Blaine and William Youatt became partners in London's leading canine veterinary practice in the early nineteenth century. Neither qualified as a veterinary surgeon. Blaine trained in medicine and Youatt for the clergy and were an unlikely partnership. Blaine was a flamboyant character who had been an army surgeon before he turned to veterinary medicine and acquired the wealth to retire to the life of a country squire. Youatt was a tragic figure, pious and melancholic, who, shamed by debt, committed suicide. Just off Oxford Street, their veterinary practice was unusual in treating dogs. They built a business that served the new fashion for keeping dogs as family pets, but also looked after sporting dogs kept in the capital. Both published ground-breaking books. Blaine and Youatt were certainly more expert than any qualified veterinary surgeon to be a 'dog doctor', the derogatory term used for their profession.

Delabere Blaine

Delabere Pritchett Blaine was born in London in 1770.[1] His father was a master baker in Moorfields. He was apprenticed to a surgeon-apothecary aged fourteen and qualified five years later, when he took a post at Borough Hospital. In his spare time, he pursued an interest in animal anatomy. This expertise gained him an ill-fated year at the London Veterinary College (LVC), which ended with dismissal after it was pointed out that he was making many errors in his lectures. Although without formal veterinary qualifications, he then ran a veterinary practice in Lewes in Sussex for a year. Needing a regular income, he returned to medicine, with a commission as a surgeon in the Horse Artillery, that conveniently allowed him to pursue human and equine studies. He then set up as a surgeon in Queen's Square in London, but gave this up after a year when he inherited 'a fortune'. Blaine retired to the life of a country gentleman, pursuing field sports and continuing his studies of animal anatomy. He was a spendthrift. The money ran out, forcing him to take further military appointments. But his career stalled, and he resigned, disgusted at favouritism in promotions. With enough saved, he took a year out, when he again devoted his time to field sports and, more significantly, completed a veterinary textbook – *The Outlines of the Veterinary Art* (1802).[2] He also published on the diseases of horses and dogs, a pamphlet on canine distemper and mange, and sold his own 'efficacious remedy'.[3]

The success of his books and medicines encouraged Blaine to start his own veterinary practice in London. His writings corrected many of the errors taught at the LVC, especially in anatomy, and covered animals other than the horse in greater detail than previous books. His reform-minded, entrepreneurial approach annoyed the veterinary establishment but brought financial success. At his premises in Argyll Street, off Oxford Street, he offered advice on the diseases and defects of horses and advised on buying and selling. Blaine also built up a practice for the pets of the rich, with a canine infirmary that offered patients 'commodious apartments for their reception, where they receive the most kind and judicious treatment'.[4] The range of patent medicines grew, with remedies for distemper, mange, worms and canker, along with purging balls. In 1817 his *Canine Pathology* was published, which set out a complete description of the diseases of dogs and an introduction to 'the moral qualities of the dog'.[5]

Blaine left the practice in 1818, when he retired to the country to enjoy writing and sports. He combined these two passions in the voluminous *Encyclopædia of Rural Sports*.[6] The publication was welcomed in the *Edinburgh Review* as 'a complete round or circle of sporting knowledge – a perfect manual for the amateur, who may turn to it with equal confidence, whether he wishes to learn how to train a fox-hound in England or to kill a giraffe in Africa'.[7] Blaine enjoyed over two decades of retirement, dying in 1845.

William Youatt

Youatt was born in Devon in 1776. He trained in Exeter to become a Nonconformist minister, then served at the Unitarian Hall in Baffins Lane, Chichester. It was there that he married Mary Payne in 1803. He moved to a new clerical post in London in 1810, but he abandoned the cloth to become Blaine's assistant just two years later. What led to this change is unknown, but both men believed that humans had a duty to avoid cruelty to domesticated animals and to promote the welfare of all God's creations (Figure 13.1).

Youatt learnt on the job, unable to study at the LVC because of his association with Blaine. He was a quick learner and they soon became partners in the business. Their work with dogs set them apart. Blaine once observed that 'my attention to the medical treatment of dogs subjected me to an imputation of want of common pride, and utter disrespect for my former character and habits'.[8] The partners advertised their services in newspapers, targeting 'every celebrated Sportsman'.

After Blaine's departure, Youatt continued to sell and distribute their medicines, but he now sought medical validation by advertising his premises as 3, Nassau-street, Middlesex Hospital – the medical hospital was on the same road. He added medicine chests to the range of products, designed 'for the convenience of gentlemen in the country, at some distance from a regular veterinarian'.

Figure 13.1 William Youatt

He developed his own brand of medicines for horses, ox and sheep, but was not good with money.[9]

Youatt attracted national attention in the late 1820s when he joined the controversy over how to deal with the new outbreak of rabies. Local authorities introduced compulsory muzzling and rounded up strays, while the public took their own measures, which often involved cruelty or summary slaughter. The Society for the Protection of Animals (SPCA) turned to veterinarians for advice on better ways to manage the problem. Edward Coleman at the LVC maintained that rabies arose spontaneously in dogs kept in filthy conditions, and control required destroying feral dogs and those owned by the poor. Youatt set out a more targeted, humane approach. He claimed that the disease never developed spontaneously – it always spread directly from bites. A meeting of the SPCA in 1825 was told that he had recently dealt with sixteen cases and that they were all in fighting Terriers. These dogs tended to have the 'furious' form of rabies and were ten times more likely to spread it than breeds which that took the milder, 'dumb' form. Youatt argued that the way to prevent rabies was to promote responsible ownership and ban dogfights. He told the meeting that these measures 'would also improve the moral habits of the lower classes, which are terribly debased and degraded by these brutal sports', which was met with applause.[10] His views were in step with the broader aims of the SPCA, which were as much about reforming the working class as protecting animals. The organisation did not campaign against the gentlemanly sports of fox and stag hunting, hare coursing and shooting. In the 1830s, Youatt became veterinarian to the SPCA, an appointment that reflected both his veterinary expertise and his principled stance on animal welfare.

Youatt set out his views on rabies and hydrophobia in a book published in 1830 – *On Canine Madness*.[11] The chapters had first appeared as articles in the *Veterinarian*, a journal he had founded in 1828. That journal was modelled on the *Lancet*, in that it combined campaigning for professional reform with the publication of new ideas and practices. As the its editor, he had become a leader of veterinary reform. One target was the LVC, where Coleman's continuing tenure as Principal was said to symbolise the backwardness of veterinary medicine in Britain. With all this going on, it is hard to see when he found time to work at Nassau Street. He also wrote chapters for *The Farmer's Series*, an encyclopaedia produced by the Society for the Diffusion of Useful Knowledge (SDUK). These chapters were expanded into books, also published by the SDUK: *The Horse* (1831), *Cattle* (1834) and *Sheep* (1837).[12]

Within Youatt's social circle was Isambard Kingdom Brunel, who contributed the chapter on draught (pulling) to *The Horse*.[13] Until the publication of *The Dog* in 1845, this book was Youatt's best-known work and regularly reprinted. Youatt also contributed to a popular farming manual, *The Complete Grazier; or Farmer and Cattle-Dealer's Assistant* (1833), becoming its editor for the revised seventh edition in 1839. The volume was published by the English Agricultural Society, later the Royal Agricultural Society, on whose committees he sat, demonstrating his connections with landed society. Youatt was an authority on breeding recognised by Charles Darwin (Chapter 14), who wrote: 'I have generally found Youatt an accurate man and a very sagacious one, for I knew him personally'.[14] They had met at London Zoo.

Youatt retained his elite connections, even though he suffered the shame of being declared bankrupt in 1832. He appeared regularly in court over the next three years to confirm payments to his creditors, and both his mental and physical health suffered. Friends helped by finding him new sources of income from publishing and his finances improved further with his appointment as veterinarian to London Zoo.[15] The role was a significant test of his expertise; the animals were exotic and unused to captivity, and they also had to acclimatise to English weather and suffered from staff inexperience. But the position presented Youatt with unrivalled material for comparative pathology and psychology.

He attributed many animal ailments to emotional states, as with jealousies amongst the lions. Combining his varied roles had always been difficult but it was even more challenging when he began to suffer from gout. The veterinary practice was increasingly run by his assistant, John Ainslie. The new partnership was advertised as Veterinary Surgeons and Shoeing Smiths, but they kept the canine infirmary, which treated 3,000–4,000 dogs each year.

In 1839, the SPCA announced a competition for the best essay on animal welfare. The Society had enjoyed success in changing public sentiment by exposing wanton cruelties; now, the principles for continuing and extending its work needed to be set out. Youatt entered and came third; most commentators said he should have won.[16] Published as *The Obligations of Humanity to Brutes, principally considered with reference to the Domesticated Animals*, the essay was popular and proved influential for many years.[17] The review in *The Times* described Youatt as 'a fearless advocate of humanity'.[18] Youatt's starting point was 'the spirit and doctrines of Christianity, and the duty of man as a rational and accountable creature'.[19] Drawing upon his clerical background, he cited the Bible to argue that humans had been made in God's image, and hence had delegated authority and responsibility for the remainder of His creation, most simply expressed as the injunction 'Love thy neighbour as thyself'. But dogs were more than neighbours – they were companions and friends. Youatt drew upon William Paley's *Natural Theology*, which argued that Nature showed God's design, to explain that everything under heaven had a purpose and that there was a harmony in nature for the 'greatest possible happiness'. This view was, of course, a long way from Darwin's then private understanding that struggle was a driving force of change in Nature, set out in the unpublished *Sketch* manuscript, which much modified and expanded, became *On the Origin of Species* (Chapter 14). Youatt did not shy away from discussing predation, disease and environmental changes but saw these as ultimately producing the greater good and harmony of nature, for example in controlling the prodigious reproductive potential of rats.

Youatt finally obtained a veterinary qualification in 1844. It was granted for his life's work when, Coleman having retired, the LVC became the Royal Veterinary College. The same year saw the creation of a professional body for veterinarians, the Royal College of Veterinary Surgeons. Youatt proposed the first toast at its first meeting. His grumpiness surprised his audience as he chose to be 'mixing … a little gall with the honey' in regretting the slow pace of reform.[20]

On dogs

Blaine began his book *Canine Pathology* with an extended essay on 'The moral qualities of the dog' (Figure 13.2). He argued that the different types of dog had come from one creation, which had been modified by human selection and the natural environment. Mental features had also been altered: 'By domestication, and cultivation, all the other admirable properties also observable in this animal, have been matured and brought to their present perfection'. Through anecdotes, Blaine elaborated on the five moral qualities of dogs: bravery, fidelity, attachment, gratitude and intelligence. Bravery came from dogs' natural ferocity, but aggression had been tempered by civilisation and, mostly, a dog's 'bark was worse than its bite'. On fidelity, Blaine told what was to become a familiar Victorian story of a tailor whose dog pined on his grave for years after his death. All dogs' moral qualities could be perverted, as was the case with dogfighting. Blaine contended that 'the contempt of pain, danger, and death, that characterise the bull-dog [was] altogether a cultivated property'.[21] Attachment was shown in dogs' general service to humankind, in many roles, and to individuals, where it followed from gratitude for care and companionship.

CANINE PATHOLOGY,

OR A
FULL DESCRIPTION
OF THE
DISEASES OF DOGS:
WITH THEIR
CAUSES, SYMPTOMS, AND MODE OF CURE:
Being the Whole of the Author's
Curative Practice,
DURING TWENTY YEARS' EXTENSIVE EXPERIENCE.
Interspersed with numerous
REMARKS ON THE GENERAL TREATMENT OF THESE ANIMALS;
AND PRECEDED BY AN
INTRODUCTORY CHAPTER
ON
The Moral Qualities of the Dog.

BY DELABERE BLAINE,
Veterinary Surgeon, and Professor of Animal Medicine in general.

P. XXXV   *Austin sc.*

London:
PRINTED FOR T. BOOSEY,
4, Broad Street, Exchange.
1817.

Figure 13.2 Title page of Delabere Blaine, *Canine Pathology, or a Full description of the diseases of dogs; with their causes, symptoms, and mode of cure … Preceded by an introductory chapter on the moral qualities of the dog* (London: T. Boosey, 1817)

On canine psychology and intelligence, Blaine wrote that humans could act by reason while animals relied on instinct. Yet, God's Providence had given dogs some reasoning faculty, which enhanced the possibilities of interactions and service to humans. Amongst the many examples of dogs' intellect was herding livestock without instruction, saving lives (rescuing people from fire or drowning) and learning to perform tricks. Finally, Blaine suggested that dogs had a 'sixth sense', mostly evident 'whereby a dog, removed to a distance, is enabled to return alone, although the intervening portions of the distance are utterly unknown to him, and that, in such return, it is evident he can neither be assisted by seeing, hearing, smelling or recollection'.[22] A striking example was a dog lost in France that allegedly found its way home to England.

Youatt also saw the dog as 'perfect in its kind', with unique faculties, instincts and propensities suited to its own being and role of human servant and companion. The term used for training dogs (and other domesticated animals) was 'breaking', which told of overcoming their instincts and spirit. He argued that the physical cruelties of dogfighting, the emotional harm of dog stealing, and the cruelty of dog carts brought 'moral degradation' to the perpetrators, as well as harm to dogs. He had no time for the physical remodelling of dogs. They were best left in their natural state and not 'improved' by cropping ears, docking tails, worming tongues or removing dewclaws.[23]

In 1845, Youatt added a fourth book to his SDUK series, *The Dog* (Figure 13.3). Whatever the populist aims of the Society, it was unaffordable for even the skilled working class. The expected buyer was likely to be amongst the wealthy and upper middle class, as is indicated by the section on the design of kennels for a hunting pack and the inclusion of the Rules of Coursing drawn up by 'Noblemen and Gentlemen'. The first third of the book was on the varieties of dogs and the remainder was on dog diseases and how owners without access to a veterinary surgeon might treat common conditions. Youatt began by stressing that the dog was a

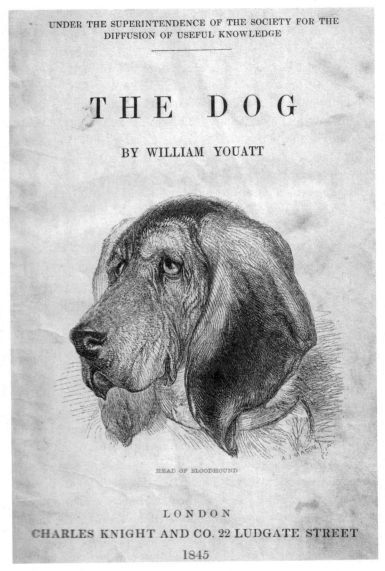

UNDER THE SUPERINTENDENCE OF THE SOCIETY FOR THE
DIFFUSION OF USEFUL KNOWLEDGE

THE DOG

BY WILLIAM YOUATT

HEAD OF BLOODHOUND

LONDON

CHARLES KNIGHT AND CO. 22 LUDGATE STREET

1845

Figure 13.3 Title page of William Youatt, *The Dog* (London: Charles
Knight and Co., 1845)

special animal, 'next to the human being, [it] ranks highest on the scale of intelligence and was designed to be the companion and friend of man'.[24] Typical of the era, he took the Genesis story as metaphorical. He saw that the variations in form and behaviour result from climate, food and crossbreeding. The Bible was also his authority for sheep being the first domesticated animal, kept by Adam's and Eve's son Abel. God had designed dogs to be adaptable and capable to be valuable assistants and friendly companions to humans, which Christian societies had taken advantage of most. Different types of dog were, then, a mark of civilisation.

Youatt divided dogs into three classes, defined principally by the shape of the skull and size of the brain, which determined intelligence and sensitivity. The Greyhound was typical of the first class, which had elongated heads and small brains. That group also included wild dogs and Wolfhounds. The second class had shorter muzzles and bigger brains, which gave them greater intelligence and scenting ability. These were Youatt's favourites, the most 'pleasing and valuable' dogs, and included gun dogs, sheepdogs, hounds and Newfoundlands. The third class had short muzzles and small brains, making them 'inferior or brutal'. Bulldogs, Terriers and Mastiffs were the main breeds.

Youatt's descriptions of the symptoms and nature of diseases were modern, focusing on localised changes in specific tissues. His treatments were humoral, involving the rebalancing the body's fluids. He detailed the signs and symptoms of different conditions, and illustrated these with stories of cases he had treated. Distemper was left till last – 'a sadly fatal disease ... [that] destroys fully one-third of the canine race'.[25] He demanded humane action – putting the dog down. 'As soon, however, as the spasms spread over him, accompanied by a moaning that increases to a cry, humanity demands that we put an end to that which we cannot cure'.[26]

Reviews suggested that *The Dog* was destined to repeat the success of his earlier books for the SDUK. As before, he 'equally entertained and instructed the most ardent sportsman and the most unsophisticated of "general readers"'.[27] Its format became a model for similar books, most notably the influential *Dog in Health and Disease* by John Henry Walsh (Chapter 9), first published in 1859, which ran to three further editions.

Two years after publication of *The Dog*, Youatt 'committed suicide under ... melancholy circumstances'. He felt disgraced with 'losses from unfortunate speculations' and could see no way of meeting his debts. The whole situation seemed so out of character that the inquest decided that he was 'in an unsound state of mind at the time of his death'.[28] He was remembered as a 'celebrated veterinarian' and as championing humane attitudes to animals. The *New Sporting Magazine* concluded its obituary by observing: 'To his friends, associates, and fellow men his loss can hardly be greater than that to the whole brute creation, who had, in his life, the most zealous of advocates and humane of masters'.[29] His name lived on in the many reprint editions of his books and in the many ways he had changed veterinary practice, not least in making small-animal practice more respectable.[30]

Chapter 14

Charles Darwin

Evolution and emotions

Charles Darwin (Figure 14.1) discussed the evolution of dogs in the first main chapter of *On the Origin of Species* (1859). He gave the different types of domesticated dogs as an example of 'artificial selection', that is, selective breeding to produce desirable traits in animals and plants for human needs. He aimed to persuade readers that, if humans could produce such variety in dogs, as seen in the difference between the Great Dane and the Pug, in just thousands of years, the greater powers of 'natural selection' could do much more over many millions of years.[1] He continued to be interested in artificial selection in his subsequent books, notably the two-volume *The Variation of Animals and Plants Under Domestication* published in 1868.[2] The first chapter of that book was entitled 'Domestic dogs and cats'.[3] Another important and perhaps surprising discussion of dogs came later, in *The Descent of Man* (1871).[4] He used evidence of similar behaviours and emotions in humans and dogs to show they were related by evolutionary descent. Humans' nearest evolutionary relations, the apes, were good candidates for this argument in terms of anatomy, but less so with behaviour and intelligence. Victorians knew them as wild, sometimes comic and impossible to train. Relations with dogs were different: they were reciprocal and cooperative, seen in working together, developing understandings and possibly reading each other's minds. Darwin's pet dogs – Nina, Spark,

Charles Darwin

Figure 14.1 Charles Robert Darwin, 1865

Pincher, Shelah, Polly, Snow, Dash, Bob and Bran – were a key resource in this thinking.[5]

Charles Darwin was born in February 1809 in Shrewsbury into a wealthy, upper-middle-class family.[6] His grandfathers were Erasmus Darwin, a doctor and poet, and Josiah Wedgwood, the pottery manufacturer. He attended Shrewsbury School and spent most of his spare time on country pursuits. So keen was the young Darwin on hunting that his father had warned him, 'You care for nothing but shooting, dogs, and rat-catching, and you will be a disgrace to yourself and all your family'.[7] As in most homes of people of their class, the Darwins kept many dogs, and Charles had a particular liking for his brother's Fox Terrier, Spark. An indication of how the family regarded its pets, Darwin's sister Elizabeth refers to Spark in letters to her brother as his 'nephew'.

Darwin's father hoped that Charles and his brother Erasmus would follow him into medicine and both went to medical school in Edinburgh. The course was not to Charles's liking and he devoted more time to natural history. He abandoned the course after two years and, in 1828, enrolled at Cambridge intending to become a clergyman, but, as at Edinburgh, his passion for nature took over. He befriended the leading naturalist John Henslow, who helped him, after graduation, to secure the post of naturalist and companion to the ship's captain on the round-the-world voyage of *The Beagle*.

The Royal Navy sailing ship set out in December 1831 on an expedition that lasted five years.[8] The primary purpose was to make geophysical measurements to aid map-making and navigation for British shipping. The route planned went down the Atlantic to South America, around Cape Horn and then across the Pacific Ocean. The ship called at many islands, went on to New Zealand and Australia, across the India Ocean to Capetown, and finally north back to England. Darwin collected rocks, plants and animals, which he shipped home at ports of call. He made detailed notes on his specimens and the peoples he met. Throughout the journey he had poor health. He was prone to seasickness and may have caught a tropical disease. He returned to Britain determined to pursue a career as a naturalist, and to take advantage of the new institutions and networks of science developing in London.

In 1838 he married his cousin Emma Wedgwood. They had a good income from the wealth on both sides of the marriage, and this enabled Darwin to pursue his desired career. They lived in central London before moving to Down in Kent in 1842. Darwin became a pillar of the local community and Justice of the Peace.[9] In the early 1840s, Darwin had a *Sketch* of a theory of evolution, then termed 'the transmutation of species'. A key question was, how is it that plants and animals are so well suited to their environment? He sought an explanation other than in God's design. His answer as that the forces of nature, particularly hereditary variation and competition for resources, 'selected' those animals and plants best suited to an environment, and in suitable conditions these flourished as new species – through survival of the fittest.

The idea of the selection of variants best suited to a particular environment suggested the analogy with the human selection of domesticated animals. Dogs were exemplars and none more so than the Greyhound. Firstly, selective breeding had made them a distinct type, which bred true, or when crossed with other breeds showed dominance and hereditary power. Second, physical form in Greyhounds showed adaptation to sighting, chasing and catching fleet-footed hares.[10] As with other working dogs, a specific form had been selected to suit their function. In the *Sketch*, Darwin portrayed nature not as a world of blind forces, where outcomes were contingent on circumstances, which was his later argument in *On the Origin of Species*, but as a 'force' with the agency to fit animals to environments and tasks. Darwin had speculated on the action of the 'force' with dogs in his notebook:

> if a being infinitely more sagacious than man (not an omniscient creator) during thousands and thousands of years were to select all the variations which tended towards certain ends, for instance, if he foresaw a canine animal would be better off, owing to the country producing more hares, if he were longer legged and keener sight – greyhound produced.[11]

The *Sketch* was not published. Darwin felt it was underdeveloped and he moved to other publications, on geology and coral reefs. Between 1842 and 1856, he settled into the life of investigator, correspondent, writer and local worthy. His family grew; there were ten children, but three died in childhood. He himself endured chronic illnesses and regularly visited health resorts.

In the mid-1850s, he returned to the *Sketch* and the 'transmutation of species' with a plan to write a big book entitled *Natural Selection*. A key task was to answer the weaknesses in his earlier *Sketch*, notably how new features emerged and exactly how advantageous ones survived to give new species. He turned to poultry and pigeon breeding to answer the first question, joining fanciers at their club meetings.[12] Breeders' experience and his investigations showed that variations in physical form occurred continuously. If not a law of nature, variation was a constant force of the natural world. The skill of fanciers lay in selecting desirable features and breeding to keep them true generation after generation. But how did nature select? How did some features persist and others die out? The answer was twofold. First, *competition* for resources led the plants and animals best-suited (the fittest) to a particular environment to survive preferentially. Second, *separation of populations* and *geographical isolation* allowed the best-suited features to accumulate and survive in discrete populations.

Work on the big book progressed slowly because of illness. It stopped altogether in 1858 with news that Alfred Russell Wallace, a plant collector working in Borneo, had independently come up with a similar theory of evolution. While having scientific priority from his earlier *Sketch*, Darwin was magnanimous and agreed that he and Wallace should announce their ideas at the same meeting of the Linnaean Society in July 1858. His publishing plans changed. He started work on a shorter book that would be accessible to the general reader. The result was published in November 1859 – *On the Origin of Species by Means of Natural Selection, or the Preservation of Favoured Races in the Struggle for Life*.

Two months before the publication of *On the Origin of Species*, what is now regarded as the first modern dog show was held, in Newcastle upon Tyne. Some writers have seen significance in the timing, because dog shows demonstrated the power of selection and led to the rapid 'evolution' of new dog breeds, where differences became so great that breeds looked like different species. But it was just a coincidence. Darwin's understanding of artificial selection went back years and derived, first and foremost, from poultry and pigeons, not dogs.

Darwin's view on the evolution of dogs was that 'they descended from several wild species', principally earlier types of wolf, hyena and jackal, with the variety of forms now seen produced by cross-breeding and selection. Most of his discussion was on behaviour, which Darwin termed 'domestic instincts'. Dogs were presented as an example of animals with inherited behavioural traits produced by selection.

> How strongly these domestic instincts, habits, and dispositions are inherited, and how curiously they become mingled, is well shown when different breeds of dogs are crossed. Thus, it is known that a cross with a bulldog has affected for many generations the courage and obstinacy of greyhounds; and a cross with a greyhound has given to a whole family of shepherd-dogs a tendency to hunt hares. These domestic instincts, when thus tested by crossing, resemble natural instincts, which in a like manner become curiously blended together, and for a long period exhibit traces of the instincts of either parent: for example, Le Roy describes a dog, whose great-grandfather was a wolf, and this dog showed a trace of its wild parentage only in one way, by not coming in a straight line to his master when called.[13]

One possible implication of Darwin's theory was that, in time, the degree of behavioural, not just physical, variation between breeds could see them becoming different species.

On the Origin of Species was a sensation in science and society. Britain's scientific elite was well prepared and supported Darwin's overall argument, though they were not always happy with the details. The book prompted discussion of humankind's place in nature and nature's place in humankind.[14] There were debates on how Darwinism, as it became known, should or should not inform religion, ethics, morality, social issues and politics.[15] Darwin did not involve himself in the public discussions, leaving that to his supporters, most notably Thomas Henry Huxley, known as 'Darwin's Bulldog' for the tenacity of his defence of natural selection.

In 1868 Darwin published the two-volume *The Variation of Animals and Plants Under Domestication.*[16] It drew upon work not used in *On the Origin of Species.* Despite the title, it was principally an opportunity to elaborate on natural selection. He used the experience of plant and animal breeders to demonstrate the sheer abundance of variations generation by generation, and to suggest how the number and repetition of even tiny variations could accumulate into marked changes across a species. Darwin also addressed the question of inheritance: how favourable features were passed on from generation to generation and retained.

The first chapter was on dogs and cats. It asked again 'whether the numerous domesticated varieties of the dog have descended from a single wild species or from several'.[17] He reviewed the historical record but also drew upon contemporary publications on natural history and dogs. He concluded again that 'the balance of evidence is strongly in favour of the multiple origin of our dogs', though he said he might be persuaded of a single origin. But how old were the different types of domesticated dog? Various writers had suggested that Greyhounds, Mastiffs, Lapdogs and other types existed 4,000–5,000 years ago, but Darwin wrote, 'there is not sufficient evidence that any of these ancient dogs belonged to the same identical sub-varieties with our present dogs'.[18] Rather, Darwin pointed to the gradual changes wrought by human selection, witting and unwitting, to make dogs fit for different roles and climates.

> There can be no doubt that the fancy bulldogs of the present day, now that they are not used for bull-baiting, have become greatly reduced in size, without any express intention on the part of the breeder … . [T]he Newfoundland dog, which was certainly brought

into England from that country, but which has since been so much modified that, as several writers have observed, it does not now closely resemble any existing native dog in Newfoundland.[19]

Selection pressures could be quite specific; for example, the British Bulldog degenerated in the Indian climate.

Another companion volume to the *On the Origin of Species* was published in 1871 – *The Descent of Man*.[20] As the title suggests, Darwin addressed the much-debated question of humans' relation to the apes but, perhaps unexpectedly, the book had a lot to say about dogs. Why? He wanted to show that humans were not unique and that differences between humans and animals were of degree, not kind. There are examples throughout the book of anatomical features and mental attributes that humans share with a variety of animals. While adult humans and dogs are physically very different, they have a similar anatomical architecture, and the striking similarities in embryos is cited as evidence of common descent (Figure 14.2). For similarities with mental traits, Darwin drew upon his experiences with pets and scientific studies.[21] He pointed to common features such as moods, kindness, humour, imagination, abstract thought, morality and even religious-type thinking. The bonds created for work, sport and companionship with dogs, whether through instinct, training or emotional communication, allowed perhaps the reading of each other's minds.

The common emotions of humans and dogs were also evident in physical responses to threats:

> Terror acts in the same manner on them as on us, causing the muscles to tremble, the heart to palpitate, the sphincters to be relaxed, and the hair to stand on end. Suspicion, the offspring of fear, is eminently characteristic of most wild animals. Courage and timidity are extremely variable qualities in the individuals of the same species, as is plainly seen in our dogs. Some dogs and horses are ill-tempered and easily turn sulky; others are good-tempered; and these qualities are certainly inherited.[22]

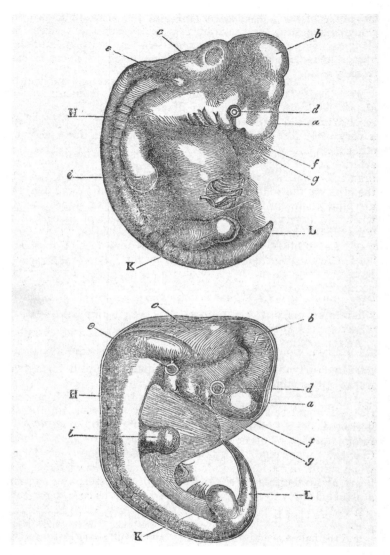

Figure 14.2 Upper figure, human embryo; lower figure, that of a dog, in Charles Darwin's *The Descent of Man* (London: John Murray, 1873), p. 15

In the second edition of *The Descent of Man*, Darwin added an example of a dog's sense of fun:

> Dogs show what may be fairly called a sense of humour, as distinct from mere play; if a bit of stick or other such object be thrown to one, he will often carry it away for a short distance; and then squatting down with it on the ground close before him, will wait until his master comes quite close to take it away. The dog will then seize it and rush away in triumph, repeating the same manoeuvre, and evidently enjoying the practical joke.[23]

While dogs learn to obey commands, there is no suggestion that they have any sense of language. Rather, individual dogs recognise the word-sounds of their master and perhaps meanings from different tones of voice.

Not content with emotions, humour and learning, Darwin went further, to explore the possible intellect of animals as the evolutionary root for the higher mental powers of humans. Observations of his own dogs convinced Darwin that they had dreams and, hence, the power of imagination.[24] What did dogs howl at in the night, if not imaginary things? And did this imply superstition and the possibility of abstract thought? Again, he drew on personal experience.

> When I say to my terrier, in an eager voice (and I have made the trial many times), 'Hi, hi, where is it?' she at once takes it as a sign that something is to be hunted and generally first looks quickly all around, and then rushes into the nearest thicket, to scent for any game, but finding nothing, she looks up into any neighbouring tree for a squirrel. Now do not these actions clearly shew that she had in her mind a general idea or concept that some animal is to be discovered and hunted?[25]

The ability to reason in 'lower' animals suggests the evolutionary root of reason in 'higher' animals.

Do dogs have a moral sense? Darwin suggested that he saw this in the behaviour of gundogs, in the tension between instinct and training.[26] The instinctual impulses to chase and bite conflict with their trained duties to obey and hold back, then return with game carried in a soft mouth. There were more profound questions. Do humans and dogs share a sense of right and wrong? Darwin can be read as suggesting that dogs have thoughts analogous to religious beliefs. First, they look upon their human masters as a God-like person, who has higher powers, which dogs depend upon, obey, revere, love and perhaps worship in their own way. Second, he supposed that dogs give spirit-like agency to strange phenomena.

> The tendency in savages to imagine that natural objects and agencies are animated by spiritual or living essences, is perhaps illustrated by a little fact which I once noticed: my dog, a full-grown and very sensible animal, was lying on the lawn during a hot and still day; but at a little distance a slight breeze occasionally moved an open parasol, which would have been wholly disregarded by the dog, had anyone stood near it. As it was, every time that the parasol slightly moved, the dog growled fiercely and barked. He must, I think, have reasoned to himself in a rapid and unconscious manner, that movement without any apparent cause indicated the presence of some strange living agent, and that no stranger had a right to be on his territory.[27]

Darwin speculated that in higher animals, 'The belief in spiritual agencies would easily pass into the belief in the existence of one or more gods'.

Dogs also appeared prominently in Darwin's *The Expression of the Emotions in Man and Animals*, published in 1872.[28] On *The Beagle*, Darwin had recorded the varied ways that different peoples in the places visited communicated their feelings. Back home, he continued to collect material on what he referred to as 'an old hobby horse'.[29] Ever the naturalist, Darwin's family, as well as his pets, provided evidence. In his children, he saw inherited, instinctual behaviours from human's evolutionary past that had been unchanged by a Victorian upbringing. Family pets allowed reflections on the differences between domesticated dogs and cats and the wild species he had seen on his travels.

Charles Darwin

Darwin suggests that many commonly observed dog behaviours can be read as preparations for 'serviceable actions', that is, those aiding survival. First, he considered responses to threats, where there were some quite human-like examples:

> When a dog approaches a strange dog or man in a savage or hostile frame of mind he walks upright and very stiffly; his head is slightly raised, or not much lowered; the tail is held erect and quite rigid; the hairs bristle, especially along the neck and back; the pricked ears are directed forwards, and the eyes have a fixed stare.[30]

The stance was illustrated by drawings of dogs with the appropriate facial expressions (Figure 14.3).

Yet, if aggression ceased and the dog found itself approaching, say, its master, the opposite behaviour (friendliness) would be seen:

> Instead of walking upright, the body sinks downwards or even crouches, and is thrown into flexuous movements; his tail, instead of being held stiff and upright, is lowered and wagged from side to side; his hair instantly becomes smooth; his ears are depressed and drawn backwards, but not closely to the head; and his lips hang

Figure 14.3 Dog approaching another dog with hostile intentions, by Mr. Riviere, in Charles Darwin's *The Expression of the Emotions in Man and Animals* (London: John Murray, 1873), p. 52

loosely. From the drawing back of the ears, the eyelids become elongated, and the eyes no longer appear round and staring. It should be added that the animal is at such times in an excited condition from joy; and nerve-force will be generated in excess, which naturally leads to action of some kind.[31]

Again, there were illustrations (Figures 14.4 and 14.5). Darwin wrote that in a drawing it was 'not a little difficult to represent affection in a dog, whilst caressing his master and wagging his tail, as the essence of the expression lies in the continuous flexuous movements'.[32] Dogs also showed affection by rubbing their bodies and licking, which Darwin saw as having their roots in the maternal love of their infant, and were again humanlike.

Indeed, a dog was able to 'express love and humility by external signs … when with drooping ears, hanging lips, flexuous body, and wagging tail, he meets his beloved master'.

Darwin's dogs also showed enjoyment and disappointment. At the end of a daily walk, he wrote that one of his pets 'showed his pleasure by trotting gravely before me with high steps, head

Figure 14.4 Dog in humble and affectionate frame of mind, by Mr. A. May, in Charles Darwin, *The Expression of the Emotions in Man and Animals* (London: John Murray, 1873), p. 53

Figure 14.5 The same caressing his master, by Mr A. May, in Charles Darwin, *The Expression of the Emotions in Man and Animals* (London: John Murray, 1873), p. 55

much raised, moderately erected ears, and tail carried aloft but not stiffly'.[33] But the dog did not like to stop, which Darwin often did, to look at his plant experiments. When Darwin turned toward the greenhouse, the dog adopted his sad 'hot-house face':

This consisted in the head drooping much, the whole body sinking a little and remaining motionless; the ears and tail falling suddenly down, but the tail was by no means wagged. With the falling of the ears and of his great chaps, the eyes became much changed in appearance, and I fancied that they looked less bright. His aspect was that of piteous, hopeless dejection; and it was, as I have said, laughable, as the cause was so slight.[34]

In these examples, Darwin expressed anthropomorphism, reading human-like feelings and emotions from his dog's demeanour and behaviour. The book on emotions was Darwin's last on animals; his subsequent publications were on plants. Nevertheless, in 1874 he was drawn into the controversy over vivisection, prompted by an experiment on a dog at the meeting of the British Medical Association in 1874. He gave evidence to the Royal Commission on Vivisection and made two points: first, 'I am fully convinced that physiology can progress only by the aid of experiments on living animals'; and second, that 'such experiments should be carried out under anaesthetic and without inflicting any pain'.[35]

Darwin died in April 1882. The family expected him to be buried at the local church in Down. A campaign by leading scientists led to his interment in Westminster Abbey, close to Isaac Newton. His work had changed biology and, for the wider public, it had transformed views of humans' place in nature and of human nature. Comparisons between humans and dogs were crucial in the presentation of his ideas on physical and mental evolution to his scientific peers and the public.

Chapter 15

Gordon Stables

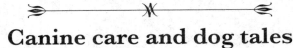

Canine care and dog tales

Gordon Stables qualified in medicine and adapted his expertise to produce do-it-yourself dog healthcare manuals for elite and popular audiences (Figure 15.1). At the same time, he was a prolific author, writing hundreds of boys' and girls' adventure novels and animal-narrated stories. In *Sable and White*, he told the story of a dog who had suffered at the hands of heartless owners and described the cruelties of dog shows.[1] These publications contributed to his public support for canine welfare, although privately he did not spare the rod with his pets. There was almost no subject on which he would not take up his pen. He was a proud Scot, often seen in full Highland dress, and curling was his favourite sport. In the twenty-first century, Stables has been recognised as the inventor of the touring caravan, an achievement that was celebrated in 2005, on the centenary of the Caravan Club.

William Gordon Stables was born in May 1837 in Aberchirder, Banffshire. He went to Aberdeen Grammar School before enrolling at Aberdeen University to read arts. He changed to medicine and graduated eight years later. It was common for local medical students to take holiday jobs as surgeons on the whaling ships that hunted off Greenland. Stables made two such voyages. Another Scottish medical student, who also switched to writing, did the same two decades later – Arthur Conan Doyle.[2]

Doggy people

Figure 15.1 Gordon Stables

Stables served in the Royal Navy as an assistant surgeon for eight years from 1862. He published an account of his experiences in his first book – *Medical Life in the Navy*.[3] The narrative is in a jaunty style that anticipates his adventure stories. Stables had decided views on three navy practices: compulsory shaving, flogging and pay. He maintained that the prohibition on moustaches led men to prefer the army and made sailors look effeminate. He asked: 'What sort of guys would the razor make of Count Bismark [*sic*], Dickens, the Sultan of Turkey, or Anthony Trollope? Shave

Tennyson, and you may put him in petticoats as soon as you please.'[4] Stables was invalided out of the service, on half pension, because he suffered from rheumatic and jungle fever.

Two years were then spent in the merchant marine, in which he claimed to have sailed twice around the world. These were lost years. He suffered melancholia and became addicted to the sedative chloral hydrate.[5] He recovered, gave up medicine and started a new career as an author and journalist. In 1874 he married Lizzie McCormack in Bristol. They settled in a house, later called The Jungle, at Ruscombe, near Twyford, in Berkshire.

How did Stables maintain his prodigious output over so many years? He wrote in a summerhouse called the Wig Wam and told a reporter of a typical day.

> He usually writes 20 folios of foolscap a day, with about 300 words on a folio. Possessed of an iron constitution, no fire is ever found in his bedroom or dressing-rooms. Usually, he begins work at seven o'clock in the morning, thinking out plans for his chapters for the day. After so engaging himself for a short time, he plunges into a cold bath, has a quick breakfast, and commences work at eight o'clock, continuing straightway till half-past one, when he partakes of dinner with Mrs. Stables and his six children, the eldest of whom, a son, is 18 years of age, and the youngest, a daughter, three. The doctor continues his old habit, acquired at sea, of sleeping after dinner, usually till about half-past four. He then has tea by himself in his study, after which he continues work till 10 or 11, and even at that hour he says is far from tired, and often reads in bed till 12.[6]

His encyclopaedic knowledge came from being a keen naturalist as a child, studying both the arts and the sciences at university, his experiences travelling around the world, a memory for facts and stories, strong opinions and a clear moral compass.

His first animal advice books were on cats and dogs. He wrote quickly, completing two books on each in two years.[7] The dog publications were on rabies and a guide to keeping and breeding.[8] Stables had no veterinary qualifications, and his only experience was likely to have been treating ships' pets and the exotic animals sailors brought on board: snakes, mongooses, lizards, monkeys, deer and birds.[9] At home, he would have administered to his pets, of which there were many.[10] There were opportunities for doctors in small-animal work, because veterinarians shunned work on pets – their professional identity was first and foremost with horses.

Stables's books on dogs were not well received.[11] He maintained rabies was caused mainly by infection but stuck to the discredited idea that it could arise spontaneously if dogs were ill-treated. He suggested that rabies most likely arose and spread among strays and street dogs, which had too much freedom to fight and lived in filth and feral packs. Well-bred, well-cared-for dogs from good homes were no danger. Going against official public health advice, he contended that confined and muzzled dogs would become agitated and aggressive, possibly leading them to become rabid.

One review of his book *The Practical Kennel Guide* did not start well.[12] It suggested that 'Dr Stables is evidently unfitted for the task which he handles with such flippancy and unbounded egotism'. Much of the material presented, over 200 pages, was described as 'superficial', the illustrations mostly 'indifferent' and his advice on kennel hygiene 'dangerous'. The book also prompted a letter to *The Country* about its description of the Gordon Terrier as 'an old man's dog'.[13] The angry correspondent accused Stables of being a 'theoretical writer' and hoped that 'If ever the doctor's book comes to a second edition, he will correct many of the blunders with which it is crammed and confine himself to facts, avoiding all his usual fancy flights which generally end in a "downer"'. Neither veterinarians nor dog aficionados thought well of his books, though this seems not to have damaged sales. Perhaps it was his fluency with the pen, alongside success at dog shows with his Newfoundlands, that saw him appointed kennel editor of the *Live Stock Journal*.

Stables's style was evident in his next dog book – *Ladies' Dogs, As Companions, Also a guide to their management in health and disease; with many stories, humorous and pathetic painted from the life*.[14] In one sense, the title says it all: fact and fiction, advice and anecdote, and hope and anguish. The early chapters are on Toy dogs and are in two parts: a description of the breed and then anecdotes, in some of which the thoughts and feelings of dogs are given in reported speech. The stories typically include episodes of sadness when the dog has been abandoned, for instance after their owner is lost at sea. Stables argued that women should not confine themselves to small breeds. Indeed, he recommended the largest of all dogs, the St Bernard, and his favourite, the Newfoundland. He had a special place for the Highland Collie and the Scotch Terrier. The story of his own Scotch Terrier Wagga-Wagga, ironically so named because he lacked a tail, reveals how he 'trained' his dogs:

> The prevailing disposition of Wagga-Wagga's mind is that of morosity, combined with bad temper. There is nothing on four legs that he won't fly at, and nothing on two either; so, instead of spending the day in the garden, he spends it out on the highway fighting with the school children or attacking other dogs. From these latter he gets, on average, three thrashings a day.[15]

He blamed the absence of a tail for Wagg-Wagga's disposition, which was allegedly changed when a squirrel's tail was fixed on to him with wire.[16]

Stables was invited to write on canine medicine and surgery for Vero Shaw's influential and authoritative *The Illustrated Book of the Dog*, published in 1881.[17] This volume competed for sales against John Henry Walsh's *The Dog in Health and Disease* (Chapter 11), and its veterinary sections were quite different. Walsh was more practical, while Stables was, surprisingly, more academic, with chapters set out as if in a veterinary medicine textbook.[18] He gave practical advice in two popular booklets: *The Common Sense of Dog Doctoring* and *The Dog: From Puppyhood to Age*. Both were sold cheaply through the offices of the dog food manufacturer Spratt's Patent Limited.

Despite its poor reviews, *The Practical Kennel Guide* sold well and was reprinted in 1883 and 1887. Another advice book, *Our Friend the Dog*, did even better, running to eight editions.[19] It had begun as a series in the *People's Friend*, a weekly magazine of stories and features that aimed to 'promote self-improvement and studious, sober habits'. Never modest, Stables said the book was 'the most complete that has ever been written on the canine race, [with] full instructions how to treat dogs properly in health and during sickness, with hints as to the most successful method of breeding them for pleasure, show or profit'.[20] He also offered advice in his journalism. In 1881, he published a series of articles on 'Boys' dogs and all about them' in the *Boy's Own Paper*, covering hounds, gundogs and other masculine breeds.[21] He wrote further columns on how to train and tame dogs. The series expanded to other pets: rats, ferrets, canaries and monkeys; and on poultry in 'Doings for boys' and 'Advice to growing lads'. In the *Girl's Own Paper*, he recommended different pets – cats and birds; in the same publication, writing as Medicus, he advised on female health and beauty.[22]

His adventure stories for boys began in 1877 with *Jungle, Peak and Plain: A Boy's Book of Adventure, etc.*, followed by *Wild Adventures in Wild Places* four years later.[23] Both were copiously illustrated and based on Stables's travels, albeit with great imaginative licence. They featured a young Scottish boy's exploits across the world, beginning in the Arctic, then on to Africa and the American West.[24] His first long serial story, told over eleven weeks, was an Arctic saga, 'The cruise of the Snowbird' (1881), published the following year as a book.[25]

Over the next two decades, Stables published nearly 100 novels. They were mostly set in his own time, though he ventured into earlier centuries and then into the future. Storylines tended to meander, with diversionary anecdotes and heroes rapidly moving from one side of the world to the other. Many stories featured wars, with heroes fighting with Nelson at Trafalgar, and action in the Crimean War, Indian Mutiny, American Civil War and Boer War.[26]

In 1884 he published his first animal-narrated stories in *Aileen Aroon*, a collection in which some chapters are about his favourite animal friends, including cats and birds, and some are told by them.[27] A decade later came his best-known book in the genre, *Sable and White*.

The hero was Luath, a Collie, who told of his many adventures and many owners, most of whom were kind, but some not so. The central theme was a canine view of dog shows. Luath found small local shows in the open air were fine, but conditions at the large indoor shows posed a danger to health. A positive aspect of shows was the opportunity to socialise and make friends, as Luath did with Professor Huxley, a large Mastiff (Figure 15.2). The canine Huxley was the alter ego of Thomas Henry Huxley, the leading promoter of Charles Darwin's theory of natural selection and a supporter of vivisection. Stables made Huxley the voice of his own views against both vivisection and the rabies vaccine. The brave Mastiff told of his torture by physiologists: 'We would be tied to a bench or stool and cut to pieces alive, and all for the supposed benefit of that proud biped the microbe man'. The 'microbe man' was a none too subtle reference to Louis Pasteur.[28]

In 1886, Stables published an adventure book of a different type. It was autobiographical and recorded his 1,300-mile journey from Twyford to Inverness in a horse-drawn caravan, or, as he termed it, his land-yacht – The Wanderer (Figure 15.3).[29] He claimed to have always been a gypsy at heart; now his wealth had enabled him to live out the dream in a purpose-built, servant-attended vehicle as a 'Gentleman Gypsy'. The two-ton vehicle was built in Bristol by a railway carriage manufacturer, with a mahogany-panelled, Pullman car-like interior. In 1892 he published a travelogue of another tour on which he took his family. They were accompanied by his groom, his valet Mr Wells (who played the fiddle at entertainment evenings Stables organised along the way) and his St Bernard. He also took his tricycle.

The benefits of open-air and frugal living prompted a new genre for Stables, of books on health, though they were little informed

IN SEARCH OF A BULL-TERRIER.

Figure 15.2 Luath meets Professor Huxley, the Champion Mastiff

by his medical training. His first such book was *Tea: The Drink for Pleasure and Health*, though this was more about the brew's history and economic geography than its disease-preventive and curative properties. He then published *Rota Vitæ: The Cyclist's Guide to Health and Rational Enjoyment* (1886). It was similar to his caravanning book: a narrative of a tricycling holiday in north-east England and southern Scotland.[30]

Figure 15.3 The Wanderer ready for the road, 1892

In the 1900s, he took up a syndicated column, 'Health and home', in regional newspapers, in which he answered readers' queries.[31] By then in his sixties, his behaviour became increasingly eccentric, not due to age but to whisky. He may have obtained free samples from Robertson's Whisky, whose malt was sold with the endorsement: 'The Oldest, and Purest and Best. Gordon Stables, M.D., R.N.'[32]

In the 1970s, the social historian Patrick Dunae interviewed people who remembered Stables as the scourge of his village. One resident remembered:

> The lads in Ruscombe were terrified of him. Many years later, they remembered him as a cantankerous recluse who perpetually wore a kilt and sported a fearsome skean-dhu (a sheath knife about 6 inches long, traditionally worn in the right sock with the handle showing); who would emerge from the 'Wig-Wam' to berate delivery boys; who could be seen staggering out of the local pub, with a cockatoo perched on his shoulder, a vicious dog in one hand, and a naval cutlass in the other, bellowing at anyone that came in the way.

He lived alone in later life. His wife had moved out and he found it impossible to find staff.

Improbably, in his final years, he took a shine to another prolific novelist – Marie Connor Leighton. She was the wife of Robert Leighton, who also wrote boys' adventure stories and books on dogs. She had other suitors, including the well-known rival adventure story author G. A. Henty. She seems to have encouraged their attentions, while keeping them at arm's length under her spell. Claire Leighton wrote a biography of her mother in which Stables appears, thinly disguised, as Alexander, a 'wild creature'.

> He seemed to smell of mothballs mingled with a whiff of Scotch Whiskey [*sic*]. He always wore Highland kilts. He had two sets – winter weight and summer weight – and because the dark green of the Gordon clan didn't show the dirt, they were rarely cleaned … . He wore those kilts in the streets of London though sometimes when he was going to a fashionable gathering like the Eton or Harrow cricket match at Lords, he would compromise with custom by wearing a top hat as well. He never seemed to know how ridiculous he looked.[33]

Stables sent Leighton flowers and wrote her poems. One summer he took his caravan to Lowestoft, where the Leightons were on holiday, to deliver his gifts in person.

Stables died in May 1910 at home and was buried in the local church. His estate was valued at £6,108, over £500,000 in 2020. He left nothing to his wife and just £50 to Mrs Leighton to buy a memorial ring.

Chapter 16

Everett Millais

Basset Hounds and breeding

Everett Millais established the Basset Hound as a breed in Britain and sought to bring a more scientific approach to dog breeding and disease control (Figure 16.1). As the eldest child of the Victorian superstar John Everett Millais and his wife Effie Gray, he enjoyed wealth and privilege. He was the first person to exhibit a Basset Hound at a British dog show and a founder member of the Basset Hound Club. He undertook scientific work in three areas: artificial insemination; 'rational breeding' using Francis Galton's theories of heredity; and the microbiology of dog distemper. His experience and expertise gave him the confidence to campaign for the reform of the dog show fancy, which made him enemies with some members of the Kennel Club.

Everett Millais was born in May 1856 in Perthshire, Scotland. His father, John Everett Millais (1829–96), was a founder of the Pre-Raphaelite Brotherhood and one of the most famous painters of the day. His mother, Euphemia (Effie) Chalmers Ruskin, née Gray, was previously married to the leading social and cultural critic John Ruskin.[1] Her marriage to Ruskin was annulled as unconsummated. The breakup caused a minor scandal at the time and the reason for the marriage's failure has excited much speculation since.[2] Effie's marriage to Millais was happy and enduring.

Figure 16.1 Everett Millais, 1886

Consummation was never in doubt. Everett arrived within a year and seven more children followed.

Everett's childhood, when he was known as Evie, was split between London and Perthshire. Unacknowledged early fame came when he was a model for the young Sir Walter Raleigh in his father's much-loved and much-reproduced painting of the famous figure's boyhood (Plate 7). Seemingly more at home in Scotland, he showed a passion for natural history, especially collecting flowers and birds' eggs, and for shooting and fishing. He was a boarder at the lower school at Rugby when the head was Frederick Temple, a future Archbishop of Canterbury. He then attended Marlborough College. When he was fifteen, he visited Paris and was seriously ill with smallpox. He recovered, but the family thereafter regarded Evie as frail. His poor health did not stop them from sending him abroad again, to Hannover and Paris, to finish his education and acquire languages. He was earmarked for a career in the diplomatic service.

In France, he visited the de Bruene family in Etrepagny, Normandy, and was given a Basset Hound named Model (Figure 16.2). Millais developed a deep affection for the dog and thought the breed 'more beautiful than Dachs', his previous favourites. The breed's French name came from their 'low' stature. They hunted with their nose to the ground, and their acute sense of smell enabled them to follow scent trails, though slowly.

Figure 16.2 Everett Millais's Basset Hound Model, 1881

The encounter with Basset Hounds started a love affair, which led to Millais becoming influential in the late-Victorian dog shows and canine affairs.

Back home, Millais entered Model into dog shows and in 1875 won a prize at Wolverhampton in the 'Any other variety class', mostly dogs from overseas.[3] Other successes followed and made Model the obvious prototype for the breed standard.[4] This status put him in demand for stud duties, but there were few Basset Hounds to breed with. To get around this, Millais made a cross with a beagle, the British dog closest in size and 'look'. He then bought a bitch from the de Breunes, breeding with her to return to the correct Basset 'look'. Millais's kennel was soon producing dogs that he could sell and take to shows around the country. Bassets grew in popularity, being regarded as novel, charming and amusing due to their comical, short-legged walk. Fanciers, most notably Lord Onslow, took up the breed and numbers soon allowed them their own class at shows. Indeed, the 'improvements' made were said to have Anglicised the breed, and it was no longer 'foreign'.[5] Millais also claimed expertise on Dachshunds but saw these as unimproved, even degenerate. He wrote 'that 90 per cent of the Dachshunds now seen in this city [of London] are no more the pure Dachshund they are represented to be than those mongrels in Paris that have the audacity to sign themselves Bull-terrier'.[6]

Millais did not follow a diplomatic career. His language proficiency was too weak, and later plans for him to work at the Stock Exchange came to nothing because of his unreliability. Following his father, he tried his luck as a freelance artist. His forte was sculpting, especially wax modelling, and in 1876 he set up a studio in Lowestoft, later moving to Swaffham. Why did he leave London? Most likely, he was sent away because his heavy drinking was causing embarrassment to the family. His never robust health was a concern too. Matters did not improve, and soon Sir John wanted him 'out of the way'. Millais was sent to the colonies, hopefully to a remote station with no alcohol. He was away for four years.

Little is known about his exile, other than that he spent time in Australia and shot big game in India and Africa.

Millais returned in 1884, seemingly reformed. The following year he met his future wife, Mary, the daughter of William Hope-Vere, a Scottish landowner. They married in Pau in April 1886 and lived at Palace Gate in Kensington. Millais re-established a kennel for his dogs at Shepperton in Middlesex, where he often stayed over.[7] He was soon recognised again as the leading authority on Basset Hounds. He judged at shows and contributed to publications such as the *Stock Keeper and Fancier's Gazette* and *The Field*.

Basset Hounds from Millais's kennel won many prizes, and he made money selling puppies. His dogs also carried the imprimatur of being products of science, as he had published a book entitled *The Theory and Practice of Rational Breeding*, in which he made available to dog fanciers the latest thinking on inheritance.[8] He mostly used the ideas of Francis Galton and the assumption that each parent contributed, on average, one half of their heredity to their young.[9] Thus, breeders could follow the inheritance of a particular dog, generation by generation, as it contributed a half, then a quarter, an eighth, a sixteenth and so on, to subsequent litters.

Millais's attempts to improve the dogs in his kennel did not run smoothly; there was a particular problem with infertility. He was concerned that inbreeding had weakened Basset Hounds in Britain. They were still relatively few in number, and there was an understandable preference to breed from champions. One possibility was that dogs had weak sperm and it was not reaching bitches' eggs. To meet this problem, he experimented with artificial insemination, adapting methods used by Lazzaro Spallanzani, an Italian priest and natural philosopher of the eighteenth century. He collected semen from a dog and then used a syringe to inject it into the vagina of a bitch. He published the results of his 'experiments' under the pseudonym 'A dog breeder' in the *Veterinary Journal*.[10] He made nineteen further 'impregnations', which were discussed in a review paper on artificial insemination, submitted by Walter Heape, a leading Cambridge physiologist, to the Royal Society in 1897.[11] The article was read by Francis Galton, whose eugenic ideas, that there should be selective breeding to preserve good human 'stock', were becoming controversial.

The twelfth 'impregnation' became famous. A female Bloodhound, appropriately named Inoculation, was crossed with a Basset Hound. The height difference made artificial insemination necessary (Figure 16.3). In this experiment, his aim was to introduce new blood to remedy degeneration in bone, stamina, size and mental ability. One stimulus was that the Regius Professor of Medicine at Cambridge, Sir Clifford Allbutt, had returned a Basset Hound that he had acquired from Millais, saying it was a 'canine idiot'. At the time, 'mental deficiency' in humans was associated with 'close inter-marriage'.

Why did Millais not bring in 'new blood' from France? He regarded French Basset Hounds as inferior, unimproved in their

Figure 16.3 Inoculation and Nicholas. If the dogs had been presented the other way round, the need for artificial insemination would be obvious!

conformation and with impure blood. British Bloodhounds, on the other hand, had enjoyed years of improvement, while their size and strength would add what breeders called 'substance'. The outcross was also an opportunity to test Galton's theory of ancestral heredity, that is, to see whether the 'influence' of the Bloodhound halved generation by generation. After four generations, there would just be one-sixteenth heredity from Inoculation.

From each litter, Millais selected puppies nearest to the Basset Hound conformation standard and then mated these with true Basset Hounds. In just three generations, he had dogs with the correct 'look', that had also been strengthened internally and hereditarily by English blood. Millais argued that there was a lesson in the experiment, not just for Basset Hound breeders but for the whole dog fancy. No one need tolerate the evils of inbreeding, nor fear remedying it by out-crossing. He demonstrated that it was possible to return to the correct standard rapidly and without damaging the integrity of a breed; indeed, such out-crosses strengthened it.

Millais presented this work in a booklet entitled *Two Problems of Reproduction* in 1895.[12] His connections amongst London's scientific elite were evident when, in 1897, Francis Galton used his data on tricolour inheritance in a paper on the theory of ancestral heredity.[13] Galton is best-known for his writings on eugenics, which he defined as 'the science of improving stock', clearly referencing selective animal breeding. In its earliest versions, he explicitly advocated positive eugenics, though negative eugenics were implied. He proposed 'judicious mating ... to give the more suitable races or strains of blood a better chance of prevailing speedily over the less suitable than they otherwise would have had'. As early as 1865, he had speculated on what might later have been termed 'dog eugenics' to produce a dog with 'general intelligence' rather than specific abilities. It is rarely put in these terms, but the whole business of fancy dog breeding, then and now, used eugenic principles.[14]

Revealing another area of scientific expertise, in 1890 Millais published an article in the *British Medical Journal* entitled 'The pathogenic microbe of distemper in dogs, and its use for protective inoculation'.[15] He had no training or qualifications in microbiology, although he had taken courses in anatomy and physiology. The breakthrough was based on investigations made as a guest in Charles Sherrington's laboratory at St Thomas's Hospital.[16] Sherrington was a leading physiologist; indeed, he was awarded a Nobel Prize in 1920 for his work in neurophysiology.

Millais set out how he had identified the germ of the disease under the microscope, cultured it in test tubes and then produced a vaccine by weakening the bacterium by heat. None of these claims stood up. Scientists and veterinarians ignored them. The identity of the dog distemper germ was not confirmed until 1906, when it was shown to be a virus, not a bacterium. If Millais had actually identified the microbe and produced a vaccine, he would have joined the Pantheon of heroes of the Bacteriological Revolution, alongside Joseph Lister, Louis Pasteur and Robert Koch.

Millais's interest in medicine and science became public when he was announced as a founding member of the Society for the Prevention of Hydrophobia and the Reform of the Dog Laws (SPH).[17] It was led by Victor Horsley, a controversial scientist who was the main target of anti-vivisection activists. The Society was prompted by Pasteur's vaccine that prevented the development of hydrophobia in humans bitten by a rabid dog. The cure was a sensation and made front-page news. It created the notion of the 'medical breakthrough'.

In France, a new research laboratory for experimental medicine, the Institut Pasteur, was established to enable Pasteur and his associates to continue and extend their work to other diseases. The SPH had two aims: first, to build an Institut Pasteur in London to treat domestic dog-bite cases; and second, to introduce dog muzzling and other controls to stop rabies spreading. As animal lovers, many dog fanciers opposed vivisection and saw muzzling as cruel and counterproductive. Millais stood with the scientists. He spoke at SPH meetings and shared a platform with leading figures in medicine and science: Joseph Lister, Michael Foster and William Roscoe.[18] With these interests and his previous French connections, reports that Millais visited Pasteur in Paris to learn microbiology are plausible, though there is no evidence. In 1890, Millais was elected to the Physiological Society, nominated by Sherrington and George Romanes, who had been a friend of Charles Darwin (Chapter 14).

Millais passed his preclinical examinations in physiology and anatomy in 1893 and moved on to hospital training. In April 1896, he presented the case history of a hernia operation in a lecture by the surgeon William Anderson at St Thomas's Hospital. Artistic networks may still have been helpful to Millais's career, as Anderson was an expert on Japanese art and his collection was the basis of the British Museum's collection.

Although his distemper 'discoveries' were ignored by scientists, Millais claimed the role of the dog fancy's expert on distemper and campaigned for better control. He bemoaned arrangements at shows and regularly wrote in the doggy press, especially the Manchester-based *Our Dogs* magazine. Disappointed with the response of the Kennel Club, he very publicly resigned his membership. He cited a catalogue of faults at shows, including the cruelty of extended opening hours, poor hygiene and feeding, and failure to ban the cropping of ears and the docking of tails. His attacks on the Club became stronger. Well known for composing a paragraph when a sentence would do, he wrote long diatribes against the Club. He was particularly irate at the toll of suffering and deaths that distemper caught at dog shows was causing. He painted the Club's leadership as a self-serving, self-perpetuating clique. He wrote that they were a new class of gentlemen 'dog dealers' who had lost their way, becoming a bureaucracy for administering shows rather than an agency for improving the nation's dogs. That role had been taken over by specialist breed clubs, like the Basset Hound Club, which, while doing good work, were prone to have narrow interests and likely to produce unhealthy dogs with exaggerated features. Millais's trenchant comments won him friends amongst other critics of the Kennel Club. He enjoyed a good reputation with some in the dog-show rank and file, who admired his willingness to speak out.

He succeeded to the baronetcy created for his father in August 1896 but held it for just a year. Millais died suddenly at home in Shepperton in September 1897 from pneumonia after a chill from sitting in wet clothes. He was buried in Hanworth churchyard. Millais had described himself in *Who's Who* as a 'Traveller and Naturalist'. This label misrepresents his work and its importance. He introduced the Basset Hound to Britain and worked tirelessly for its improvement. As a gentleman scientist with eclectic interests, in an era when professionalisation and specialisation had become the norm, he brought science to the dog fancy and his ideas on breeding remained influential long after his death.

Campaigners and politicians

17. Mary Tealby (1801–1865)   Dogs' homes
18. Frances Power Cobbe (1822–1904)   Sentient creatures
19. John Cumming Macdona (1836–1907)   St Bernards
20. Sewallis Shirley (1844–1904)   The Kennel Club

Reform and improvement were common themes in Victorian Britain, pursued through voluntary actions and government legislation. In founding a home for stray and lost dogs, Mary Tealby extended the longstanding work of the RSPCA against animal cruelty, with the typical Victorian response of a welfare institution. Frances Power Cobbe's campaigning against experiments on live animals tested the limits of the RSPCA's appetite for reform, as she took on the medical profession and its supporters. She was a radical feminist who claimed a particular empathy with dogs' suffering. She wanted a complete ban on vivisection, but succeeded in achieving only its regulation. John Cumming Macdona brought the St Bernard breed to Britain and was a founder member of the Kennel Club, but his reforming ventures were in human affairs: for his parishioners early in his career when a clergyman and later on for his constituents when a Member of Parliament. Sewallis Shirley, who also served as an MP, was a reformer of a different type. He was an establishment figure whose mission was the improvement of dog shows, for which he led the creation of the Kennel Club. Their reforms were in part for the welfare of dogs, but mainly to improve the standing of the promoters, breeders, exhibitors and judges at shows, rescuing them from the taint of 'trade' and financial losses, and from accusations of cheating and bias.

Chapter 17

Mary Tealby

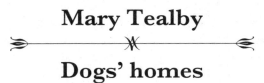

Dogs' homes

Mary Tealby founded the world's first dogs' home in Holloway, London, in 1861. The Temporary Home for Lost and Starving Dogs, now known simply as Battersea Dogs' Home, became a model for dog rescue homes across the country. It gave new expression and material form to the growing concern with animal welfare, first seen in the creation of the Society for the Protection of Cruelty to Animals in 1824 (and then its rise in status to Royal in 1840). With dogs, this new sensibility was expressed in the changing status of family pets and the emotional investment in man's and woman's best friend.[1] As in the different attitudes to the 'deserving' and 'undeserving' poor, the Home differentiated between valued pets, expected to be rehomed, and valueless curs; the latter were largely London's strays, and the Home took responsibility for disposing of them.

Mary Tealby was born Mary Bates in December 1801 in Huntingdon. Her father was a druggist and the family enjoyed moderate wealth. Typical of the time, money was spent on the education of the first son, her younger brother Edward. He went to Uppingham School and Clare College, Cambridge, where he read divinity. Tealby's education was modest, designed to prepare her for a good match. Aged twenty-eight, she married Robert Tealby, who worked in his father's timber-importing company in Hull. It is unclear how the couple met, but they settled in Hull, close to the docks area. The Tealby family had some notoriety. Robert's father's first marriage had been controversially annulled in 1812 on the grounds that his first wife, Mary, was underage when they had married twenty-eight years earlier. To add to the scandal, just three weeks after the annulment, Robert married again. His first wife kept her married name, so there were two Mary Tealbys in the town.

There is speculation that Mary Tealby, after her respectable small-town upbringing, found the Tealby family and the docks area rough and tough. Nonetheless, she stayed for over twenty years, until the mid-1850s. There were no children. Her departure was prompted by a call to look after her ailing mother, who was living in London. Her husband died in 1862 and left nothing in his will for his wife, suggesting they were estranged.

The origin of the Holloway dogs' home reportedly came from a chance encounter.[2] One day in 1860, Tealby visited her wealthy friend Mrs Sarah Major, whom she found in the kitchen looking after a sick, scrawny stray dog found abandoned in the street. Tealby took the dog home and tried to nurse it back to health, by giving it hot port wine every thirty minutes. But the dog died. Tealby decided to continue to care for distressed street dogs. Word spread of her work, and she was soon overwhelmed due to the number of strays and lost dogs on the streets of the capital.[3] The demand was such that she decided a dedicated site was needed for what she called a 'canine asylum'. At that time, 'asylums' were where 'lunatics' were kept and had a poor reputation, but Tealby used the word in its general sense of a benevolent institution affording shelter and support to the unfortunate or afflicted.[4] The word 'Home' was ultimately chosen for use in the name in order to point to a domestic, familial setting, and the assumption that 'lost and strays' were or could be pet companions.[5]

Premises were found in stables in a mews off nearby Hollingworth Street. But this meant money was needed for rent and staff. Initially, the venture was supported by donations from her network of female friends, but Tealby wanted it to have a more secure future. With her brother, she founded the Dogs' Home Society. Its prospectus stated:

> The lady who is endeavouring to organise this society has in one suburb only found that so many [dogs emaciated and even dying from starvation] that she cannot help feeling that the aggregate amount of suffering among those faithful creatures throughout London must be very dreadful indeed.[6]

News of the venture spread. Many rallied to the cause with donations, but it was ridiculed in the press. An editorial in *The Times* observed: 'There is a lady residing in Islington whose zeal we venture to say out runs her discretion'.[7] The work of the RSPCA in stopping cruelty to animals was welcomed as a sign of England's high place amongst civilised nations, but the editorial saw a dogs' home as a move 'from the sublime to the ridiculous'. The Home's supporters were said to have 'taken leave of their senses', implying it was they who should be in an asylum. In typically misogynist fashion, the editorial concluded that the roots of such a misguided venture lay in the fact that 'most of the subscribers are ladies'. Other press reactions were similar, with headlines like 'The last freak of the dog' and 'The latest absurdity', which contrasted with claims that every town needed 'a canine asylum'.[8]

Tealby and her brother Edward went ahead. The Society's first meeting was chaired by Lord Raynham, who was well known for his support of anti-cruelty measures, and the Society gained the backing of the RSPCA. Donations secured the rent, kennels for forty dogs and the hiring of a keeper, James Pavitt. Running costs were anticipated to be a problem and one suggestion was to offer boarding kennels for the pets of the wealthy when they travelled out of town. Demand was high and fourteen days was set as the limit for reclaiming a lost dog, after which strays were sold, given away or put down. The Tealbys rejected the approaches of scientists seeking live animals for vivisection and dead ones for dissection.

Sentiment in the periodical press was more positive than that in the daily papers. For example, William Kidd, the author of *Our Domestic Pets*, praised Tealby's venture in an article in *Leisure Hour*, a weekly periodical published by the Religious Tract Society. He offered 'all honour to her name' and agreed with her principles: 'I cannot understand that morality which excludes animals from human sympathy, or releases man from the debt and obligation he owes to them'.[9] In August 1862, the Home received the endorsement of none other than Charles Dickens, who empathised with suffering dogs as he had with the Victorian poor.[10] In his magazine *All Year Round*, he compared 'Two dog shows' he had recently visited. He had, perhaps, been prompted by adjacent advertisements on the front page of the *Islington Gazette* of 21 June 1862 for the Monster Show of Sporting and Other Dogs and a bazaar to raise funds for Tealby's Home for Lost and Starving Dogs (Figure 17.1).

Dickens wrote that at the former, the aristocracy of Dogdom competed to be best in breed; at the latter, its lower classes waited to be claimed or cured. He had 'discern[ed] a great moral difference' between the two sites. He mocked the Monster Show, suggesting that the dogs on display had 'a slight tendency to give themselves airs', and 'As to any feeling for, or interest in each other

Figure 17.1 Notices for what Charles Dickens called 'The two dog shows', 1862

the prosperous dogs were utterly devoid of both'. At Holloway, 'on the other hand, here seemed a sort of fellowship of misery, whilst their urbane and sociable qualities were perfectly irresistible'. Dickens described a visit to the Home:

> As you enter the enclosure of this other dog show ... you find yourself in a queer region, which looks, at first, like a combination of playground and muse. The playground is enclosed on three sides by walls and under fourth by a screen of iron cage-work. As soon as you come within sight of this cage some 20 or 30 dogs of every conceivable and inconceivable breeding, rush towards the bars and flattening their poor snouts against the wires, ask in their own peculiar and most forceful language whether you are their master come at last to collect them?[11]

Welcoming the efforts of the 'band of humane-disposed persons' who had established the Home, Dickens encouraged donations, as he doubted it would divert monies from other charities. He concluded that the Home told of 'the remarkable affection with which English people regard the race of dogs' and that it was 'evidence of that hidden fund of feeling which survives in some hearts even in the rough ordeal of London life in the nineteenth century'. John Colam, the secretary of the RSPCA, later wrote that Dickens's support was crucial in turning public opinion in favour of the Home.[12]

Nonetheless, finances remained precarious, making fund-raising a continuing priority. The annual bazaar was the leading money-raising event; by the summer of 1863, it boasted an array of aristocratic patronesses. Now staged in St James's Hall in Regent Street, it was advertised on the front page of *The Times*.[13] Such events, along with endowments and large donations, allowed a mortgage to be taken out on the Hollingsworth Street premises. By then, around 2,000 dogs were accepted each year, with holding centres in Westminster, Chelsea and Bethnal Green. For the first time, a veterinary surgeon was appointed to 'superintend the sanatory condition of the home'.[14]

The bazaar of 1864 was the last that Mary Tealby attended. Her father died in August that year and she became less active as her health declined. The following year she moved to the home of her relative Robert Weale, an assistant commissioner of the Poor Law who had a large house in Biggleswade. Unable to attend committee meetings, she instead wrote in with her ideas. She died on 3 October 1865 and was buried at St Andrew's Church in Biggleswade. Her passing received no other acknowledgement than a notice of death in local newspapers. Later in the year, her work was recognised, but with concerns for its future.

> The joyous bow-wow of the dogs provided for in Mrs Tealby's 'Home' will now sink into a howl of despair at the sad fall before them, for it is feared that the 'Home for Sick and Starving Dogs' will be annihilated now its founder and patroness is no more.[15]

But the Home was secure, with loyal supporters, solid finances and a permanent staff.

In 1867 the Home's position was strengthened when it gained a regular income from receiving dogs seized by the police under the new Metropolitan Streets Act. The legislation had been brought in to improve public safety on the streets by controlling road traffic, the dumping of waste and livestock movements, and by the rounding up of strays, which were now squarely associated with 'dirt, disorder, danger and disease'.[16] Any dog taken off the street had to be claimed within three days, otherwise it was sold or put down, but the numbers had overwhelmed the police, who therefore turned to the Home, which essentially became its dog pound (Figure 17.2).[17]

More dogs meant more noise and smell. There were complaints from neighbours and a prosecution claiming that the Home had caused ill-health amongst Holloway residents. The Home won, but its committee decided to look for new premises, in a non-residential area. They chose land close to Battersea Park, adjacent to railway lines, where the noise of trains would be greater than that of barking dogs (Figure 17.3). Acquiring the site, building kennels and

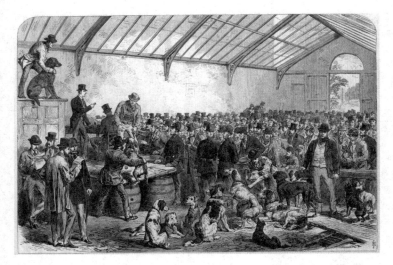

Figure 17.2 Sale at Chelsea of vagrant dogs seized by the police, 1868

making a move put the Home in financial straits again. It moved in 1871 and opened with cages for 150 to 200 dogs.[18] The number of dogs received varied, but could be very high when rabies threatened, as in 1885, when 25,000 dogs were brought in; the following year there were even more – 40,000.[19] The government refused to cover the extra cost, arguing that support should come from public subscription and sales.

In 1885, the Home received a small but significant donation, £10, from Queen Victoria (Chapter 1). Her sons, the Prince of Wales and Prince of Leopold, had visited the Home and given their support, but there was further delight when the Queen agreed to be its patron. As with her support for other charities, not least the RSPCA, the Queen often sent letters to the Home expressing her views. For example, she threatened to reduce her subscription when the Home proposed to dispose of the increased number of euthanised dogs with the new technology of cremation.[20]

In 1897, to mark the Queen's Diamond Jubilee, the Home's committee proposed the opening of a country branch, in order

Figure 17.3 'Home for Lost and Starving Dogs, Battersea', 1876

to help counter its reputation for slaughtering unfortunate strays and the dogs of the poor. The 'sanatorium' at Hackbridge in Surrey had large paddocks, a surgery and 'commodious kitchens', giving the 'better class' of dog time to recover from the stresses of separation and to be claimed. The country home was opened by the Duke and Duchess of Portland in October 1898 and was described by the Duke as 'A Dogs' Paradise'.[21]

Tealby's Dogs' Home, along with the RSPCA, was and still is widely cited as evidence that Britain is a nation of dog lovers. She created a typically Victorian institution. Its values and operation were informed by concerns about cruelty and suffering, the ideals of philanthropy, the assumptions of class and the goal of improvement. Endeavours to prevent cruelty to animals, in personnel and values, were linked to the campaigns against slavery and child labour. Yet, the Dogs' Home was founded nearly a decade before the first Doctor Barnardo's Home, and the RSPCA was founded over half a century before the National Society for the Prevention of Cruelty to Children.

Chapter 18

Frances Power Cobbe

➣ ———————— ✕ ———————— ➣

Sentient creatures

Frances Power Cobbe regarded dogs as her fellow sentient beings, with feelings, emotions and consciousness (Figure 18.1). These deeply held views led her to become the leader of the British anti-vivisection movement.[1] She argued that women had a unique relationship with dogs, which came from emotional empathy and common experiences of subordination. She was a prolific author of books, pamphlets and journal articles, and wrote for national newspapers. A strong advocate of women's rights, she campaigned for the admission of women to universities, reform of the marriage laws, and for women's suffrage.[2] While she believed in women's autonomy, she did not believe in sexual equality. For Cobbe, women were the 'mother sex', whose role was caring for their family or, if unmarried, other people and creatures. She wrote an essay on 'How a dog thinks and feels' in which she concluded that there were more similarities than differences in mental attributes between humans and dogs.

Cobbe was born in Newbridge, County Dublin, in December 1822. She was the fifth child and only daughter of an established couple in the Anglo-Irish gentry, Charles Cobbe, a landowner, and his wife, Frances Conway. She was educated at home, apart from two years at a private school in Brighton. She left when her mother's illness demanded extra hands at home and they became close, sharing many interests. After her mother died in 1847, tensions

Figure 18.1 Frances Power Cobbe, 1894

with her father grew, mainly over religion. She was for a time a non-believer but found new faith in the 1860s in the Unitarianism of the American Theodore Parker.[3] His writings shaped her emerging feminism, as his creed was that God was 'not a King but a Father and Mother, infinite in power, wisdom, and love'.

Her troubled relationship with her father continued until his death in 1857, after which she embarked on a Mediterranean tour. In Italy, she met the sculptor Mary Lloyd and they became lifelong companions. Cobbe at various times called Mary her 'husband', 'wife' and the 'old woman'.

On her return to Britain, Cobbe worked with Mary Carpenter, the founder of ragged schools, in Bristol and then moved to London, settling down with Mary Lloyd. She then embarked on a hectic, multifaceted career. She was active in women's rights, education, women's suffrage and animal welfare, in words and deeds. Her social and correspondence networks included many of the leading intellectuals of the Victorian era, including scientists such as Charles Darwin (Chapter 14), T. H. Huxley and Herbert Spencer.[4]

She enjoyed the respect of all, even her critics, for her principled stance on the issues she campaigned upon. Her friend the Reverend John Verschoyle gave this description of her:

> Above the mighty girth emphasised by the dress rose a strong, intellectual face, backed by a great leonine head with a mane of strong shortcut hair. A frank, straight gaze of penetrating eyes that seem to read one's unspoken thoughts carried the impression of intellectual power and absolute truthfulness; and then in another moment her face beamed with humour and wit, or shone with the radiance of a great goodwill and kindliness, the natural language of a big human heart.[5]

She was formidable.

Her earliest essays, published in influential periodicals, were on celibacy versus marriage for women, what to do with 'old maids', and women's education. She joined a group of active proto-feminists, including Millicent Fawcett, Lydia Becker, Emily Davies (the founder of Girton College, Cambridge) and John Stuart Mill. Her feminism was unique. She asserted women's rights, but not equality, though women's loyalty to God and themselves had precedence over their duty to husbands or parents. Sexual differences shaped the specific roles of women and men, with the innate maternal instincts of caring evident in the family or, in spinsters, caring more widely. Women were 'the mother sex'.

Cobbe's first essay on animals was 'The rights of man and the claims of brutes', published in 1863, the same year as her book *Essays on the Pursuits of Women*.[6] Although about the whole of creation, dogs featured strongly. She contrasted humans, who were moral beings with free will and a sense of right and wrong, with brutes which were inferior and instinctual, yet sentient and capable of emotions. Humans had *rights*, while brutes had *wants*, which they often pursued with ferocity.

Her prime example of animal sentience was the affectionate dog, where the relationship was not master–servant or owner–possession, but rather 'pure, disinterested, devoted love'. She cited examples of dogs being subject to torture and willing to die rather than abandon fidelity to their 'master' or 'mistress'. Cobbe speculated that such 'wonderous instincts' implied dogs may have some form of emergent moral faculty, as 'consciousness and self-consciousness are mysterious powers working upwards through all orders of existence'.[7] These beliefs led to the conclusion that dogs and other animals had to be treated humanely or, rather, as 'human-like'. The essay ended with a possible analogy: perhaps dogs' love of humans was akin to humans' love of God.

In 1867 Cobbe published an extended essay entitled 'The consciousness in dogs' and a short, limited-edition book, *The Confessions of a Lost Dog: Reported by Her Mistress*. The former was aimed at the head, the latter at the heart. Both told of the strong emotional bonds between dogs and humans, especially women. The essay was published as a review of twelve of the most influential dog books of the era, but these received scant attention as Cobbe dwelt on her views on 'How a dog thinks and feels'. The narrative took readers on a journey where they had to think like a dog. First, readers had to think with a dog's body:

[W]e must imagine ourselves inhabiting a diminutive and prostrate form, without hands, without speech, and destined to die of old age as we enter our teens; also, as having for our special endowments a remarkable power of finding our way, and a preternaturally acute nose, accompanied by unconquerable propensity for Ubomi (carrion), and all abominable things.[8]

Wittily, Cobbe mentioned the tail: 'A peculiar caudal appendage, serving, so effectually, as a "vehicle for emotions" that instead of availing, like language, "to conceal our thoughts," it should constantly and involuntarily betray our joy, sorrow, alarm, or rage'. She reiterated her view that dogs had very similar passions and emotions to those of humans: anger, hatred, jealousy, envy, gluttony, love, fear, pride, vanity, magnanimity, chivalry, covetousness, avarice, shame, humour, gratitude, regret, grief, maternal love, courage, fortitude, hope and, 'lastly, faith in a beloved superior is perhaps the most beautiful and affecting'.[9] Dogs had memory, and the ability to learn and follow instructions; indeed, they enjoyed being governed, like children and 'savages'.

But what about the differences with humans? Cobbe maintained that there was no evidence that dogs were capable of abstract thought. The absence of language meant they had no culture, as there was no accumulation of knowledge from generation to generation. Dogs had no moral sense of right and wrong but learned their 'values' from humans, for good or ill. Once again, this pointed to their devotion and fidelity, and when this was betrayed, dogs felt the pain of rejection. Cobbe was impressed by stories of dog suicides, which showed 'high mental faculties', will power and loyalty. This assumption was evident in the retellings of Greyfriars Bobby's fourteen-year mourning at his owner's graveside.[10] On balance, she concluded that the differences between humans and dogs were those of degree rather than kind:

The elementary machinery of the human mind is present and active in the brain of the dog. There are Memory, Reflection, Combination, Forethought, Association of ideas, and that process of arguing from cause to effect which we are want to consider as Reasoning, strictly so called.[11]

Cobbe ended up wondering if this meant dogs enjoyed an after-life. She saw no reason why not. If a baby or young child who had no knowledge or understanding of God and morality went to heaven, why not a dog at a similar level of psychological develop-ment? While Darwin saw the similarities between humans and dogs as evidence of common descent, for Cobbe they came from God's creation.

Cobbe's book *The Confessions of a Lost Dog* was narrated by a Pomeranian, Hajjin, as told to its mistress.[12] The novel was pub-lished as a gift to subscribers of the Lost Dogs' Home then in Holloway, where the story concludes.[13] Born in Lausanne, Hajjin was taken to London and found herself living in a large house with a mistress who 'loved me'. But her mistress suffered from poor health and often travelled abroad to convalesce, leaving Hajjin to endure harsher treatment, often below stairs. Though there were some pleasures, including a 'marriage' to the Retriever next door. But sadness followed. Hajjin had two puppies that, as often with the children of unmarried mothers in the Victorian era, were taken away and found new homes.

Good times with devoted care and fine foods returned every time the mistress came home. The devoted couple enjoyed many days out, and on one such day Hajjin saved her mistress from drown-ing, though the dog suspected the danger was feigned, designed to test her love. Out walking one day, Hajjin was separated from her mistress and became truly lost. She suffered many of the physical and mental cruelties common to London's street dogs. All abuses were by unthinking, unfeeling males: a bricklayer kicked her; she was nearly run over by a wildly driven omnibus, chased by a dog stealer and stoned by boys claiming she was a rabid 'mad dog'. Eventually, when found cowering in a doorway to avoid further ill-treatment, Hajjin was rescued by a woman and taken to the Lost

Dogs' Home. One day she spotted her mistress amongst visitors, which led to a happy reunion after she called 'Here I am! – Here I am! – I'm so glad! – Let me out! – Wow!-wow! Wough!'

If, for Cobbe, Battersea Dogs' Home represented the best in human feeling towards dogs, vivisection represented the worst – cold, calculated cruelty. Cobbe played a leading role in attempts to control and ban experiments on live animals in Britain. Indeed, it became the primary focus of her writing and campaigning. The RSPCA had been agitating about cruelty in physiology laboratories since the 1860s but had not initiated any legal action.[14] The situation changed after the Norwich meeting of the British Medical Association in September 1874. Eugene Magnan, a French physiologist, demonstrated the differential effects of high doses of alcohol and absinthe on two dogs.[15] Several doctors present objected that the procedures were cruel and unnecessary; the uproar was reported in several newspapers. The RSPCA was emboldened and brought a prosecution under the Cruelty to Animals Act, not against Magnan, who had returned home, but instead the local organisers of the Norwich meeting. The case was heard that December and failed. The verdict was that while the experiments were cruel, the defendants had no direct involvement, so there was no case to answer.

Cobbe was furious and believed that the RSPCA had not pursued the matter determinedly. She wrote a memorandum to the RSPCA's committee urging action, which gained 1,000 signatories, and she published two pamphlets: *Reasons for Interference* and *Need for a Bill*. She joined forces with Dr George Hoggan to call for legislation to regulate vivisection. In February 1875, Hoggan wrote a much-quoted letter to the *Morning Post* relating his observations of cruelty and the suffering in sentimental terms:

> I think the saddest sight I ever witnessed was when the dogs were brought up from the cellar to the laboratory for sacrifice. Instead of appearing pleased with the change from darkness to light, they seemed seized with horror as soon as they smelt the air of the place,

divining, apparently, their approaching fate. They would make friendly advances to each of the three or four persons present, and as far as eyes, ears, and tail could make a mute appeal for mercy eloquent, they tried it in vain.[16]

The RSPCA set up an investigation, but Cobbe and Hoggan wanted action. In December 1875, they set up a Society for the Protection of Animals Liable to Vivisection. It became known as the Victoria Street Society (VSS), after the location of its offices. Its president was none other than the leading social reformer Lord Shaftsbury, and other leading Victorian politicians and intellectuals leant their support. Cobbe ran the Society's lobbying and publicity campaigns, serving as honorary secretary from 1876 to 1884. The Society's emblem featured a St Bernard dog in the pose immortalised in Edwin Landseer's 1838 painting *A Distinguished Member of the Humane Society* (Figures 6.1 and 18.2). The choice of a breed renowned for saving human lives captured Cobbe's views on the mutuality of relations between humans and dogs.

A vital claim in scientists' defence of vivisection was its utility: medical research saved human lives. This view cut no ice with Cobbe, for whom vivisection was a moral issue, where 'mercy

Figure 18.2 Emblem of the Victoria Street Society, 1889

and sympathy' for fellow creatures were paramount. She had a particular distrust of medical men. Unimpressed by the examples they gave of the discoveries that had come from vivisection, she asked: what could be learned about the real experience of human ill-health from such unnatural procedures on other creatures? Experiments on live animals by students were said to dull their sensibilities, likely making them unsympathetic, hard-hearted doctors. In turn, the almost exclusively male medical profession was likely to place the health of the body above that of the mind and the soul, and value knowledge above love.

Cobbe's attitudes on cruelty to animals were complex. She was very protective of companion animals, but less so with farm and wild animals. It was cruelty and pain that always stood out. A swift, necessary death in the abattoir was acceptable and even God-ordained. She opposed vegetarianism, arguing that God had provided certain animals for humans to eat. Like the RSPCA, she tolerated field sports, accepting that the death of the game, hares and foxes was quick and without suffering. Her companion Mary Lloyd was a relation of Richard Lloyd Price, famed for his ability in field sports and game shoots (Chapter 10). Scientists, particularly physiologists, were styled as 'professionals' engaged in cold, calculated, unnecessary cruelty. The title page of *The Modern Rack*, a collection of her critiques of science, included a poem that contrasted old and new cruelties.

> Savage Tormenters of old
> Rested with thumbscrew and rack
> Secrets of crime and blood and guile
> From traitors and murderers black –
> Lives there now in the world a man so bold
> Would call those torturers back?
>
> Baser Tormentors to-day
> Grope out with scalpel and knife
> In gruesome wound of faithful hound
> Fair Nature's secrets of life –

Lives there yet in our land a man will say
These meaner tormentors shall have their way?[17]

Cobbe worried that vivisectors' 'impassive pitilessness' would
likely spread if science continued to gain cultural influence. She
epitomised the close links between feminism and anti-vivisection:
'both were fighting to protect defenceless creatures from the limit-
less powers of men'.[18]

Lobbying by the VSS and many others, including Queen
Victoria, for controls on vivisection led the government to appoint
a Royal Commission to investigate and make recommendations.
It had the challenging brief of reconciling the opposed demands
of anti-vivisectionists for tight controls, if not abolition, and scientists' wish that their research and teaching be unhindered. The
result was an Act, passed in 1876, to regulate rather than ban
vivisection. Cobbe saw this as a defeat. She continued to lobby
for tighter restrictions and for monitoring as required by the Act
to be taken out of the hands of scientists, whose work she claimed
had not changed, as they worked around the regulations. She
was most active with her pen, editing the VSS's journal, *The
Zoophilist*, and writing regularly for leading weekly and monthly
periodicals, as well as new books. A constant barrage of letters
to newspapers pointed out the abuses that were still tolerated,
as well as breaches of the legislation.[19] These interventions usually prompted replies from both sides of the issue.[20] In May
1881, she crossed swords with Charles Darwin and led the VSS's
unsuccessful prosecution of David Ferrier for causing pain to
monkeys.[21]

The VSS produced numerous pamphlets and popular tracts
every year, many of which were in fact reprints of her periodical articles. The new books included *The Anti-vivisection Question*
(1884), *Science in Excelsis* (1885) and *Vivisection in America* (1890),
with Benjamin Bryan. She took on leading scientists and a particular *bête noire* was the French physiologist Claude Bernard.

Figure 18.3 Claude Bernard's apparatus for suspending a dog's body, with tubes for the collection of stomach or liver fluids, 1889

Bernard's illustrations of dogs attached to experimental equipment and his descriptions of procedures were reproduced to shock her readers; one example was a device that suspended a dog for feeding experiments, where stomach and liver fluids were collected in tubes from the organs (Figure 18.3).

Not only did vivisection continue, but the number of experiments grew with the development of bacteriology and immunology. Those on cats and dogs did not escalate due to the bureaucracy of the licensing requirements, and scientists switched to smaller mammals, mainly mice and rats, which were better suited to experiments in the new fields.[22] Anti-vivisectionists found it harder to raise sympathy for the suffering of vermin.

Cobbe also campaigned against the muzzling of dogs to control rabies.[23] She argued that the cure was worse than the disease, as muzzling caused epilepsy and fits, which left the dogs unable to eat or drink. Worse still, these symptoms were mistaken for rabies, and so innocent dogs were summarily despatched. For Cobbe, killing was bad enough, but the methods used were horrific. She asked that 'the police be henceforth furnished with poleaxes, or other weapons suitable to the performance of this butchery, and be no longer limited to the use of their short truncheons'.[24] She had, though, also a more fundamental objection to the new laws:

> [Muzzles] are teaching the British public to regard with suspicion, dread, and finally hatred animals whose attachment to mankind has been a source of pure and humanising pleasure to millions, in which is formed a link (surely not undesigned by the Creator?) between our race and all the other tribes of earth and air. A creature gagged and fettered in the street inevitably suggests the idea of danger. He is no longer the playful companion of his master's ride or walk, the vigilant watchman of his owner's cart or coat, the herald of his mistress's carriage, the guardian of the children and the perambulator.[25]

And that was not all. The alternative to muzzling was the vaccine developed by Pasteur, produced by an extensive programme of experimental research that relied on vivisection.

In 1884, Cobbe resigned as honorary secretary of the VSS and left London to live in Hengwrt in North Wales with Mary Lloyd. She continued to write on women's issues and anti-cruelty and published an autobiography.[26]

Frustrated at the failure to control vivisection, in 1898 she sought a complete ban on the practice and founded the British Union for the Abolition of Vivisection (BUAV). She was its president, wrote new pamphlets and oversaw the creation of twenty branches across the country. She continued to be concerned about medical competence. Consequently, her will stated: 'On my body the operation of completely and thoroughly severing the arteries of the neck and the windpipe, nearly severing the head altogether, so as to render any revival in the grave absolutely impossible'.[27] Lloyd died in 1896, and Cobbe continued to live at Hengwrt until her death in 1904. Her obituary in *The Times* observed: 'Although, too, her work in the anti-vivisection crusade provoked much hostile criticism and was regarded in many quarters as showing rather more of zeal than of discretion, the perfect sincerity of Miss Cobbe herself was never to be doubted'.[28]

Chapter 19

John Cumming Macdona

St Bernards

John Cumming Macdona created the St Bernard breed. This involved importing Alpine Mastiffs and reimagining them as the famous rescue dogs from the hospice on the St Bernard Pass in Switzerland. He ended his career as a Member of Parliament, before which he had been a Church of England vicar and Queen's counsel. A founding member of the Kennel Club, his standing saw him invited to judge at the first big dog show in New York, in 1877. While there, he led a service at the Church of the Holy Trinity in Manhattan.[1] The *New York Times* reported that his sermon was 'a revelation'. He arrived 'wearing a tweed suit and smoking a cigar … robed in flowing black silk with a regulation white neckband'. He had a friend and soulmate in the equally colourful Charles Cruft (Chapter 12), and served as chairman of Cruft's Dog Show for over twenty years. He was enough of a celebrity to be featured in Spy's portraits in *Vanity Fair* with the title 'St Bernards' (Figure 19.1).

Macdona was born in Dublin in April 1836. His father, George de Landre Macdona, was a textile merchant and regular visitor to the United States, who eventually became a naturalised citizen. The family owned a townsite eighteen miles west of San Antonio, Texas, where a small town called Macdona developed at an important railroad junction. The eldest of eight children, John was brought up in Dublin and stayed in the city to read divinity at Trinity College. Ordained in 1859, he took his first post

Figure 19.1 John Cumming Macdona, 1894

in Mossley, near Manchester. He was popular and his reputation grew through his relief work during the Cotton Famine and his support of schooling.[2]

In 1863 he moved to be curate of Sefton, near Liverpool. Again, he was a parish favourite. When the rector, Roger

John Cumming Macdona

Dawson-Duffield, went on two years' leave, Macdona abandoned the usual High Church format for more down-to-earth services.[3] When the Rector returned, worshippers rebelled against the resumption of old ways, withdrew from the choir and locked the organ. There followed weeks of 'disgraceful disturbances' at Sunday services, allegedly stoked by Orange Order men.[4] Macdona resigned and was missed by the congregation. The following year, parishioners presented him with a silver casket and a letter that thanked him for having led 'warm … hearty and devotional' services, improving church music, establishing a choir and boosting attendances.[5]

In February 1865, he married Esther Ann Milne, daughter of the late James Milne, who had been a partner in the Oldham textile firm of Milne, Travis and Milne. She was heiress to a considerable fortune. The couple moved to Ireland when Macdona became a rector in Mullingar in Westmeath. Family wealth enabled them to enjoy a lifestyle unthinkable for most clergy. They bought a seventy-acre country estate, Hilbre House, at West Kirby on the estuary of the River Dee, where he bred dogs for shows and field trials.

Macdona returned to England and held a temporary position as Queen's chaplain at Sandringham before becoming rector of St Mary's in Cheadle. He split his time between his parish and Hilbre House, where his father took up residence to supervise the kennel. During his tenure in Cheadle, he raised £10,000 (£900,000 in 2020) to restore the church building.

A keen sportsman, Macdona was a good skater in his youth and a keen yachtsman. Hilbre House was ideally situated for sailing, which he pursued with his usual enthusiasm. He favoured 'canoes', which were then small one-person, sea-going boats with sails, not paddles. Macdona had strong opinions on their design, having his own made with watertight compartments to give buoyancy after capsizing. He often told the story of setting out on a day's cruising, with his pet monkey Tom for company, and running into a storm.

The rough seas panicked Tom, who jumped on to Macdona's head and the canoe capsized. With its watertight compartments it stayed afloat and, after many struggles and going under three times, Macdona righted his now mast-less canoe. Lying prostrate on the deck, he paddled slowly ashore, 'black in the face and frothing at the mouth'. Tom's fate was never mentioned; presumably he was lost at sea.

Time and money enabled Macdona to become a leading dog fancier.[6] He was best known for Tell, the foundation of the St Bernard breed. When first imported, the dog was excluded from shows as being foreign, but within a few years fanciers accepted that Macdona had made it a 'British breed'. In Walsh's *The Dogs of the British Islands*, the first handbook of conformation standards, Tell featured as exemplifying the breed standard. It proved to be a controversial choice. Tell was unlike the famous Barry, who had saved the lives of travellers lost in snowdrifts. A photo of Barry appeared in the press in 1892; he did not have a heavy coat nor the large head and thick mane that became characteristic of the breed (Figure 19.2). Today, Barry can be seen in Bern Natural History Museum, where his taxidermied body has been kept since his death in 1815.[7]

Barry-type rescues had been imagined in several paintings by Edwin Landseer, but his dogs were Alpine Mastiffs (see Chapter 6). As the name suggests, they were large, heavy dogs unsuited to work in deep snow, but they were the type Macdona went to Switzerland in 1866 to acquire. There were many contradictory stories about the dogs of the hospice, with local sources suggesting that there was not a specific physical type. Instead, they were a variable bunch, valued for their ability and bravery, not their anatomy. Lighter dogs with shorter coats were better in snow, less likely to sink into drifts and become weighed down by ice. Macdona's choice of Tell was seemingly more influenced by Landseer than by what he might have found on his travels. The influence of the British dog fancy and its breed standards internationally was

Figure 19.2 Barry – the original taxidermied exhibit, 1892

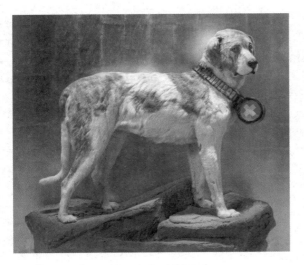

Figure 19.3 Barry – the taxidermied exhibit today

evident when visitors to the Bern Museum kept complaining that Barry was not a St Bernard! In response, staff remodelled him to the Macdona type. They made him taller by lengthening his legs, lifted his head to give greater nobility and added a barrel of brandy to match Landseer's painting (Figure 19.3).

Macdona went back to Switzerland and bought similar dogs, building up a large breeding kennel. His role in establishing the breed was evident when more than half of the St Bernards in the first Kennel Club studbook had their ancestry in his kennels. Macdona's royal connection continued, with Tell the sire of the Prince of Wales's St Bernard Hope.

Mount St Bernards, to give their full name, were first entered in dog shows in 1862, but there was no agreement on the correct physical type until Tell set the breed standard, by sweeping all before him at the Islington show in 1865. As the numbers at shows increased, judges split the breed into rough- and smooth-coated classes. Tell still set the standard for the roughs, while Macdona's Monarque, Victor and Jungfrau defined the smooth-coated breed.

Tell became a canine celebrity. He allegedly caused a 'St Bernard boom' and shows were built around his appearances. For Macdona, he was much more: a representative of a hallowed, saintly breed. Many dog breeds killed, but only St Bernards (and Newfoundlands, with which there were similarities) saved human lives.[8] Reportedly, Macdona had discussed with William Gladstone whether there was another animal in the world created for this purpose.[9] When Tell died in 1871, Macdona had a small stone mausoleum built at the foot of a round tower in the grounds of Hilbre House, which became a coastal landmark still known as Tell's Tower. Macdona wrote the following epitaph for a stone plaque: 'He was majestic in appearance, noble in character, affectionate in dispositions, and of undaunted courage'.[10] There is no evidence that he was ever involved in a rescue, but he looked the part. In the twentieth century, a reimagined Barry became a character in popular culture, featuring in advertisements for many products and in cartoons.[11]

Macdona also bred and exhibited other breeds. He was very successful with his Setters and Pointers in field trials, while at shows he competed with Skye Terriers, Dandie Dinmonts, Fox Terriers, Irish Setters, Gordon Setters and Siberian Wolfhounds.

He championed the Clarke strain of Skye Terriers from the estate of the Duke of Argyll. These were later called the Roseneath Terrier and are now regarded as precursors of the popular West Highland Terrier. Macdona's experience and expertise were in demand at dog shows, and he added weight to the first cat show by agreeing to be a judge. He had charisma and a talent for self-promotion.

The controversies over St Bernards continued, with some aficionados claiming he had put the breed on the wrong course with the large, long-coat type. His harshest critics were in the United States and none more than James Watson, who wrote that Macdona was 'the great English exploiter of the breed', helped by the fact that he 'was a very conspicuous figure at the leading dog shows'.[12] Watson lampooned Macdona's 'mountain rescuers':

> It is popularly believed that every stormy night the monks of St. Bernard send out a dog to save travelers. It carries a blanket, two bottles of hot water, a mustard plaster, two coarse towels, a basket filled with roast chicken and three kinds of vegetables, and a liquor case containing rum, lemon peel, sugar, and water. ... On coming up with the traveler, who is always lying insensible, half-covered with snow, the dog clears away the snow, removes the traveler's clothes, places the hot water bottles at his feet, the mustard plaster on his stomach, rubs the insensible man with the coarse towels until his circulation is restored, then the dog dresses his patient and wraps him in the blanket.[13]

Watson added that in some versions, the dog mixed a hot toddy and served dinner before returning to the monastery at a gallop with the victim on his back.[14]

Macdona was also seen as a 'dog dealer'. On his trip to the big show in New York in 1877, he brought to sell: 'two English Setters, two magnificent St. Bernard dogs, a black retriever, a red-and-white Irish Setter puppy, a Fox Terrier puppy and a black Skye Terrier'.[15] Macdona's standing in America was eventually redeemed from attacks by Watson by two imports of other breeds: the Fox Terrier puppy Tim, which began a fad for the breed on the East Coast; and a Pointer called Croxteth, which greatly improved the performance of the breed in American field trials.

Macdona was a great traveller and usually travelled in some style.[16] In 1886 he summarised his travels and adventures. He was particularly proud of having eaten some strange foods: 'snails ... in Paris, sour crouts [sic] in Prague, frogs and blue fish in Delmonico's in New York, hedgehogs in South America, and taken Rioga [sic] on the top of Vesuvius, the rarest of Madre at Xeres, the driest Amontillado at Madrid, and the blackest of coffee with the Arabs in Africa'. His South American trip (featuring hedgehogs) had been in 1881. He had spent several months travelling around, beginning in Uruguay, where he visited the Liebig Extract of Meat Saladero at Fray Bentos. An enthusiast for technological innovations, he marvelled at the production line, with men stripping carcases and the mechanical rendering down of the flesh, which reduced a 300-pound bullock to seven pounds of meat extract. He then travelled across the Pampas to start his journey across the Andes from Mendoza in Argentina to Santa Rosa in Chile. His party travelled by mule and took generous provisions: 'boxes of bread, biscuits, tinned tongues, roast chickens, German sausages, Yarmouth bloaters, anchovy paste and mixed pickles, salt, pepper, sugar, tea, coffee, cocoa, mustard, soup, candles, pâté de foie gras, ... beer, and in case of illness a bottle of brandy; also, a small barrel of Mendoza red wine'. *The Field* published letters with descriptions of his adventures and he collected these into a small book.[17]

Macdona resigned his post at Cheadle in 1883, taking advantage of the Clerical Disabilities Act. He sold most of his dogs to American buyers, though he 'saved for the nation' Bayard, his best-known St Bernard at the time.

Macdona's next calling was the law. He bought a house in London and joined chambers at the Middle Temple, where he qualified as a barrister in 1889. Golf and racehorses replaced dogs as his sporting recreations. He played regularly at the Royal Liverpool Golf Club at Hoylake, just a mile from Hilbre House. On his travels, he played at courses across England and promoted the course at Pau in the Pyrenees, where the Macdona Cup was a regular event. He visited Beijing in 1899 and found no golf course. Typically enterprising, he set out to establish one, and allegedly succeeded with one laid out on the city's racecourse.[18] He had two Arab mare racehorses, Zuleika and Hadji, which mated with the Duke of Westminster's famous stallion Bend Or. There were hopes for one of the fillies intended for participation in the Oaks, but, unbeknown to Macdona because he was 'far away in the wild Western American States', she was withdrawn.

Life in the courts was not enough for Macdona: he aspired to a parliamentary career as a Liberal. Unhelpfully, he soon left the party over the government's Egyptian policy and its treatment of General Gordon. However, his profile and personality saw him welcomed by the Conservatives.[19] He stood unsuccessfully for Chesterfield in 1885, after campaigning for the expansion of the Empire to bring trade and jobs to north Derbyshire. The following year he travelled to the East Coast of the United States and reported his observations in the *Derbyshire Times*.[20] He did not like what he saw economically, and he criticised monopolies such as Standard Oil and Bell Telephone. He did, though, find support there for tariff reform and preference for Empire trade; he claimed that 'Every intelligent American I have yet met here professes to be amazed at our stupid policy of Free Trade in preference to Fair Trade'. He went on to Texas to see the land he had recently inherited from his father. He gave an exhibition of golf and is said to have introduced the sport into the state.[21] He had hopes for the economic development of the town of Macdona, as it was served by two railroads. In a letter published in the local newspaper, he looked to old, not new industries, seeing opportunities for blacksmiths, other handicraft workers and weavers.[22]

Macdona was adopted as the prospective Conservative candidate for Rotherhithe in 1890 and became active in the constituency. He won the seat in the June 1892 election. In his early years in Parliament, he lobbied on many issues. His initial interests were local, especially the importation of diseases through the Port of London and the welfare of Thames watermen. He published a booklet in 1902 on their history, which he had compiled for the Royal Commission on the Manning of the Navy.[23] Perhaps due to his many crossings of the Atlantic, he was concerned with the dangers posed by floating shipwrecks in the oceans and the Thames.[24] Dogs featured only once in his parliamentary career, when he asked a question about rabies.

Macdona supported women's suffrage. He moved the second reading of the Votes for Women Bill in 1896 and supported the Parliamentary Franchise (Women) Bill in 1897. His support of women extended to the social sphere, to include women cycling and driving cars.[25] Both activities showed his love of new technologies. He was a founding member of the Self-Propelled Traffic Association, which promoted cycling and motoring, and was essentially anti-horse. The Association lobbied for improved roads and the development of vehicle manufacturing industries. Speaking at the Association's launch in 1895, Macdona warned that car manufacturing in France, Germany and America was leaving Britain behind.[26]

Arthur Balfour's Conservative government resigned in December 1905, prompting an election which resulted in a Liberal landslide. Macdona lost his seat and retired from politics, whereafter he spent his time at Hilbre House and his London home in Chelsea. One connection with dogs endured, chair of Cruft's Dog Show Society, a position Macdona had held since the Society's creation in 1886. He died in May 1907. His obituarists had little or nothing to say about his political career, but instead remembered his good work in the Church and his role in establishing the St Bernard breed.[27]

John Cumming Macdona

Macdona remained a public figure in death. He wanted to be buried at the abbey in Sligo, believing he was a descendent of Bryan MacDonagh, who had restored building. His request was refused, causing a controversy at a time of rising political tensions, but the issue was religious, not political. The Church of Ireland did not accept cremation, so ashes could not be buried in consecrated ground. Instead, Macdona's ashes went to the municipal cemetery. That was not the end of the story. In 1912, his grave was desecrated by, it was assumed, Nationalists.

239

Chapter 20

Sewallis Shirley

The Kennel Club

Sewallis Shirley was the first chairman of the Kennel Club, and led its rise to be the dominant dog organisation in Britain and a model for canine governance internationally. The Club's aim was typically Victorian: 'improvement' of the nation's dogs, dog shows and field trials. A profound, though unintended consequence of its work was the remodelling of Dogdom into distinct and discrete breeds. Shirley specialised in many breeds over his fancying career, including Bull Terriers, Collies and Retrievers. He was born into a landed family with estates in Warwickshire and Ireland, and his position and wealth led into service with local agencies and, in time, in national politics.

Sewallis Evelyn Shirley was born in London in July 1844 into a family related to the Earls Ferrers. He was brought up at Ettington (previously Eatington) Park, Warwickshire, where the family had lived for 800 years. He was educated at Eton, where he kept a pack of Beagles, and at Christ College, Oxford, though he did not graduate. His father and grandfather had been Conservative MPs. At Shirley's coming of age, a reporter assumed that the same career was inevitable, as 'heavy duties in England belonged to wide possessions and ancient descent'.[1] As well as Ettington Park, the family had a large estate at Lough Fea in County Monaghan (Figures 20.2 and 20.3).

Figure 20.1 Sewallis Shirley

Figure 20.2 Ettington (formerly Eatington) Park, built in 1858 for Shirley's father in the Gothic Revival style

At just twenty-four years of age, Shirley was elected to sit in Parliament for the Southern Division of Monaghan. He served from 1868 to 1880, but was largely invisible in the House of Commons, though he opposed Home Rule and supported the Protestant constitution. After his re-election in 1874, a petition was lodged by Nationalists claiming bribery and intimidation of the electorate, but nothing came of it.[2] Though a typical absentee landlord, Shirley continued the family tradition of trying to be an improving estate owner, for example in supporting the Shirley Estate Farming Society, which held an annual agricultural show.[3] Tensions with Nationalists continued, usually prompted by disputes when tenants were evicted. Deteriorating relations were reflected in the 1880 election, in which Shirley came bottom. He stood again in 1885 with no success. At the same time, he had public roles in Warwickshire, serving as a Justice of the Peace, Deputy Lieutenant, and High Sheriff. in 1884.

Shirley kept and rode to hounds in Ireland and Warwickshire. The Warwickshire Hunt often met on his estate, where he also shot rabbits and game. He was a crack marksman, competing in pigeon shooting contests at the Hurlingham Club. Typical of Victorian gentlemen, he had a natural history collection, including taxidermied birds and a supposed dog-fox hybrid, plus an egg of the extinct Great Auk. Gamekeepers kept the estate well-stocked for sport and helped with his large kennel, where he maintained a pack of hounds and his show dogs.[4] Money and connections allowed him to acquire breed champions. At the very first show he entered, in Birmingham in 1867, Shirley won the Fox Terrier class with Jack.[5] The Birmingham Dog Show Society had begun its events in 1860, with classes just for sporting dogs as part of the annual agricultural show. Non-sporting dogs were added the following year in what was styled a 'National Exhibition'. The Society went from strength to strength, supported by noblemen, gentlemen and newly wealthy industrialists from across the Midlands. In 1865 it opened its own building – named after its patron, Lord Curzon.

Figure 20.3 Lough Fea House, Carrickmacross, Co. Monaghan

Shirley's win with Jack was questioned over issues that had beset dog shows and which, seven years later, the Kennel Club was established to remedy. First, the report in *The Field* described Jack as only 'a fair average dog', but this was readily challenged as there was no agreed conformation standard. The result with Fox Terrier bitches was similarly disputed, as the winner was said to be too Bulldog-like and probably a crossbreed. Second, results relied upon the preferences of individual judges, who might not be expert, honest or fair. At shows like that in Birmingham, where exhibitors and judges were local and knew each other, there were accusations of favouritism and bribery. Third, Shirley had to refute allegations that Jack's ears had been 'tampered with' or cropped, that is, cut to make them drop. This insinuation was a particular affront to a gentleman. Cropping was the type of 'alteration' allegedly practised by working-class fanciers on their 'little beauties' in preparation for contests in public houses. If conformation dog shows were to prosper, their social level needed to be raised, with rules and regulations policed by gentlemen.[6] In turn, such improvements would attract 'a better sort' of exhibitor and better dogs. In the short term, the cross-class character of shows remained. Indeed, Shirley bought his next champion Bull Terrier, Dick, from James Hinks, a member of the Birmingham Fancy, so he likely came from dogfighting stock.

From 1870 Shirley led the promotion and organisation of dog shows in London.[7] The Birmingham show, held every December, remained the premier event, and previous attempts to mount similarly grand events in the capital had foundered. They had lost money and been tainted with speculation and trade. The aim of Shirley and his fellow reformers was to put dog shows on a new footing. He called together a 'Committee of Gentlemen' who had 'no motive but the improvement of the dog' and 'a sincere love of the canine race'. Their first venture was a new-style Crystal Palace Dog Show, for which they put up the money and provided superior facilities. The report in *The Field* claimed it had 'the very best collection of sporting and non-sporting dogs ever grouped together'.[8] It had a mixed reception. There were protests about judging, especially complaints that its organisers took most of the prizes, including Shirley, with his dog Dick. The Committee of Gentlemen was back the following year with the best dogs, but not the social mix they had wanted. One reporter found that 'Pretty girls and stately dowagers, cold beauties and laughing damsels, the frank open-hearted fellow and the cynical abomination, the swell and the snob, the well-dressed gentleman and the Whitechapel rough, meet on common ground where dogs are concerned'.[9] There were complaints that the Committee operated as a clique and again took more than their fair share of prizes.[10]

The Committee's third show, in 1872, attracted a 'monster entry' of 1,000 dogs and, to up the tone, a high entry fee – five shillings – was charged on the first day, though it was reduced on subsequent days. The number and range of Shirley's own entries showed his enthusiasm and the depth of his kennel: Clumber Spaniels, Curly-coated Retrievers, Bull Terriers, Smooth Terriers and, in the class 'Yard dogs', 'a nondescript', probably a mongrel.[11] The following year, just before the event, Shirley led the Committee's rebranding as the Kennel Club and was elected its first chairman. High status was secured when the Prince of Wales agreed to be its patron and exclusivity was achieved when its membership was capped at 100. Needless to say, it was men only. While there was talk that it might have its clubhouse with facilities for meeting, dining and drinking, lack of funds meant that it established only offices. Nevertheless, when the office was moved to Pall Mall in 1877, it was close to the Carlton and other clubs patronised by members.

The Club's first rule was a noble one: 'it shall endeavour in every way possible to promote the improvement of dogs, dog shows, and dog trials'. In practice, it concentrated on regulation. Following the Jockey Club, it published an open studbook, based on registrations, pedigrees and records of show and trial performances. Many breeders and exhibitors claimed these were the most significant reforms, promising to end the chaos and misinformation around a particular dogs' identity, ancestry and accomplishments. Showing very Victorian values, the improvement of dogs was to be achieved by competition. In part, it was the competition of the market, not least because winning dogs gave owners prestige and prize money and an income from sales and stud fees. It followed that top dogs would be the favoured parents of the next generation, continuing, eugenic-like, to guarantee the preservation and perpetuation of 'good stock' and 'good blood'.[12] But the Club did not want the cut-throat competition of trade, but rather the fair play found in sports, especially rural sports, with their gentlemanly ethos and conduct. These were to be promoted and protected by rules, fairly applied by trusted men of experience, wealth and principle, whose favour could not be bought and who were only guided by the goal of canine improvement.

Shirley and the Club Committee decided not to set breed standards. They maintained that defined points would become fixed and stifle the improvement of breeds and Dogdom overall. Two developments came from this choice, which determined how the modern dog was made. Firstly, show promoters increased the number of breeds by creating more competition classes at shows to accommodate owners' and judges' tastes and attract more entries. Most commonly, breeds were split by size, colour, coat or anatomy, or a combination of these. For example, the separation of Smooth and Curly-Coated Retrievers into distinct breeds was led by Shirley. Secondly, the vacuum created by the Kennel Club's attitude to standards was filled by breed clubs. Again, Shirley was involved, serving as chair of the Collie Club, which defined standards for Smooth and Rough Collies, and enforced these my monopolising judging at shows. Led by enthusiasts, some said fanatics, breed club standards became ever 'fancier', with exaggerated features. Many were creations of fashion and seen as artificial because they required technical maintenance, as in the clipping and grooming of long coats. Critics called for the power of breed clubs to be reined in, but the Kennel Club was unmoved. One suggestion was that the Club become a parliament, with breed club presidents as its members. Shirley rejected the idea, wishing to keep the Club elite and select, concerned with the higher calling of 'improvement', not serving any constituency.

The Club also claimed authority over field trials, which had developed since the mid-1860s to test the ability of gun dogs. Initially set up to be run in conjunction with dog shows in order to link good ability and good anatomy, the events soon took separate tracks, leading to predictions that it would not be long before there two types of Pointers and Setters – 'show' and 'field'. Shirley believed this separation could be avoided. He judged at both events, including the first Kennel Club trial in 1873. The Club's second field trial, the following year, saw Shirley and the Club at odds with John Henry Walsh and the influential *Field* newspaper (on Walsh and *The Field*, see Chapter 9). An editorial by Walsh claimed that the paper had previously backed the Club in its moves to improve the 'morals and manners of the admirers of the canine race' and banish 'the objectionable proceedings of "doggy" men'. Dissent now was over what seemed a quite trivial matter: what notice had been given about an event's rules?[13] The Club was accused of unfairness in its denial of appeals on all aspects of shows and trials. Shirley replied, asking Walsh to withdraw, which he did in part but he still felt he 'must adhere to the general tenor' of his complaint.[14] Underlying 'this unpleasant business' was the continuing view that the Club's Committee remained a self-serving clique. Much of Shirley's time was taken up with Club bureaucracy, as the Committee acted as a court of appeal for complaints after shows and trials. Shirley's name was never out of the sporting and doggie press, where he often had to defend the Club's actions. Always in demand as a judge at shows and trials, he enjoyed celebrity status in canine affairs at all levels.

Shirley continued to compete at conformation shows, even when he was judging other breeds at the same event. He had a particular impact on shaping two breeds: Retrievers and Collies. In his book *The Sportsman's Library* (1845), John Mills wrote that 'It is not necessary for me to say much about retrievers, as any dog can be taught to fetch game'.[15] Others agreed that 'There is no true type of them. Every person has a peculiar fancy regarding them.'[16] What was required in a dog was a 'good nose' to find game and 'a soft mouth' to bring it back unharmed. They were dogs defined by their behavioural characteristics, not their form, but this was changed by dog shows. Exhibitors and judges chose a specific type to be *the* Retriever. It was said by its breeders to have its origins in a cross between British gundogs and black Newfoundlands, including the St John's dog, from which the modern Labrador also descended. By the 1870s, black dogs with long coats were the favoured look for *the* Retriever, and at the first Kennel Club show Shirley won second prize with Statesman, which he had bought from Battersea Dogs' Home. The breed was soon divided into smooth (flat) and curly (wavy) coats, with Shirley owning the most successful wavy-coated dogs.[17] In 1879, Hugh Dalziel, a leading authority, wrote, with men like Shirley in mind, that 'The idea of which these dogs are the embodiment was conceived in the minds of certain sportsmen years ago and has been slowly worked out, every succeeding year seeing some fault bred out and desirable points developed'.[18]

Shirley also owned a breed-defining Collie, called Hornpipe, who was chosen by Vero Shaw to illustrate the rough-coated variety in his encyclopaedic book in 1881. Like his Retrievers, it had both good blood and good looks.[19] 'Collie' became the accepted name for the breed, and the abandonment of 'Sheepdog' at shows was another sign of the abandonment of function in dogs' names. The change was aided when Collies became popular and fashionable pets, encouraged by the example of Queen Victoria's Sharp (Chapter 1).

The Kennel Club had success in making dog shows more respectable. A report on the Club's fourth show remarked upon 'an almost entire absence of the rough element, and hardly any but well-dressed ladies and gentlemen parading the long dog avenues'.[20] The move of shows upmarket was reflected in the prices paid after the event for prize winners: 100 guineas for a Bloodhound puppy or a Black-and-Tan Manchester Terrier, ninety guineas for a St Bernard puppy and many others over forty guineas.[21] Shows became ever larger and grander, taking over the big London venues – the Crystal Palace, the Westminster Aquarium and Alexandra Palace. Shirley was less optimistic about progress in the north of England. His views revealed the prejudices of his class, as seen in the snobbish condescension with which he ridiculed the validity of competitions in the north-east, where dogs had names such as 'Wag, Roy, Bobs, Bangs, Jets, Nettles, Vics &.c.'[22]

The Club's Committee continued to be plagued by post-show complaints, which were surprisingly acrimonious, given that prizes at shows were largely token. Money was a factor because of anticipated stud fees and puppy sales, but more important was the sense that gentlemanly values had been flouted. Complaints remained about Committee members monopolising prizes, which they answered by claiming that they (and their dogs) were the cream that naturally rose to the top. Regional rivals, led by the Birmingham Dog Show Society, resisted London's domination and kept to their own rules. The Club hit back. From 1880, members were permitted to exhibit or judge only at shows held under its rules.[23] Its opponents called it a boycott, a politically sensitive term for Shirley at this time. It had been coined the previous year from events on the estate of a fellow absentee Irish landowner, Lord Erne, whose agent, Captain Charles Boycott, was ostracised over the eviction of tenants in a protest organised by the Irish Land League.[24]

Within the closed circle of the Club, Shirley enjoyed a reputation for attention to detail and quiet diplomacy. In 1880 he began private publication of the Club's own journal, the *Kennel Gazette*, ownership of which he passed to the Club the following year. In 1885, he negotiated a rapprochement with the Birmingham Dog Show Society, by allowing its representation on the Club's committees. In the controversy over the cropping of dogs' ears, Shirley held the increasingly unfashionable view that it was desirable in some breeds, and he led the opposition to reform, but changed sides after the infamous Carling ear-cropping case in 1895 revealed the extent of popular sentiment against cruelty.[25]

Shirley retired as chairman of the Club in 1899 and was immediately elevated to the new post of president (Plate 8). He spent more time in Ireland in his later years, where he was a successful breeder and owner of thoroughbred racehorses. His interest and involvement in dog shows did not wane with age; for example, in 1898 and 1903, he judged in Moscow.

Shirly died suddenly after a brain haemorrhage in March 1904. There were many tributes; all stressed the reforms he had led to improve shows and trials.[26] Typical was that of Sidney Turner, who had succeeded him as chairman:

> To speak of Mr Shirley in his connexion with dogs would be to write a history of the past 35 years or more when his guiding mind first conceived of the idea of evolving law and order out of the nebulous chaos which then surrounded the exhibition of dogs. The success which has attended this undertaking has been, and is, largely due to the tact, discretion and judgement which are so necessary to a leader of men.[27]

In the twentieth century, the Kennel Club expanded its ambition from the governance of shows and trials to meet its first original aim – the improvement of the nation's dog. The Club moved to define breed standards and campaign for canine health and welfare more generally. Paradoxically, in the early twenty-first century, the health and welfare consequences of certain breed standards were the reason for most of the criticism it received.

Afterword

Pedigree chums

One of the most popular dog food brands in the twentieth century was Pedigree Chum. The name nicely captures the lasting ways that Victorians changed the dog. It was advertised with the slogan 'Top breeders recommend it', inviting dog owners to associate with an elite of Doggy People who had champion pedigree-bred dogs and fed them the best food. At the same time, it showed you cared for your best friend, your chum. One of our Victorian Doggy People, Charles Cruft, contributed most to this view, with his high-profile dog shows, which encouraged not only the ownership of pedigree dogs but also an emotional – and economic – investment in pets.

Victorian Doggy People left a powerful legacy, and the story of dogs in the twentieth century was largely one of continuities with the changes they made. Their enduring influence can be seen through my headings for the five parts of the book: high society, low society; celebrities and millionaires; sportsmen and showmen; doctors and scientists; and campaigners and politicians.

In high society, the Royal Family continued to be very public pet lovers in the twentieth century, none more so than Queen Elizabeth II with her Corgis and then Dorgis (Corgis crossbred with Dachshunds). From the ranks of the aristocracy came one of the earliest criticisms of the new fashions in ownership and fancy breeds. In 1911, Judith Neville-Lytton, sixteenth Baroness

Wentworth, published her book *Toy Dogs and Their Ancestors*; she looked back to old ways and standards. She wrote that 'People can be silly over pet dogs and bring ridicule on them by making them wear motor goggles and goloshes', but went on to defend pet ownership for all classes:

> The keeping of pet dogs is sometimes decried as a degrading, disgraceful, ridiculous, and, indeed, immoral practice confined to an effete aristocracy or a still more detestable plutocracy. This I strenuously deny. I repeat that a sensible boy and a sensible dog are the best education for each other and the results of the companionship will remain long after the little dog has been forgotten under the grass in some corner of the garden.

On breeds, she was severe on changes to Toy Spaniels:

> The tendency of exhibitions is, of course, to encourage exaggeration of special points, and this should be strenuously fought against by judges. Fashion says the ears should be set low but there should be moderation in all things and it makes a dog look ridiculous to have his ears off way down his neck giving him a silly goose like expression.

Attacks on fancy standards continued throughout the twentieth century but remained within the Doggy World until the BBC broadcast the documentary *Pedigree Dogs Exposed* in 2008. The furore that followed forced a review of breeding practices and standards, although critics claim that little has changed.

Celebrities continued to publicly associate with dogs, which contributed to their image. Stars parading with their dogs became a feature of Hollywood, where a favourite was the Sealyham Terrier. Owners included Elizabeth Taylor, Bette Davis, Cary Grant, Gary Cooper and Alfred Hitchcock, who made his usual cameo appearance in *The Birds* with two dogs. Princess Margaret also kept the breed. Amongst millionaires, the Rockefellers bred Bullmastiffs on their estate in the Pocantico Hills in kennels as luxurious as those built by J. P. Morgan. The father-and-son chocolate and candy magnates Frank and Forrest Mars were responsible for an important shift in dog foods. In 1930, Forrest, who had invented the Milky Way, split from his father and moved to England. One of his first investments was to acquire Chappel Brothers, which made tinned dog food. The company was the British branch of an American company that had started with horsemeat as its main ingredient. Chappie was marketed as more nutritious than the dry biscuits sold by Spratts and other companies. The business allowed Forrest to acquire the capital to move back to the United States and launch his own food company, with leading pet brands Pal, Whiskas, Kit-E-Kat and Pedigree Chum.

A novel feature in the twentieth century was dogs becoming celebrities. The first dog movie star was Blair, who played the hero in the 1905 silent movie *Rescued by Rover*, where the dog tracks down a kidnapped baby. The most famous celebrity was a German Shepherd, Rin Tin Tin, the stage name of Rinty, a First World War soldier's pet, taken from France to the United States in 1918. The dog first appeared in *Where the North*, the commercial success of which allegedly saved the small start-up Warner Brothers from bankruptcy. Star status was confirmed with his celebrity endorsement of the dog food Ken-L Ration. He died in 1932, having appeared in twenty-seven films. He started a Hollywood dynasty, succeeded by his son Rin Tin Tin Jr. and Rin Tin Tin III. In 1943, the film *Lassie Come Home* launched the career of the famous Collie, whose character was based on the dog of the same name in Elizabeth Gaskell short story 'The half brothers'. Played by a dog called Pal, Lassie had a brief movie career of just seven films, but lived on in novels and on television and radio. Other stars followed: Benji, Old Yeller, Toto, Marley and Beethoven, and a new genre – animated films – inspired by *Lady and the Tramp*.

I have already mentioned the impact of the Great Showman, Charles Cruft. One significant change happened in 1942, when commercialism and gentlemanly values were combined: the Kennel Club bought the right to the Cruft's name for its shows. Field sports and coursing continued; although the latter was

banned in 2004, it continues to this day in the form invented in
the 1920s – Greyhound racing. In 1926, the Belle Vue Stadium
in Manchester held Britain's first meeting, with technology
imported from the United States. Six Greyhounds chased an
electrically powered 'hare' around an oval track. The sport was
thereby democratised and commercialised in a single move.
Unlike on the old straight courses, spectators could follow the
whole race, and the new venues provided opportunities for
betting and socialising. The sport was an instant success and
attracted large crowds, rising from 5 million in 1927 to 16 million
two years later. The old Wembley Stadium in London was kept
solvent by hosting Greyhound meetings. Indeed, it was so important that during the football World Cup in 1966, a match was
moved to the White City Stadium because it clashed with a
Greyhound night.

Scientists continued to experiment on dogs, with regulations
less restrictive in most countries than those in Britain. Dogs were
key model animals for several famous winners of the Nobel Prize
in Physiology or Medicine: Pavlov on reflexes in 1904 and Banting
and Macleod on insulin and diabetes in 1923. Trial procedures on
dogs gave surgeons the skills for heart transplantation. Christiaan
Barnard, a South African surgeon, transplanted forty-eight dog
hearts before operating on a human patient in 1967; this was 250
fewer than his American rival, Norman Shumway.[1] Infamously, in
1975, *The People* newspaper shocked Britain with the revelation that
Beagles, heads held in restrictive frames, were smoking thirty a day
to test 'safe cigarettes'.[2]

Dogs' health benefited from spin-offs in developments in
human health, from antiseptic and aseptic surgery to antibiot-
ics, but innovations were slow to travel from doctors to vets. In
the first half of the twentieth century, little veterinary research
was directed at dogs' health. An exception was the development
of a vaccine for dog distemper, which was funded by a public
subscription organised by *The Field* newspaper with an appeal to

a nation of dog-lovers. Then, with the rise of motor transport, the number of horses in the country fell rapidly and urban veterinarians redirected their professional work and identity at treating dogs and other pets.

Although it was not until 1952 that a small number of enthusiasts created the British Small Animal Veterinary Association, animal welfare campaigners took up the veterinary care of pets sooner. In 1917, Maria Dicken had founded the People's Dispensary for Sick Animals (PDSA) to provide free treatment for the sick and injured animals of the working class.[3] Another aim was to educate the poor on the everyday care of their pets. Dicken called her treatment centre a 'dispensary', a term from the Victorian era associated with charitable medical aid for the poor. Veterinarians opposed the charity and saw Dicken as 'an animal nut', but the service met a demand, and by the mid-1920s there were over fifty clinics. Over the 1930s, the veterinary professionals recognised the potential boost to their income and reputation and agreed to work with the PDSA. Cooperation continued after the Second World War, but the PDSA was increasingly marginalised by the growth of large urban, pet-focused veterinary practices.

Dogs were absent from British politics for most of the twentieth century and largely ignored by politicians, apart from regular complaints about the suffering caused by the six-month quarantine imposed on dogs brought into the country. Dogs were of such a low profile that there was barely a whimper when the government, as part of its agenda of cutting bureaucracy, abolished the Dog Licence in 1987. Soon after, following vociferous campaigning, the government changed tack and introduced new regulations to control 'dangerous dog' breeds and new fines for pet owners not picking up their dog's poo. In the late 1990s, an action group led by Lady Mary Fretwell led another campaign, to abolish the six-month rabies quarantine. With the new Labour government more willing to align with the European Union's veterinary regime, vaccination replaced quarantine in 2000. The change had benefited from the support of Chris Patten, a senior Conservative who, returning from governorship of Hong Kong, had stayed in France rather than endure a six-month separation from his two Norfolk Terriers. No other senior politicians engaged in the debate; perhaps, like most British prime ministers during their residency at 10 Downing Street, they preferred cats. The White House was and is different. An unbroken succession of Presidents have brought their dogs to the Office or quickly acquired pets, like the Obama family. Donald Trump broke the tradition, but it was re-established by Joe Biden with two German Shepherds, although one had to be rehomed after biting staff.

Continuities persisted through the COVID-19 pandemic. As more people worked from home, they acquired pet dogs for companionship, and chose specific breeds to suit their lifestyle and tastes. One estimate was that over a third of young adults became new pet owners, with 70 per cent choosing a dog. Researchers found that amongst new owners there were benefits to human emotional wellbeing from having a dog around and to think about, while dogs also gained from less isolation, with people forced to work from home.[4] But those planning to buy a dog were warned to avoid unscrupulous puppy farms, the modern counterpart of Victorian dog dealers. The Dogs Trust worried about people not being attuned to their dog's emotions, as Charles Darwin had said. The Trust encouraged owners to get out – their dog not only needed exercise but the opportunity to socialise with other dogs – and to be aware that on return to work after the COVID lockdowns were lifted, separation anxiety might be particularly severe. The many breeds created by Victorians meant that there was a dog for every taste and, as then, there were fashionable favourites. Increased demand pushed up prices, doubling for Border Collies and rising by half for French Bulldogs. There was surprise at the Kennel Club that many of the fastest-growing registrations were for large breeds. Some owners chose new designer breeds, like Cockerpoos, while others chose twentieth-century creations, like the Labrador and Golden Retriever, but the most popular breeds, Bulldogs (albeit of the small French type) and Collies, would have been familiar to Victorian Doggy People, although they would have certainly have disapproved of the many 'improvements' to their physical form.

Plates

1 *Windsor Castle in Modern Times*, by Edwin Landseer,
   1841–43. Royal Collection Trust © Her Majesty Queen
   Elizabeth II 2022
2 An early dog show, Queen's Head Tavern, 1855.
   © Kennel Club
3 *The Hunting Parson*, by J. Loder, 1841. Courtesy of Blundell's
   School, Tiverton, Devon
4 *The Connoisseurs: Portrait of the Artist with Two Dogs*, by Edwin
   Landseer, 1865. Royal Collection Trust © Her Majesty Queen
   Elizabeth II 2022
5 Richard Lloyd Price, 'Pointers', *Vanity Fair*, 10 October
   1885, opp. p. 205 © The University of Manchester
6 Charles Cruft, *Canine World and Sportsmen*, 13 February
   1891, cover © Kennel Club
7 *The Boyhood of Raleigh*, by John Everett Millais, 1870. Presented
   by Amy, Lady Tate in memory of Sir Henry Tate 1900.
   Photo: Tate
8 Sewallis Evelyn Shirley. © Kennel Club

Figures

0.1 *The Old Shepherd's Chief Mourner*, by Edwin Landseer, 1837.
From Estelle M. Hurll, *Landseer: A Collection of Fifteen Pictures
and a Portrait of the Painter with Introduction and Interpretation*
(Boston, MA: Houghton, and Company, 1901), p. 81   6

0.2 Principal points of the dog, 1922. From R. Leighton, *The
Complete Book of the Dog* (London: Cassell and Company
Ltd, 1922), p. xiv   10

0.3 The Poodle, 1845. From W. Youatt, *The Dog* (London:
Charles Knight & Co., 1845), p. 45   12

0.4 Corded Poodles, 1889. From R. Lee, *Modern Dogs:
Non-Sporting Division* (London: The Field & Queen, 1899),
opp. p. 187   13

1.1 Queen Victoria with Sharp, 1866. Royal Collection
Trust © Her Majesty Queen Elizabeth II 2022   18

1.2 Her Majesty's pet dog 'Looty', 1863. From *The Field*, 23
May 1863, p. 496. © British Library Board,
MFM.MLD49   22

1.3 The Islington Dog Show, 1893. From *Graphic*, 18
February 1893, p. 159. © British Library Board,
HS.74/1099   25

1.4 Funeral procession of King Edward VII, with the
King's charger and Caesar, May 1910. Royal Collection
Trust © Her Majesty Queen Elizabeth II 2022   27

List of figures

2.1 Bill George. From Edgar Farman, *The Bulldog* (London: Stock Keeper Co., 1899), opp. p. 21   30

2.2 Wallace (the lion), Tinker and Ball. From *Pierce Egan's Anecdotes: original and selected, of the turf, the chase, the ring, and the stage: the whole forming a complete panorama of the sporting world, uniting with it a book of reference and entertaining companion to the lovers of British sport* (London: Knight & Lacey, 1827). © The University of Manchester   31

2.3 *Punch*'s 'visit to a very remarkable place'. From *Punch*, 28 November 1846, p. 222. © British Library Board, HIU.LD34A   32

3.1 Jemmy Shaw and his talented ratter dog Jacko. From *Illustrated Sporting News*, 16 December 1865, p. 645. © British Library Board, Mic.A.2580–2585   39

3.2 Tiny the Wonder. A souvenir handkerchief. © Museum of London. ID no. 99.44   42

3.3 'In memory of Jacko, the Champion Terrier, 14 lb Weight.' Image © Dominic Winter Auctioneers   43

3.4 Pet shop, Seven Dials, London. From 'The toilet', *Illustrated London News*, 5 September 1874, pp. 231–32. © British Library Board, MFM.MLD47   45

4.1 The Duchess of Newcastle and her Borzois. From Charles Lane. *Dog Shows and Doggie-People* (London: Hutchinson, 1902), frontispiece   49

4.2 The Duchess of Newcastle, Lady Nora Hastings, and the Clumber Harriers. From 'Lady Masters of Hounds', *Sketch*, 27 November 1901, p. 212. © British Library Board, HIU.LD52   51

4.3 The Duchess of Newcastle with a Borzois and Smooth-Haired Fox Terrier. From 'The Duchess of Newcastle, a leading personality in the kennel world', *The Field*, 2 February 1935, p. 207. © British Library Board LOU.LD49   58

List of figures

5.1   Jack Russell in later years. Photograph courtesy of
      Sir Hugh Stucley   70
6.1   *A Distinguished Member of the Humane Society*, by Edwin
      Landseer, 1838. From Estelle M. Hurll, *Landseer: A
      Collection of Fifteen Pictures and a Portrait of the Painter with
      Introduction and Interpretation* (Boston: Houghton, and
      Company, 1901), p. 52   77
6.2   *Dignity and Impudence*, by Edwin Landseer, 1839.
      From Estelle M. Hurll, *Landseer: A Collection of Fifteen
      Pictures and a Portrait of the Painter with Introduction and
      Interpretation* (Boston: Houghton, and Company, 1901),
      p. 33   78
6.3   *Suspense*. From *British Workman*, 90, June 1862, p. 358.
      Courtesy of the BLT19 project: 19th-century Business
      Labour, Trade and Temperance periodicals   81
7.1   Harry Panmure Gordon with his Bearded Collie. From
      Country Gentleman, 1891, p. 1052. © Mary Evans Picture
      Library, Picture 10159774   86
7.2   John Pierpont Morgan, 1892. Courtesy of Library of
      Congress, Washington, DC   86
7.3   Mrs Panmure Gordon and her sister. From 'An
      eccentric collector', *Tatler*, 10 September 1902, p. 419.
      © British Library Board, ZC.9.d.561   88
7.4   Cragston Kennels. From *Harper's Weekly*, 22 February
      1896, p. 172. Image produced by ProQuest LLC as
      part of ProQuest® HarpWeek Archive   93
8.1   Miss Alice Cornwell, later Mrs Stennard Robinson.
      From 'Interview', *Women's Penny Paper*, 19 October
      1889, p. 1. © British Library Board, LOU.LON 297   97
8.2   Miss Mortivals aged five years, with three Black Pugs.
      From *Westminster Budget*, 2 November 1894, p. 3.
      © British Library Board, MFM.MLD29   102
8.3   'The Championship Open Class of the Ladies Kennel
      Association at Earl's Court.' From *Illustrated London News*,

List of figures

23 November 1901, p. 6. © British Library Board, MFM.
MLD47   104

8.4   Mrs Stennard Robinson, was the Secretary of the
Ladies Kennel Association, Mrs Dealtry – The
Plaintiff. From 'Sequel to a dog show', *Penny Illustrated
Paper*, 17 June 1905, p. 6. © British Library Board.
MFM.M40515   107

9.1   John Henry Walsh. From J. H. Walsh, *A Manual
of Domestic Medicine and Surgery* (London: George
Routledge, 1858), frontispiece   112

9.2   John Henry Walsh with his wife and daughter at the
All-England Croquet Club. From *Illustrated London
News*, 9 July 1870, front page. © British Library Board,
MFM.MLD47   116

9.3   All England Lawn Tennis Championship at
Wimbledon. From 'All England Lawn Tennis
Championship', *Illustrated Sporting and Dramatic News*,
14 July 1877, p. 405. © British Library Board, MFM.
MLD47   117

9.4   Mr Smith's Pointer, Major. From Stonehenge. *The
Dogs of the British Islands* (London: Horace Cox, 1867),
opp. p. 31   120

10.1 National sheepdog trials at Bala. From 'National
sheepdog trials', *Graphic*, 5 December 1874, p. 545.
© British Library Board, HS.74/1099   126

10.2 Sheepdog trials at Alexandra Palace, 1882. From 'Sheep
dog trials at the Alexandra Palace', *Graphic*, 24 June 1882,
p. 632. © British Library Board, HS.74/1099   128

11.1 John Henry Salter, 1875. From E. W. Jaquet, *The
Kennel Club: A History and Record of Its Work* (London:
Kennel Gazette, 1905), p. 17   135

11.2 Stages of a coursing event. From 'Public Coursing at
Kempton Park'. *Graphic*, 24 February 1883, p. 201.
© British Library Board, HS.74/1099   137

List of figures

11.3   John Henry Salter stalking game birds with his favourite
       dogs. From 'Dr Salter with three of his famous dogs –
       Mike, King Koffee and Romp', in J. O.
       Thompson (compiler), *Dr Salter, of Tolleshunt D'Arcy in the County of
       Essex, Medical Man, Freemason, Sportsman, Sporting-Dog
       Breeder and Horticulturalist: His Diary and Reminiscences,
       from the Year 1849 to the Year 1932* (London: John Lane,
       1932), pp. 132 and 402   141
11.4   John Henry Salter in his Masonic robes. From J. O.
       Thompson (compiler), *Dr. Salter, of Tolleshunt D'Arcy in
       the County of Essex, Medical Man, Freemason, Sportsman,
       Sporting-Dog Breeder and Horticulturalist: His Diary and
       Reminiscences, from the Year 1849 to the Year 1932* (London:
       John Lane, 1932), frontispiece   143
12.1   Winners at Cruft's First Great Show of All Kinds of
       Terriers. From *Illustrated Sporting and Dramatic News*,
       20 March 1886, p. 9. © British Library Board,
       HIU.LD53   150
12.2   Queen Alexandra greeting her prizewinning Basset
       hounds at Cruft's. From 'Royal pets recognised
       during a parade of prize-winners: Queen Alexandra
       and her "entries" at Cruft's', *Illustrated London News*,
       21 February 1914, pp. 296–97. © British Library
       Board, MFM.MLD47   153
13.1   William Youatt. Wellcome Collection,
       NonCommercial 4.0 International (CC BY-NC 4.0)   160
13.2   Title page of Delabere Blaine, *Canine Pathology, or a
       Full description of the diseases of dogs; with their causes,
       symptoms, and mode of cure … Preceded by an introductory
       chapter on the moral qualities of the dog* (London: T. Boosey,
       1817). Wellcome Collection, NonCommercial 4.0
       International (CC BY-NC 4.0)   165
13.3   Title page of William Youatt, *The Dog* (London:
       Charles Knight and Co., 1845)   167

List of figures

14.1 Charles Robert Darwin, 1865. Photograph by the London Stereoscopic & Photographic Company. Wellcome Collection, NonCommercial 4.0 International (CC BY-NC 4.0)   171

14.2 Human embryo; that of a dog, in Charles Darwin's *The Descent of Man* (London: John Murray, 1873), p. 15. From the Wellcome Collection. NonCommercial 4.0 International (CC BY-NC 4.0)   178

14.3 Dog approaching another dog with hostile intentions, by Mr. Riviere, in Charles Darwin's *The Expression of the Emotions in Man and Animals* (London: John Murray, 1873), p. 52. Wellcome Collection. NonCommercial 4.0 International (CC BY-NC 4.0)   181

14.4 Dog in humble and affectionate frame of mind, by Mr. A. May, in Charles Darwin, *The Expression of the Emotions in Man and Animals* (London: John Murray, 1873), p. 53. Wellcome Collection. NonCommercial 4.0 International (CC BY-NC 4.0)   182

14.5 The same caressing his master, by Mr A. May, in Charles Darwin, *The Expression of the Emotions in Man and Animals* (London: John Murray, 1873), p. 55. From the Wellcome Collection. NonCommercial 4.0 International (CC BY-NC 4.0)   183

15.1 Gordon Stables. From Gordon Stables, *Leaves from the Log of a Gentleman Gypsy: In Wayside Camp and Caravan* (London: Jarrold & Sons, London, 1892), frontispiece   186

15.2 Luath meets Professor Huxley, the Champion Mastiff. From Gordon Stables, *Sable and White: The Autobiography of a Show Dog* (London: Jarrold & Sons, 1893), opp. p. 42   192

15.3 The Wanderer ready for the road. From Gordon Stables, *Leaves from the Log of a Gentleman Gypsy: In Wayside Camp and Caravan* (London: Jarrold & Sons, London, 1892), opp. p. 12   193

List of figures

16.1 Everett Millais, 1886. Family photograph courtesy of
Dr Roger Bowdler   196

16.2 Everett Millais's Basset Hound Model. From V. Shaw,
The Illustrated Book of the Dog, (London: Cassell, Petter,
Galpin & Co., 1881), p. 338   197

16.3 Inoculation and Nicholas. From E. Millais, *Two
Problems of Reproduction* (London: Dog Owners' Annual,
1895), p. 9   200

17.1 Notices for what Charles Dickens called 'The two
dog shows'. From the *Islington Gazette*, 21 June 1862,
p. 1. © British Library Board, MFM.M72992
[1862]   210

17.2 Sale at Chelsea of vagrant dogs seized by the police.
From 'Police sale of stray dogs at Chelsea', *Illustrated
London News*, 14 November 1868, p. 478. © British
Library Board, © British Library Board,
MFM.MLD47   213

17.3 'Home for Lost and Starving Dogs, Battersea'. From
Graphic, 24 June 1876, p. 464. © British Library Board,
HS.74/1099   214

18.1 Frances Power Cobbe. From F. P. Cobbe, *The Life of
Frances Power Cobbe, by Herself*, vol. I (London: Bentley,
1894). Wellcome Collection, NonCommercial 4.0
International (CC BY-NC 4.0)   217

18.2 Emblem of the Victoria Street Society. Cover of
Edward Berdoe, *The Futility of Experiments with Drugs on
Animals* (London: Victoria Street Society, 1889)   223

18.3 Claude Bernard's apparatus for suspending a dog's
body. From F. P. Cobbe, *The Modern Rack* (London:
Swan Sonnenschein, 1889), p. 193. Wellcome
Collection, NonCommercial 4.0 International
(CC BY-NC 4.0)   226

19.1 John Cumming Macdona. From 'Saint Bernards',
Vanity Fair, 8 February 1894, opp. 85   230

List of figures

19.2 Barry – the original taxidermied exhibit. From
'A celebrated Swiss St. Bernard breeder', *Stock Keeper
and Fancier's Chronicle*, 14 August 1892, p. 158. British
Library Board, LOU.LON 22 [1892]   233

19.3 Barry – the taxidermied exhibit today. Courtesy of
Lisa Schäublin, Naturhistorisches Museum, Bern   233

20.1 Sewallis Shirley. From C. H. Lane, *Dog Shows and
Doggy People* (London: Hutchinson & Co., 1902),
p. 213   241

20.2 Ettington (formerly Eatington) Park. From C. L.
Eastlake, *A History of the Gothic Revival* (London:
Longmans, Green; New York: Scribner, Welford,
1972), opp. p. 261   241

20.3 Lough Fea House, Carrickmacross, Co. Monaghan.
Courtesy of National Library of Ireland, Call number
L.ROY_07125   243

Notes

Notes to Introduction

1 The term Doggy People was used widely for canine enthusiasts throughout the Victorian period, for example in the title of Charles H. Lane's *Dog Shows and Doggy People* (London: Hutchinson, 1902).

2 A. Oliver, *From Little Acorns: The History of Birmingham Dog Show Society, Est. 1859* (Birmingham: Birmingham Dog Show Society, 1998), pp. 7–8.

3 Idstone, *The Dog, With Directions for His Treatment* (London: Cassell, Petter and Gilpin, 1872); Idstone of "The Field", *The "Idstone" Papers: A Series of Articles and Desultory Observations on Sport and Things in General* (London: Horace Cox, 1872).

4 Oliver, *From Little Acorns*, pp. 10–25.

5 Lane, *Dog Shows*, pp. 178–80.

6 H. Ritvo, 'The emergence of modern pet-keeping', *Anthrozoös* 1 (1987), pp. 158–65; J. Hamlett and J-M. Strange, 'Animals in the family mini-special issue: introduction and historiographical review', *History of the Family* 26 (2021), pp. 173–85.

7 J. Hamlett and J.-M. Strange, *Pet Revolution: Animals and the Making of Modern British Life* (London: Reaktion Books, 2023).

8 P. Howell, *At Home and Astray: The Domestic Dog in Victorian Britain* (Charlottesville, VA: University of Virginia Press, 2015); N. Pemberton and M. Worboys, *Rabies in Britain: Dogs, Disease and Culture, 1830–2000* (London: Palgrave, 2012).

9 P. Howell, 'Between the muzzle and the leash: dog walking, discipline and the modern city', in P. Atkins (Ed.), *Animal Cities: Beastly Urban Histories* (London: Routledge, 2016), pp. 221–42.

10   E. Russell. *Greyhound Nation: A Coevolutionary History, 1200–1900* (New York: Cambridge University Press, 2018).

11   H. Ritvo, *The Animal Estate: The English and Other Creatures in the Victorian Age* (Cambridge, MA: Harvard University Press, 1987); M. Worboys, J-M. Strange and N. Pemberton, *The Invention of the Modern Dog: Breed and Blood in Victorian Britain* (Baltimore, MD: Johns Hopkins University Press, 2018).

12   'National sports', *Illustrated London News*, 12 July 1862, p. 63; 'International Dog Show', *York Herald*, 28 June 1862, p. 7.

13   Stonehenge, *The Dogs of the British Islands* (London: Horace Cox, 1867).

14   M. Brandow, *A Matter of Breeding* (Boston, MA: Beacon Press, 2015).

15   W. Youatt, *The Dog* (London: Charles Knight and Co., 1845), pp. 101–04.

16   Youatt, *The Dog*, p. 48.

17   H. Dalziel, *British Dogs* (London: L. Upcott Gill, 1888), vol. 2, p. 457.

Notes to Chapter 1, Queen Victoria

1   'The last day', *Daily Mail*, 23 January 1901, p. 5; 'The Queen asks for her pet dog', *Sunderland Daily Echo*, 22 January 1901, p. 6.

2   E. Longford, *Queen Victoria RI* (London: Weidenfeld and Nicolson, 1964); C. Hibbert, *Queen Victoria: A Personal History* (London: Harper Collins, 2001); J. Baird, *Victoria: The Queen. An Intimate Biography of the Woman Who Ruled an Empire* (London: Random House, 2016).

3   'The Queen and her pets', *Figaro in London*, 3 March 1838, p. 35.

4   *Queen Victoria's Journal*, 4 May 1838, p. 151. http://www.queenvictoriasjournals.org/search/displayItemFromId.do?FormatType=fulltextimgsrc&QueryType=articles&&filterSequence=0&PageNumber=5&ItemID=qvj02079&volumeType=ESHER#transcript (accessed 28 January 2022).

5   '*Eos*, signed and dated 1841', Royal Collection Trust. https://www.rct.uk/collection/403219/eos (accessed 19 October 2020).

6   *Windsor Castle in Modern Times*, etch dated 1848, made by Frederick Stacpoole, with mezzotint added by T. L. Atkinson.

7   *Victoria, Princess Royal, with Eos*, 1841, Royal Collection Trust. https://www.rct.uk/collection/401548/victoria-princess-royal-with-eos (accessed 12 September 2022).

8   Centrepiece hallmarks 1842/43, Royal Collection Trust. https://www.rct.uk/collection/1570/centrepiece (accessed 12 September 2022).

9   S. Gordon, *Noble Hounds and Dear Companions: The Royal Photograph Collection* (London: Royal Collection, 2007).

10   'The Queen's Staghounds', *The Field*, 23 November 1872, p. 520, 30 November 1872, p. 545. Also see: C. Armstrong, 'Her Majesty's Staghounds', *The Field*, 4 March 1893, p. 309.

Notes

11 'Her Majesty's pet dog Looty', *The Field*, 23 May 1863, p. 496. Also see A. Robson, *Dogs and Domesticity Reading the Dog in Victorian British Visual Culture*, PhD thesis, University of Plymouth (2017).

12 'Queen Victoria, 1819–1901', Border Collie Museum website at http://www.bordercolliemuseum.org/QueenVictoria/QueenVictoria.html (accessed 11 January 2022).

13 H. Rappaport, *Queen Victoria: A Biographical Companion* (London: ABC-CLIO, 2003).

14 H. Rappaport, *Magnificent Obsession: Victoria, Albert, and the Death That Changed the Monarchy* (London: Hutchinson, 2011), p. 36.

15 E. B. Simpson, 'The Queen's dogs', *Art Journal*, July 1887, p. 242.

16 Hibbert, *Queen Victoria*, p. 496.

17 Simpson, 'The Queen's dogs', p. 243.

18 'Dog show at the People's Palace', *The Field*, 28 August 1888, p. 354.

19 'Dog show at the People's Palace', *The Field*, 13 October 1888, p. 525.

20 'Dog show at the Agricultural Hall', *The Field*, 13 February 1892, pp. 214–15; 'Dog show at the Agricultural Hall', *The Field*, 11 February 1893, pp. 215–16.

21 'International Dog Show Paris', *The Field*, 6 July 1878, p. 21.

22 'Ladies Kennel Association's Dog Show', *The Field*, 13 June 1896, pp. 913–14; M. Worboys, J-M. Strange and N. Pemberton, *The Invention of the Modern Dog: Breed and Blood in Victorian Britain* (Baltimore, MD: Johns Hopkins University Press, 2018), pp. 207–09 and 211.

23 A. Brown, *Who Cares For Animals: 150 Years of the RSPCA* (London: Heinemann, 1974).

24 N. Pemberton and M. Worboys, *Rabies in Britain, 1830–2000, Dogs, Disease and Culture* (London: Palgrave 2012).

25 Benjamin Ward Richardson, 'The painless extinction of life', *Popular Science Monthly*, 26:3 (1885), pp. 641–52; P. Howell, *At Home and Astray: The Domestic Dog in Victorian Britain* (London: University of Virginia Press, 2015).

26 'The royal dogs', *The Field*, 12 June 1902, p. 3.

27 'Pathetic note in the funeral of King Edward', *Penny Illustrated Paper*, 28 May 1910, p. 685.

Notes to Chapter 2, Bill George

1 Stonehenge, *The Dogs of the British Islands* (London: Horace Cox, 1867), p. 71. Also see D. Flaim, 'By George: remembering Bill George, England's famous dog dealer and Mastiff contributor', *Modern Molosser Magazine*, October 2019.

2 H. Cowie, *Exhibiting Animals in Nineteenth-Century Britain: Empathy, Education, Entertainment* (London: Palgrave Macmillan, 2014), pp. 132–39; H. Cowie,

Notes

"'A disgusting exhibition of brutality": animals, the law and the Warwick lion fight of 1825', in S. Cockburn and A. Wells, eds, *Interspecies Interactions* (Abingdon: Routledge, 2017), pp. 149–68.

3   'Dogs and their days', *All Year Round*, 15 (1876), pp. 374–79.

4   'Always on sale', *The Field*, 18 August 1858, p. 98. Also see 'The author of *Fur and Feathers*' and 'A visit to "Canine Castle"', *Bell's Life*, 25 March 1860, p. 10.

5   F. Mason, 'More leaves from an old sketch book', *Fore's Sporting Notes and Sketches*, 24 (1907), pp. 100–01.

6   'Nolan and Thomas', *Bell's Life*, 27 April 1862, p. 7, 6 July 1862, p. 7.

7   '"Old Bill George" and dogs', *Westminster and Chelsea News*, 26 August 1882, p. 5.

8   E. Farman, *The Bulldog* (London: Stock Keeper Co., 1899), pp. 24–25.

9   George quoted by Captain Garnier in Stonehenge, *The Dogs of the British Islands*, 3rd edition (London: Longman, Green and Co., 1878), pp. 166–67.

10 Gelert, 'Country practice, no. II', *Sporting Review*, 23 (1850), p. 114.

11 Ex-gamekeeper, 'Judging dogs', *The Field*, 9 July 1864, p. 30.

12 Old Towler, 'Breeding up to defects', *The Field*, 9 July 1862, p. 56.

13 Bulldog, 'The London dog show', *The Field*, 12 April 1862, p. 325.

14 'North of England show of sporting dogs', *The Field*, 28 June 1862, p. 579.

15 'Crystal Palace Dog Show', *The Field*, 13 July 1878, p. 58.

16 T. B. Macaulay, *The History of England from the Accession of James II, Volume IV* (London: George Routledge and Sons, 1855), p. 588. Also see M. Storry and P. Childs (eds), *British Cultural Identities* (London: Routledge, 2017), pp. 33–36.

17 Denise Faim, 'By George', *Modern Molosser*. https://www.modern molosser.com/bill-george-victorian-dog-dealer-and-breeder-of-early-ma stiffs (accessed 22 November 2019).

18 Farman, *The Bulldog*, p. 29.

19 Dalziel, *British Dogs* (London: L. Upcott Gill, 1888), vol. 2, p. 81.

20 'A delicate question', *Morning Post*, 9 March 1865, p. 3.

21 'A curious dog case', *Reynold's News*, 6 August 1871, p. 5.

22 J. Grebe, 'History of the French Bulldog Club', at https://frenchbulldog club.org/history (accessed 22 November 2019). Also see Farman, *The Bulldog*, p. 52.

23 'Funeral of Bill George', *Sporting Life*, 11 June 1884, p. 1.

24 'Bill George's widow subscription fund', *Sporting Life*, 2 September 1884, p. 1.

25 'Bill George', *Kennel Chronicle*, 30 June 1884, p. 61.

26 'Death of Bill George', *Kennel Gazette*, June 1884, p. 124.

Notes

Notes to Chapter 3, Jemmy Shaw

1 He was registered as James John at birth but christened John James and was known throughout his adult life as Jemmy, a diminutive of James.
2 *Bell's Life*, 5 August 1849, p. 7.
3 D. Brailsford, *Bareknuckles: A Social History of Prizefighting* (Cambridge: Lutterworth Press, 1988).
4 J. Anderson, 'Pugilistic prosecutions: prize fighting and the courts in nineteenth-century Britain', *Sports Historian*, 212 (2002), pp. 35–53.
5 'The Dwarf and the Giant', *Bell's Life*, 23 May 1841, p. 4. A report in *The Era* stated that bouts between men of such different sizes were a farce and that it was no surprise that it never came off. 'Jemmy Shaw and Lawes', *The Era*, 18 April 1841, p. 9, and 23 May 1841, p. 11.
6 'The late fatal fight in Westminster', *Daily News*, 19 October 1866, p. 6; 'The late fatal fight at the West End', *Lloyd's Weekly Newspaper*, 4 November 1866, p. 5.
7 'Central Criminal Court', *Daily News*, 22 November 1866, p. 3; 'The fatal glove fight at Billy Shaw's', *Bell's Life*, 24 November 1866, p. 7.
8 D. Fleig, *History of Fighting Dogs* (Hampshire: T. F. H. Publications, 1996), pp. 105–02.
9 'Aristocratic cock fighting', *Royal Cornish Gazette*, 28 April 1865, p. 7.
10 P. Howell, 'Flush and banditti: dog-stealing in Victorian London', in C. Philo and C. Wilbert, eds, *Animal Spaces, Beastly Places* (London: Routledge, 2000), pp. 35–55.
11 'Canine', *Bell's Life*, 1 October 1843, p. 4. 'Tyke' was a term for curs and mongrels.
12 *Bell's Life*, 26 March 1848, p. 7.
13 *Bell's Life*, 2 April 1848, p. 6.
14 Jan Bondeson, *Amazing Dogs: A Cabinet of Canine Curiosities* (Stroud: Amberley, 2011), pp. 213–20.
15 H. Mayhew, *London Labour and the London Poor* (London: Dover, 1860), vol. III, pp. 9–11.
16 Mayhew, *London Labour*, p. 11.
17 *Bell's Life*, 27 April 1872, p. 12.
18 *Bell's Life*, 4 May 1862, p. 6.
19 'The Spaniel Fancy', *Hampshire Advertiser and Salisbury Guardian*, 21 March 1840, p. 2.
20 'The toilet', *Illustrated London News*, 5 September 1874, 231–32.
21 *Bell's Life*, 22 March 1863, p. 7, 29 March 1863, p. 7, 5 April 1863, p. 7, and 19 April 1863, p. 3.
22 Editorial, 'The "DAWG" show', *The Field*, 28 February 1863, p. 190.
23 'The "Dawg" Show', p. 189.

24 'Jemmy Shaw', *Bell's Life*, 29 April 1882, p. 11.
25 'Dog show at the Dramatic College, at the Crystal Palace', *The Era*, 15 July 1866, p. 4.
26 *Bell's Life*, 11 January 1886, p. 2.
27 'Jemmy Shaw funeral', *Illustrated Sporting and Dramatic News*, 16 January 1886, p. 443.

Notes to Chapter 4, Duchess of Newcastle

1 Lady Violet Greville, *Ladies in the Field* (London: Ward and Downey, 1894), pp. 61–70.
2 'Crystal Palace Dog Show', *The Field*, 1 November 1890, pp. 643–44.
3 Stonehenge, *The Dog in Health and Disease* (London: Longman, Green and Co., 1879), pp. 45–46.
4 H. Dalziel, *British Dogs: Their Varieties, History, Characteristics, Breeding, Management, and Exhibition. Illustrated with Portraits of Dogs of the Day* (London: 'The Bazaar' Office, 1879), p. 130.
5 'The Russian Wolfhounds', *Pall Mall Gazette*, 11 February 1892, p. 7.
6 'National Dog Show', *Birmingham Daily Post*, 28 November 1892, p. 12.
7 R. Lee, *A History and Description of the Modern Dogs of Great Britain and Ireland: Non-sporting Division* (London: Horace Cox, 1897), pp. 308–09.
8 R. Leighton, *The Complete Book of the Dog* (London: Cassell and Co., 1922), pp. 142–43.
9 J. R. Maguire, *Ceremonies of Bravery: Oscar Wilde, Carlos Blacker, and the Dreyfus Affair* (Oxford: Oxford University Press, 2013), p. 29.
10 See Alan Hollinghurst's 2008 review of *Belchamber* 'Don't ask Henry', *London Review of Books*, 30:19 (9 October 2008). https://www.lrb.co.uk/the-paper/v30/n19/alan-hollinghurst/don-t-ask-henry (accessed 19 January 2022).
11 P. Grayson, *The Ladies Kennel Association: The First Hundred Years* (Ashford: Dog World, 2004).
12 Quoted in 'K. Newcastle and the L.K.A.', *Ladies Kennel Journal*, 1 June 1895, pp. 23–24.
13 K. Newcastle, 'The Ladies' Show at Ranelagh', *Stock Keeper and Fancier's Chronicle*, 21 June 1895, p. 483.
14 The Kennel Club, *Treasures of the Kennel Club* (London: Kennel Club, 2000), pp. 69–70.
15 R. Lee, *A History and Description of the Modern Dogs of Great Britain and Ireland: Terriers* (London: Horace Cox, 1894), p. 133.
16 'Ladies news', *Illustrated London News*, 18 January 1919, p. 88.
17 S. Castle and T. Marples, *A Monograph on the Fox-Terrier: Smooth-Coated and Wire-Haired* (Manchester: Our Dogs, 1923).

Notes to Chapter 5, Jack Russell

1   'The late Rev. John Russell', *Illustrated London News*, 12 May 1883, p. 464.

2   'Death of Parson Russell: the last of the old school of reverend English sportsmen', *Washington Post*, 27 May 1883, p. 7; 'The Rev. Jack Russell', *New York Times*, 20 May 1883, p. 10.

3   'Death of the Rev. John Russell', *Bell's Life*, 5 May 1883, p. 7.

4   M. Worboys, 'Inventing dog breeds: Jack Russell Terriers', *Humanimalia: Journal of Human/Animal Interface Studies*, 10:1 (2018). https://www.depauw.edu/site/humanimalia/issue%2019/worboys.html (accessed 10 September 2020).

5   C. Noon, *Parson Jack Russell: The Hunting Legend, 1795–1883* (Tiverton: Halsgrove, 2000).

6   E. W. L. Davies, *A Memoir of the Rev. John Russell and His Out-of-Door Life* (London: Chatto and Windus, 1902), p. 53.

7   On Russell's hunting with Templer, see T. L. Pridham, *Devonshire Celebrities* (Exeter: Henry S. Eland, 1869), pp. 212–20.

8   *Nimrod's Hunting Tours, Interspersed with Characteristic Anecdotes, Sayings, and Doings of Sporting Men* (London: M. A. Pittman, 1835), p. 159.

9   'Devon county assizes', *North Devon Journal*, 25 March 1841, p. 3.

10 N. Gash, *Robert Surtees and Early Victorian Society* (Oxford: Clarendon Press, 1993).

11 H.H.S.P., 'Death of the Reverend John Russell', *Illustrated Sporting and Dramatic News*, 3 May 1883, pp. 192–93.

12 Linton, 'The South Devon Hounds and the South Devon Country', *New Sporting Magazine* 24 (1854), pp. 136–37.

13 'Biography: the Reverend John Russell', *Bailey's Monthly Magazine*, 19 (1870), p. 112. The author continues: 'Steady on the line, prompt in his cast, and rapid and cheery in chase, Russell was ever and is safe to give a good account of his Fox. To these excellences in the field may be added a fund of good humour and a pleasant word that under the most trying circumstances, is calculated to dispel and disarm any hasty sign of Fox antagonism'.

14 Davies, *Memoir of the Rev. John Russell*, p. 44.

15 Davies, *Memoir of the Rev. John Russell*, p. 224.

16 Davies, *Memoir of the Rev. John Russell*, p. 54.

17 'The Crystal Palace dog show', *The Field*, 18 June 1874, pp. 574–75.

18 'Barnstable dog and horse show', *The Field*, 1 July 1871, p. 2; 'Tiverton dog show', *The Field*, 27 May 1874, p. 597; 'Tiverton dog show', *The Field*, 26 May 1877, p. 611.

19 'Bideford and North Devon dog show', *The Field*, 29 July 1871, p. 98.

20 'The Reverend John Russell', *North Devon Journal*, 11 December 1873, p. 5.

Notes

21 'The visit of H.R.H. the Prince of Wales', *North Devon Journal*, 28 August 1879, p. 5; F. F. Whitehurst, 'Down in Devonshire: a royal stag-hunt', *Illustrated Sporting and Dramatic News*, 30 August 1879, p. 575.

22 *North Devon Journal*, 9 February 1882, p. 5.

23 'The aged sporting parson', *North and South Shields Daily Gazette and Shipping Telegraph*, 4 May 1883, p. 4; 'The late Rev. J. Russell', *The Standard*, 4 May 1883, p. 2. 'The Rev. John Russell', *The Field*, 5 May 1883, p. 574.

24 Lee, *Modern Dogs: Terriers*, p. 147.

25 R. Leighton, *Dogs and All About Them* (London: Cassell and Co. 1910), p. 188.

26 S. Dangerfield, 'We don't want to join that Club', *Daily Express*, 31 January 1970, p. 4.

27 M. Huxham, *All About the Jack Russell Terrier* (London: Pelham Books, 1975), pp. 30–31.

28 V. Bartlett, 'Recognition is the only way to ensure the old type's future', *Our Dogs*, 3 November 1983, p. 7.

29 R. Killick, 'Jack Russells: working dogs first and foremost', *Our Dogs*, 6 November 2015, p. 9.

30 Killick, 'Jack Russells'.

Notes to Chapter 6, Edwin Landseer

1 R.H., 'Spring gardens exhibition', *The Examiner*, 26 April 1818, p. 269.

2 R. Trethewey, *Mistress of the Arts: The Passionate Life of Georgina, Duchess of Bedford* (London: Review, 2002).

3 Stonehenge, 'The Newfoundland dog', *The Field*, 28 July 1877, p. 97.

4 R. B. Lee, *A History and Description of the Modern Dogs of Great Britain and Ireland: Non-sporting Division* (London: Horace Cox, 1894), p. 99.

5 Edwin Landseer, *High Life*, 1829, Tate Britain. https://www.tate.org.uk/art/artworks/landseer-low-life-a00703 (accessed 7 April 2020).

6 Edwin Landseer, *Low Life*, 1829, Tate Britain. https://www.tate.org.uk/art/artworks/landseer-low-life-a00702 (accessed 7 April 2020).

7 J. R. Cohen, *Charles Dickens and His Original Illustrators* (Columbus, OH: Ohio State University Press, 1980), pp. 174–76.

8 C. Lennie, *Landseer: The Victorian Paragon* (London: Hamish Hamilton, 1976), pp. 85–87.

9 Lennie, *Landseer*, p. 85.

10 'Exhibition at the Royal Academy', *New Sporting Magazine*, June 1837, p. 416; 'Exhibitions – the Royal Academy', *Blackwood's Edinburgh Magazine*, 42 (September 1837), p. 337.

11 'The pets', *Ladies' Treasury*, 1 June 1857, p. 97.

12 *British Workman*, 90 (June 1862), p. 358.

13 'North of England show of sporting and other dogs', *The Field*, 28 June 1862, pp. 578–79.

14 'One who has gone to the dogs', *The Times*, 1 July 1862, p. 14.

15 'Going to the dogs', *The Field*, 5 July 1862, p. 5.

16 E. Landseer, 'To the editor of the Times', *The Times*, 11 July 1862, p. 9.

17 J. K. Cronin, 'Popular affection: Edwin Landseer and nineteenth-century animal advocacy campaigns', in J, Castricano and L. Corman, eds, *Animal Subjects, 2.0* (Waterloo, ON: Wilfrid Laurier University Press, 2016), pp. 81–108; J. K. Cronin, *Art for Animals: Visual Culture and Animal Advocacy, 1870–1914* (University Park, PA: Penn State University Press, 2018).

18 R. Ormond, *Sir Edwin Landseer* (London: Thames and Hudson, 1981), p. 22.

19 'Sir Edwin Landseer', *The Times*, 13 October 1873, p. 12.

20 'The influence of Landseer', *Bell's Life*, 18 October 1873, p. 6.

21 'The influence of Landseer'.

Notes to Chapter 7, Harry Panmure Gordon and J. P. Morgan

1 H. Panmure Gordon, *The Land of the Mighty Dollar* (London: Warne, 1892), pp. 148–50.

2 'Brighton dog show', *The Field*, 28 October 1876, p. 518.

3 'The new Colley Club', *Stock Keeper and Fancier's Chronicle*, 9 September 1891, p. 9.

4 H. Panmure Gordon, 'Brighton Dog Show', *The Field*, 4 November 1876, p. 534.

5 'Mr. Pierpont Morgan's Collies', *Harper's Weekly*, 3 March 1894, p. 215.

6 D. Kynaston, *The City of London: Volume 1, A World of its Own, 1815–1890* (London: Chatto and Windus, 1994), p. 339.

7 'The Collie Club show', *The Field*, 8 April 1893, p. 523.

8 'Scottish Kennel Club Show at Glasgow', *The Field*, 20 June 1885, p. 824; 'Edinburgh dog show', *The Field*, 2 October 1886, pp. 484–85.

9 'Glasgow Dog Show', *The Field*, 29 July 1882, pp. 160–61.

10 V. Shaw, *The Illustrated Book of the Dog* (London: Cassell, Petter, Galpin and Co., 1881), p. 77.

11 H. Dalziel, *British Dogs: Their Varieties, History, Characteristics, Breeding, Management, and Exhibition. Illustrated with Portraits of Dogs of the Day* (London: 'The Bazaar' Office, 1879), p. 195.

12 M. Worboys, J-M. Strange and N. Pemberton, *The Invention of the Modern Dog: Breed and Blood in Victorian Britain* (Baltimore, MD: Johns Hopkins University Press, 2018), pp. 217–19. Also see A. Skipper, 'The "dog doctors"'

of Edwardian London: elite canine veterinary care in the early twentieth century', *Social History of Medicine*, 33 (2020), pp. 1233–58.

13 Worboys et al., *Invention of the Modern Dog*, p. 172.

14 'The Kennel', *Illustrated Sporting and Dramatic News*, 11 January 1902, pp. 734–35.

15 'Death of Mr. Panmure Gordon', *Financial Times*, 3 September 1902, p. 3; 'Mr. Panmure Gordon: remarkable career of a well-known man', *Daily Mail*, 3 September 1902, p. 3; 'A striking personality', *Daily Mail*, 3 September 1902, p. 5; 'Personal: death of Mr. Panmure Gordon', *Illustrated London News*, 13 September 1902, p. 378.

16 'J. P. Morgan's prize dog dead', *New York Times*, 17 July 1898, p. 9.

17 W. F. Stifel, *The Dog Show: 125 Years of Westminster* (New York: Westminster Kennel Club, 2001), pp. 57–60.

18 Quoted in M. Derry, *Bred for Perfection: Shorthorn Cattle, Collies, and Arabian Horses since 1800* (Baltimore, MD: Johns Hopkins University Press, 2003), p. 82.

19 'Morgan and Untermyer in the show ring', *New York Times*, 14 January 1907, p. 9; 'Untermyer's dogs beat J. P. Morgan's', *New York Times*, 31 May 1907, p. 11.

20 'Pure blood Collies; Samuel Untermyer adds a \$3,5000 dog to his kennels', *New York Tribune*, 2 April 1905, p. 9; 'Another high-priced Collie', *The Field*, 2 February 1907, p. 155. This was not Untermyer's most expensive dog – the St Bernard Sapho of Tytton had cost him more.

Notes to Chapter 8, Alice Stennard Robinson

1 'Interview', *Men and Women of the Day*, 2 (1889), p. 80.

2 'Sydney W. Carroll', *Oxford Reference*. https://www.oxfordreference.com/view/10.1093/oi/authority.20110803095551695 (accessed 19 January 2022).

3 'Victorian gold: Midas', *Sunday Times*, 29 January 1888, p. 3.

4 'London gossip', *Nottingham Evening Post*, 22 November 1887, p. 2.

5 'A miner in petticoats', *Southland Times*, 2 January 1888, p. 4.

6 H. Manning, *Henry Lawson: The Man and the Legend* (Melbourne: Melbourne University Press, 1991).

7 L. Sussex, 'Madame Midas and Henry Lawson', *Notes and Furphies*, 2 (1988), p. 18.

8 Quoted in 'London gossip', p. 2.

9 *Sheffield Independent*, 23 November 1887, p. 8.

10 'Miss Alice Cornwell: the Princess Midas on New South Wales mining', *Sunday Times*, 26 August 1888, p. 7.

11 *The Age* (Melbourne), 13 May 1889, p. 5.

Notes

12 *Men and Women of the Day*, 2 (1889), p. 80.

13 'At-home', *Sunday Times*, 23 June 1889, p. 6.

14 *Leeds Mercury*, 20 February 1890, p. 5.

15 'Mr. Herman Klein: music critic, teacher and writer', *The Times*, 12 March 1934, p. 19; W. R. Moran, *Herman Klein, and the Gramophone* (London: Amadeus, 1990).

16 'Miss Denise Robins', *The Times*, 3 May 1985, p. 16. Also see the auto-biography: Denise Robins, *Stranger Than Fiction* (London: Hodder and Stoughton, 1965).

17 *Sydney Morning Herald*, 11 February 1890, p. 6; *The Age* (Melbourne), 27 May 1890, p. 2.

18 Cited in the 'Excitement in Wall-street', *Melbourne Argus*, 4 March 1893, p. 13.

19 F.F.L., 'The kennel', *Sydney Morning Herald*, 18 June 1900, p. 12.

20 R. Lee, *A History and Description of the Modern Dogs of Great Britain and Ireland, Non-sporting Division* (London: Horace Cox, 1894), pp. 277–78.

21 'Black Pugs', *Hearth and Home*, 21 April 1892, p. 730.

22 'A ladies dog club', *The Field*, 26 May 1894, p. 745.

23 *Hearth and Home*, 1 November 1894, p. 893; 'Rules and regulations', *Ladies Kennel Journal*, 1 December 1894, p. 7.

24 P. Grayson, *The Ladies Kennel Association: The First Hundred Years* (Ashford: Dog World, 2004), p. 4.

25 'Whispers of the Fancy', *Stock Keeper and Fancier's Chronicle*, 14 June 1895, pp. 453–54.

26 Interview with Mrs Stennard Robinson, 'In the witness box: the Ladies' Kennel Association', *Sunday Times*, 9 June 1895, p. 2.

27 'Women in the kennel world', *British Fancier*, 12 December 1896, pp. 590–91.

28 'Women in the kennel world', p. 590.

29 Quoted in 'Miss Slaughter and the L.K.A. Committee', *Stock Keeper and Fancier's Chronicle*, 21 August 1896, p. 153.

30 'The new reign of terror – or "a reign of courtesy"', *Stock Keeper and Fancier's Chronicle*, 17 July 1896, p. 41; 'The new reign of terror: the Robinson joke', *Stock Keeper and Fancier's Chronicle*, 21 August 1896, p. 156.

31 'The Ladies Kennel Association', *The Field*, 21 May 1898, p. 776.

32 'Ourselves and the Kennel Club', *Ladies Kennel Journal*, 4 July 1896, p. 42.

33 'The scurrilous attack on the Hon. Sec. and the LKA published by *Our Dogs*', *Ladies Kennel Journal*, 3 June 1896, pp. 345–46; 'Cerberus', 'The LKA v. the Kennel Club', *Our Dogs*, 13 June 1896, p. 564, 20 June 1896, p. 599.

34 'Professional's pets', *The Era*, 18 December 1897, p. 20.

35 'The dogs of celebrities', *Strand Magazine*, July 1894, pp. 396–404.

Notes

36 'Fashionable dogs: Ladies' Kennel Association show at Earl's Court', *Daily Mail*, 16 December 1897, p. 3.

37 'Actresses day', *Illustrated Sporting and Dramatic News*, 8 July 1899, p. 753.

38 E. W. Jaquet, *The Kennel Club: A History and Record of Its Work* (London: Kennel Gazette, 1905), pp. 207, 229, 236 and 239; 'Kennel Club Ladies Branch', *The Field*, 17 July 1897, p. 124, and 24 July 1897, p. 153.

39 *The Times*, 7 June 1905, p. 4.

40 'High Court of Justice', *The Times*, 10 June 1905, p. 5. The trial was reported in *The Times*, 7 June 1905, p. 4; 8 June 1905, p. 3, 9 June 1905, p. 3, 10 June 1905, p. 5, 28 June 1905, p. 3, and 30 June 1905, p. 3.

41 'King's Bench Division', *The Times*, 28 June 1905, p. 3.

42 'Supreme Court adjudicature', *The Times*, 3 March 1906, p. 3.

43 Grayson, *The Ladies Kennel Association*, pp. 5–6.

44 L. Peskett, *The Fearless and the Fabulous: A Journey Through Brighton and Hove's Women's History* (Brighton: Brighton and Hove Museums, 2021).

Notes to Chapter 9, John Henry Walsh

1 P. Bartrip, *Mirror of Medicine: A History of the* British Medical Journal (Oxford: Oxford University Press, 1990).

2 R. N. Rose, *The Field, 1853–1953* (London: Michael Joseph, 1953), p. 73.

3 Rose, *The Field*, pp. 21–35 and 53–62.

4 Rose, *The Field*, pp. 36–44.

5 W. W. Greener, *The Gun and Its Development* (London: Cassel and Co., 1881).

6 'The government proof of rifles', *The Field* (8 December 1860), p. 467.

7 'In Memoriam', *The Field* (18 February 1888), pp. 205–06.

8 D. E. Hall (ed.), *Muscular Christianity: Embodying the Victorian Age*, (Cambridge: Cambridge University Press, 1994).

9 N. Smith, *Queen of Games: The History of Croquet* (London: George Weidenfeld and Nicolson, 1991).

10 A. Lillie, *Croquet: Its History, Rules and Secrets* (London: Longmans, Green, 1897).

11 D. Birley, *Sport and the Making of Britain* (Manchester: Manchester University Press, 1993), pp. 311–14.

12 'Lawn Tennis, Badminton and Croquet', *The Field*, 24 April 1875, p. 399.

13 J. Barrett, *Wimbledon: The Official History of the Championships* (London: CollinsWillow, 2001).

14 'Lawn Tennis Championship', *The Field*, 9 June 1877, p. 689.

15 'The Laws of Lawn Tennis', *The Field*, 11 May 1878, p. 573.

16 '"The Field" tricycle', *The Field*, 4 November 1877, p. 533.

17 'The Monster Dog Show', *The Field*, 28 June 1862, p. 588.

18 'The "Dawg" Show', *The Field*, 28 February 1863, pp. 189–90.
19 M. Worboys, J-M. Strange and N. Pemberton, *The Invention of the Modern Dog: Breed and Blood in Victorian Britain* (Baltimore, MD: Johns Hopkins University Press, 2018), pp. 95–111.
20 E. C. Ash, *This Doggie Business* (London: Hutchinson and Co., 1934), p. 206.
21 Stonehenge, *The Dog in Health and Disease*, 4th edition (London: Longmans, Green and Co., 1887), p. vi.
22 Worboys et al., *Invention of the Modern Dog*, pp. 146–54.
23 Editorial, 'Dog shows and the Kennel Club', *The Field*, 14 January 1888, p. 55.
24 'Dr Walsh', *County Gentleman*, 18 July 1888, p. 229.
25 'The late Mr Walsh', *The Field*, 18 February 1888, p. 231.

Notes to Chapter 10, Richard Lloyd Price

1 'The coming-of-age of Richard Lloyd Price: great rejoicing in Bala', *North Wales Chronicle*, 23 April 1864, pp. 4–5.
2 'Coming of age of Richard John Lloyd Price', *Wrexham Advertiser*, 23 April 1864, p. 6.
3 The Corwen to Bala railway opened in July 1866, and Bala to Dolgelly in August 1868. See W. G. Rear and N. Jones, *The Llangollen Line – Ruabon to Barmouth* (Stockport: Foxline, 1990).
4 R. J. Lloyd Price, *Dog Tales* (London: Sands and Co., 1901).
5 A. Urdank, 'The rationalisation of rural sport: British sheepdog trials, 1873–1946', *Rural History: Economy, Society, Culture*, 17 (2006), pp. 65–82.
6 'Sheep dog trials at Alexandra Palace', *Illustrated London News*, 8 July 1876, pp. 17–18. Also see *Bell's Life*, 1 July 1876, p. 11.
7 R. Lloyd Price, 'Sheep dog trials: an interesting question', *The Field*, 7 October 1916, p. 537.
8 R. Lloyd Price, 'Sheep dog trial at Alexandra Palace', *The Field*, 8 July 1876, p. 44, and 22 July 1876, pp. 114–15.
9 'Sheep dog trials at the Alexandra Palace', *Graphic*, 24 June 1882, p. 626.
10 'Moors, manors and forests', *The Field*, 25 October 1884, p. 586.
11 Committee on Laws Relating to Dogs, *Report of the Departmental Committee Appointed by the Board of Agriculture to Inquire into and Report upon the Working of the Laws Relating to Dogs with Copy of the Minute Appointing the Committee*, Minutes of Evidence, Parl. Papers, 1897, xxxiv. C.8378 (London: HMSO), paras 2134–96.
12 R. Lloyd Price, *Dogs Ancient and Modern, and Walks in Wales* (London: Eglinton and Co., 1893); F.R.A. (R. Lloyd Price), *The History of Rulacc, or Rhiwlas: Ruedok, or Rhiwaedog; Bala, Its Lake; the Valley of the Dee River; and much more of Merionethshire and counties adjacent thereto* (London: Pewtress

and Co., 1899); R. Lloyd Price, *Dogs' Tales, Canina Facundia, Wagged by R. J. L. Price: A Book for Middle-Aged Children* (London: Sands and Co., 1901).

13 *Saturday Review*, 22 July 1893, p. 105.

14 Lloyd Price, *Dogs Ancient and Modern*, p. 15.

15 'Our library table', *Athenaeum*, 20 January 1900, p. 82.

16 'Reviews and notices of new books', *Antiquary*, 35 (1899), p. 319.

17 *Bye-Gones, Relating to Wales and the Border Counties*, New Series (Oswestry: Wodall, Minshall, 1901), p. 129; *Bailey's Magazine of Sports and Pastimes*, 76 (1901), p. 44.

18 Quoted in Charles Maclean, 'Whisky woe in Wales', *Whisky Magazine*. https://whiskymag.com/story?whisky-woe-in-wales (accessed 16 January 2020).

19 Maclean, 'Whisky woe in Wales'.

20 *Morning Post*, 19 March 1900, p. 7.

21 *North Wales Chronicle*, 10 March 1900, p. 5; *The Times*, 3 March 1900, p. 3.

22 Lloyd Price was a director of the Tasmanian Land and Exploration Company, Limited. See *Mining Journal*, 26 September 1891, p. 1089.

23 'A North Wales company's liquidation', *Financial Times*, 28 November 1901, p. 5.

24 In his will, Lloyd Price's left his 'Effects' to his widow Evelyn. They were valued at £55,098 10s 6d, equivalent to £3 million in 2022.

Notes to Chapter 11, John Henry Salter

1 Salter's diaries were destroyed in a fire started by an incendiary bomb in the Second World War. A highly selective edited version was published just after his death as J. O. Thompson, *Dr. Salter, of Tolleshunt D'Arcy in the County of Essex, Medical Man, Freemason, Sportsman, Sporting-Dog Breeder and Horticulturalist: His Diary and Reminiscences, from the Year 1849 to the Year 1932* (London: John Lane,1933).

2 A. Croxton-Smith, 'A figure in the kennel world', *Illustrated Sporting and Dramatic News*, 30 April 1932, p. 267.

3 Thompson, *Dr. Salter*, p. 295.

4 E. Russell, *Greyhound Nation: A Coevolutionary History of England, 1200–1900* (Cambridge: Cambridge University Press, 2018), pp. 55–100.

5 H. Dalziel, *British Dogs: Their Varieties, History, Characteristics, Breeding, Management and Exhibition* (London: 'The Bazaar' Office, 1879), pp. 13–14 and pp. 26–27.

6 'The poultry mania', *Leisure Hour*, 31 March 1853, pp. 221–23; J. Driver, 'Poultry mania', *History Today*, 41:8 (1991), pp. 7–8.

7 See Caleb Robert Stanley's painting *Windsor Home Park: The Aviary and Poultry Farm*, 1845. Royal Collection Trust, RL 19772. https://www.

Notes

royalcollection.org.uk/collection/919772/windsor-home-park-the-avi
ary-and-poultry-farm (accessed 4 May 2017).

8 L. Wright, *The Illustrated Book of Poultry: With Practical Scheduals for Judging,
Constructed from Actual Analysis of the Best Modern Decisions* (London: Cassell,
Petter and Galpin, 1873), pp. 279–83.

9 'Sussex Spaniels', *The Field*, 5 December 1874, p. 596, 12 December 1874,
pp. 639–40, 19 December 1874, p. 662.

10 'Sussex Spaniels', *The Field*, 31 October 1874, p. 476.

11 E. W. Jaquet, *The Kennel Club: A History and Record of Its Work* (London:
Kennel Gazette, 1905), p. 3 and p. 22.

12 'T.W.B.', 'Trial of dogs in the field', *The Field*, 8 July 1865, p. 50.

13 Down Charge, 'Trial of stud Setters and Setters in the field', *The Field*,
15 April 1865, p. 256.

14 J. H. Salter, 'Judging at field trials', *The Field*, 14 May 1881, p. 665.

15 J. H. Salter, 'The "heat" versus the "spotting" system', *The Field*,
10 December 1881, p. 984.

16 A. F. Hochwalt, *Bird Dogs: Their History and Achievements* (Cincinnati, OH:
Sportsman's Digest, 1922), Ch. 3.

17 'The late Dr John Henry Salter', *Kennel Gazette*, May 1932, p. 329; 'A
figure of note in the kennel world', *Illustrated Sporting and Dramatic News*,
30 April 1932, p. 169; W. Day, 'The amazing Doctor Salter', *Country Life*,
23 December 1954.

18 Margaret Allingham, *Dancers at Mourning* (London: Heinemann, 1937),
p. 61 and p. 108.

Notes to Chapter 12, Charles Cruft

1 F. Jackson, *Cruft's: The Official History* (London: Pelham Books, 1990),
pp. 11–32.

2 Spratt was an inventor in the true nineteenth-century sense of the term.
His other inventions were a mousetrap, methods of hermetically sealing
foodstuffs in containers, multi-tool penknives and corkscrews.

3 'Spratt's Fibrine biscuits', *The Field*, 3 June 1871, p. 458.

4 'Alexandra Palace Dog Show', *The Field*, 17 June 1882, p. 827.

5 'Spratt's Patent', *Bell's Life*, 3 July 1880, p. 11.

6 G. Dalziel and E. Dalziel, *The Brothers Dalziel* (London: Methuen, 1901),
p. 272.

7 Jackson, *Cruft's*, pp. 53–61.

8 'The dog show', *The Times*, 12 February 1891, p. 10.

9 'Cruft's Dog Show', *Saturday Review*, 13 February 1892, p. 196.

10 'Dog show at the Agricultural Hall', *Horse and Hound*, 14 February 1891,
p. 6.

11 'Dog show at the Agricultural Hall', *The Field*, 14 February 1891, p. 215.
12 Jackson, *Cruft's*, pp. 62–83.
13 Jackson, *Cruft's*, p. 89.
14 'Some of the champion dogs and prizewinners at Cruft's show', *Daily Mirror*, 11 February 1905, p. 9.

Notes to Chapter 13, Delabere Blaine and William Youatt

1 M. Christy, 'The author of Blaine's Rural Sports – I', *The Field*, 9 December 1916, pp. 897–98, and 'The author of Blaine's Rural Sports – II', *The Field*, 16 December 1916, p. 940.
2 D. Blaine, *The Outlines of the Veterinary Art* (London: T. N. Longman and O. Rees and T. Boosey, 1802).
3 D. Blaine, *Domestic Treatise on the Diseases of Horses and Dogs* (London: T. Boosey, 1803); D. Blaine, *Dogs: The public attention is called to the following most efficacious animal remedies, discovered and prepared by Mr. Blaine … his powder, for the distemper in dogs … and never failing ointment, for the cure of mange in dogs, etc.* (London: Sorrell, c.1805).
4 Advertisement in Blaine, *Domestic Treatise*, p. 1.
5 D. Blaine, *Canine Pathology, or a Full description of the diseases of dogs; with their causes, symptoms, and mode of cure. … Preceded by an introductory chapter on the moral qualities of the* dog (London: T. Boosey, 1817), pp. xlix–x.
6 D. Blaine, *An Encyclopædia of Rural Sports; or, a Complete account, historical, practical, and descriptive, of hunting, shooting, fishing, racing, and other field sports and athletic amusements of the present day* (London, Longman and Co., 1840).
7 'British field sports', *Edinburgh Review*, 74 (1841), pp. 69–70.
8 Blaine, *Canine Pathology*, 1817, pp. i–iii.
9 'Meeting of creditors', *Morning Post*, 21 November 1835, p. 4.
10 'Society for Preventing Cruelty to Animals', *Bells' Life*, 3 July 1825, p. 2.
11 W. Youatt, *On Canine Madness: comprising the symptoms, post-mortem appearances, nature, origin, and preventive and curative treatment of rabies in the dog, and other domestic animals* (London: Longmans, 1830).
12 W. Youatt, *The Horse: With a Treatise on Draught and a Copious Index* (London: SDUK, 1831); W. Youatt, *Cattle: Their Breeds, Management and Diseases* (London: SDUK, 1834); W. Youatt, *Sheep: Their Breeds, Management and Diseases. To Which Is Added, the Mountain Shepherd's Manual* (London: SDUK, 1837).
13 T. K. Ewer, 'Youatt and Brunel', *Veterinary History*, 6:4 (1991), pp. 120–24.
14 C. Darwin to W. B. Dawkins, 16 January 1875, Darwin Correspondence Project, Letter no. 9819F. https://www.darwinproject.ac.uk/letter/DCP-LETT-9819F.xml (accessed 3 September 2020).

15   A. Woods, 'Doctors in the zoo: connecting human and animal health in British zoological gardens, c.1828–1890', in A. Woods et al., eds, *Animals and the Shaping of Modern Medicine: One Health and Its Histories* (London: Palgrave, 2018), pp. 27–69. Also see: T. Ito, *The London Zoo and the Victorians, 1828–1859* (London: Boydell and Brewer, 2014), p. 40.

16   Review, *Christian Reformer*, 6 (1838), pp. 591–92.

17   W. Youatt, *The Obligations of Humanity to Brutes, principally considered with reference to the Domesticated Animals* (Longmans and Co., 1839).

18   *The Times*, 3 November 1839, p. 4.

19   Youatt, *Obligations*, p. 4.

20   *The Era*, 5 May 1844, p. 11.

21   Blaine, *Canine Pathology*, p. xvi.

22   Blaine, *Canine Pathology*, p. xliv.

23   Youatt, *Obligations*, pp. 165–71.

24   W. Youatt, *The Dog* (London: Charles Knight and Co., 1845), p. 1.

25   Youatt, *The Dog*, p. 231.

26   Youatt, *The Dog*, p. 240.

27   'Obituary', *New Sporting Magazine*, February 1847, p. 147.

28   'Suicide of Mr. Youatt the veterinary surgeon', *Illustrated London News*, 16 January 1847, p. 39. Also see: *The Times*, 14 January 1847, p. 8; *Veterinarian*, 20 (1847), pp. 105–06; *Farmer's Magazine*, 15 (1847), p. 195.

29   'Obituary', *New Sporting Magazine*, February 1847, p. 147.

30   B. V. Jones, 'A short history of British small animal practice', *Veterinary History*, 15:2 (2010), pp. 93–135.

Notes to Chapter 14, Charles Darwin

1   C. Darwin, *On the Origin of Species by Means of Natural Selection, or the Preservation of Favoured Races in the Struggle for Life* (London: John Murray, 1859).

2   C. Darwin, *The Variation of Animals and Plants Under Domestication*, vols I and II (London: John Murray, 1868).

3   Darwin, *The Variation of Animals and Plants*, vol. I, pp. 15–48.

4   C. Darwin, *The Descent of Man* (London: John Murray 1871).

5   E. Townshend, *Darwin's Dogs: How Darwin's Pets Helped Form a World-Changing Theory of Evolution* (London: Francis Lincoln, 2009). Also see D. L. Feller, *The Hunter's Gaze: Charles Darwin and the Role of Dogs and Sport in Nineteenth-Century Natural History*, PhD thesis, University of Cambridge (2010).

6   J. E. Browne, *Charles Darwin: Voyaging – Volume I of a Biography* (London: Jonathan Cape, 1995), Ch. 1.

Notes

7   N. Barlow (ed.), *The Autobiography of Charles Darwin, 1809–1882* (London: Collins, 1958), p. 28.

8   Browne, *Charles Darwin*, pp. 7–14.

9   J. van Wyhe and C. Chua, *Charles Darwin: Justice of the Peace* (published independently, 2022).

10 P. H. Barrett, 'Early writings of Charles Darwin', in H. E. Gruber, ed., *Darwin on Man: A Psychological Study of Scientific Creativity; Together with Darwin's Early and Unpublished Notebooks* (London: Wildwood House, 1974), pp. 414–22.

11 F. Darwin, ed., *The Foundations of* The Origin of Species, *a Sketch Written in 1842* (Cambridge: Cambridge University Press, 1909), p. 6.

12 J. A. Secord, 'Nature's fancy: Charles Darwin and the breeding of pigeons', *Isis*, 72 (1981), pp. 162–86.

13 Darwin, *Origin of Species*, p. 214.

14 R. M. Young, *Darwin's Metaphor: Nature's Place in Victorian Culture* (Cambridge: Cambridge University Press, 1985).

15 P. J. Bowler, *Charles Darwin: The Man and His Influence* (Cambridge: Cambridge University Press, 1996).

16 Darwin, *The Variation of Animals and Plants Under Domestication* (London: John Murray, 1868).

17 Darwin, *The Variation of Animals and Plants*, vol. I, p. 15.

18 Darwin, *The Variation of Animals and Plants*, vol. I, p. 18.

19 Darwin, *The Variation of Animals and Plants*, vol. I, p. 42.

20 C. Darwin, *The Descent of Man* (London: John Murray, 1871).

21 P. White, 'Darwin wept: science and the sentimental subject', *Journal of Victorian Culture*, 16 (2011), pp. 195–213.

22 Darwin, *The Descent of Man*, pp. 39–40.

23 C. Darwin, *The Descent of Man*, 2nd edition (London: John Murray, 1874), p. 71.

24 Darwin, *The Descent of Man*, 2nd edition, p. 74.

25 Darwin, *The Descent of Man*, 2nd edition, p. 83.

26 Darwin, *The Descent of Man*, 2nd edition, p. 61.

27 Darwin, *The Descent of Man*, 2nd edition, p. 67.

28 C. Darwin, *The Expression of the Emotions in Man and Animals* (London: John Murray, 1872).

29 Darwin Correspondence Project, 'Letter no. 5330'. https://www.darwinproject.ac.uk/letter/DCP-LETT-5330.xml (accessed 3 August 2020).

30 Darwin, *The Expression of the Emotions*, p. 50.

31 Darwin, *The Expression of the Emotions*, p. 51.

32 Darwin, *The Expression of the Emotions* p. 51.

33 Darwin, *The Expression of the Emotions*, p. 57.

34 Darwin, *The Expression of the Emotions*, p. 60.

35 Darwin, *The Expression of the Emotions*, pp. 590–91; D. A. Feller, 'Dog fight: Darwin as animal advocate in the antivivisection controversy of 1875', *Studies in History and Philosophy of Biological and Biomedical Sciences*, 40 (2009), pp. 265–71.

Notes to Chapter 15, Gordon Stables

1 G. Stables, *Sable and White: The Autobiography of a Show Dog* (London: Jarrold and Sons, 1893).

2 G. Stables, 'Dr Gordon Stables and his new serial story', *Boy's Own Paper*, 30:1525 (1908), p. 432; A. Conan Doyle, 'Life on a Greenland whaler', *Strand Magazine*, 13:73 (1897), pp. 16–26. Also see D. W. Wamsley, 'Tales of the far north; Dr William Gordon Stables and the Arctic adventure story in the late Victorian era', *Polar Record*, 54 (2018), pp. 245–54.

3 G. Stables, *Medical Life in the Navy* (London: Robert Hardwicke, 1868).

4 Stables, *Medical Life in the Navy*, p. 58.

5 G. Stables, 'The confessions of an English chloral-eater', *Belgravia*, June 1879, pp. 179–90.

6 'For love or money', *Merthyr Times*, 24 October 1895, p. 8.

7 The books on cats were: G. Stables, *Domestic Cat* (London: G. Routledge and Sons, 1876); G. Stables, *Cats: Their Points and Characteristics, with Curiosities of Cat Life* (London: Dean and Son, 1877).

8 G. Stables, *Dogs in Their Relation to the Public: Social, Sanitary and Legal* (London: Cassell, Petter and Galpin, 1877); G. Stables, *The Practical Kennel Guide: With Plain Instructions How to Rear and Breed Dogs, etc.* (London: Cassell, Petter and Galpin, 1877).

9 G. Stables, 'Blue-Jackets' pets', *Chambers's Journal*, 26 July 1873, pp. 465–68.

10 S. Graham, *An Introduction to William Gordon Stables*, 2nd edition (Berkshire: Twyford and Ruscombe Local History Society, 2006).

11 'Reviews', *Sanitary Record*, 8 (1878), p. 142.

12 'Review', *Illustrated Sporting and Dramatic News*, 10 March 1877, p. 582.

13 Glendeonach, 'Doctor Gordon Stables on the Gordon Setter', *The Country*, 3 May 1877, p. 540.

14 G. Stables, *Ladies' Dogs, As Companions: Also a guide to their management in health and disease; with many stories, humorous and pathetic painted from the life* (London: Dean and Son, 1879).

15 Stables, *Ladies' Dogs*, pp. 127–28.

16 Stables, *Ladies' Dogs*, p. 129.

17 V. Shaw, *The Illustrated Book of the Dog* (London: Cassell, Petter, Galpin and Co., 1881), pp. 532–660.

18 J. Woodroffe Hill, *The Management and Diseases of the Dog* (London: Baillière and Co., 1878).

19 G. Stables, *Our Friend the Dog: A Complete Practical Guide with an Appendix on the Latest Breeds*, edited by E. B. Joachim (London: Dean and Son, 1903).

20 'Our friend the dog', *People's Friend*, January 1881, pp. 2–3.

21 For example see advice in the spring of 1880. G. Stables, 'Boys' dogs and all about them', *Boy's Own Paper*, 3 April 1880, p. 425, 24 April 1880, p. 471, 1 May 1880, p. 486, 8 May 1880, p. 500, 15 May 1880, p. 515, and 22 May 1880, p. 531.

22 G. Stables, 'Our mutual friend, puss', *Girl's Own Paper*, 16 April 1881, p. 457, and 14 May 1881, p. 518; G. Stables, 'Girls' own pets', *Girl's Own Paper*, 12 November 1881, p. 107. The series continued to 23 June 1883. On the wider context of girls' healthy pastimes see H. Marland, *Health and Girlhood in Britain, 1874–1920* (Houndmills: Palgrave Macmillan, 2013), pp. 75–84.

23 G. Stables, *Jungle, Peak and Plain: A Boy's Book of Adventure, etc.* (London: Cassel, 1877); G. Stables, *Wild Adventures in Wild Places* (London: Cassell, 1881).

24 Wamsley, 'Tales of the far north', pp. 245–46.

25 G. Stables, 'The cruise of the Snowbird', *Boy's Own Paper*, 19 March 1881, pp. 398–401. The novel was published with the same title: G. Stables, *The Cruise of the Snowbird: A Story of Arctic Adventure* (London: Hodder and Stoughton, 1882).

26 G. Stables, *How Jack Mackenzie Won His Epaulettes: A Story of the Crimean War, etc.* (London: Nelson and Sons, 1895); G. Stables, *On War's Red Tide: A Tale of the Boer War* (London: J. Nisbet and Co., 1900).

27 G. Stables, *Aileen Aroon, a Memoir, With Other Tales of Faithful Friends and Favourites* (London: Partridge and Co., 1884).

28 Stables, *Sable and White*, p. 263.

29 G. Stables, *The Cruise of the Land-Yacht 'Wanderer': or, Thirteen Hundred Miles in My Caravan* (London: Hodder and Stoughton, 1886). The journey was first serialised in the periodical *Leisure Hour*.

30 G. Stables, *Rota Vitæ: The Cyclist's Guide to Health and Rational Enjoyment* (London: Illiffe and Sons, 1886); G. Stables, *Health upon Wheels; or, Cycling as a Means of Maintaining the Health, etc.* (London: Illiffe and Sons, 1887).

31 His column appeared in the *Cheltenham Chronicle*, *Burnley Express* and *Blackburn Standard*.

32 *Illustrated London News*, 28 April 1894, p. 29.

33 C. Leighton, *Tempestuous Petticoat: The Story of an Invincible Edwardian* (London: Victor Gollancz, 1948), p. 47.

Notes to Chapter 16, Everett Millais

1 S. Fagence Cooper, *Effie: The Passionate Lives of Effie Gray, John Ruskin and John Everett Millais* (London: St Martin's Publishing Group, 2011).
2 R. Brownell, *Marriage of Inconvenience: John Ruskin, Effie Gray, John Everett Millais and the Surprising Truth About the Most Notorious Marriage of the Nineteenth Century* (London: Pallas Athene, 2013).
3 'Wolverhampton dog show', *The Field*, 23 January 1875, p. 75.
4 V. Shaw, *The Illustrated Book of the Dog* (London, Cassell, Petter, Galpin and Co., 1881), pp. 333–39.
5 N. Pemberton and M. Worboys, 'The invention of the Basset Hound: breed, blood and the late Victorian dog fancy, 1865–1900', *European Review of History*, 22 (2015), pp. 726–40.
6 Shaw, *Illustrated Book*, p. 327.
7 E. Millais, 'My kennels', *Dog Owners Annual* (Manchester: Our Dogs, 1896), pp. 65–87.
8 E. Millais, *The Theory and Practice of Rational Breeding* (London: Fancier's Gazette, 1889).
9 M. Bulmer, 'Galton's law of ancestral heredity', *Heredity*, 81 (1998), pp. 579–85.
10 'A dog breeder', 'An artificial impregnation', *Veterinary Journal*, 18 (1884), pp. 256–58.
11 W. Heape, 'The artificial insemination of mammals and subsequent possible fertilisation or impregnation of their ova', *Proceedings of the Royal Society of London A*, 61 (1897), p. 52. Communicated by Francis Galton, F.R.S. Received January 15, – Read February 11, 1897.
12 E. Millais, *Two Problems of Reproduction* (London: Our Dogs, 1895).
13 F. Galton, 'The average contribution of each several ancestor to the total heritage of the offspring', *Proceedings of the Royal Society of London*, 61 (1897), pp. 401–13.
14 J. Homans, *What Are Dogs For? The Surprising History, Science, Philosophy, and Politics of Man's Best Friend* (London: Penguin, 2013).
15 E. Millais, 'The pathogenic microbe of distemper in dogs, and its use for protective inoculation', *British Medical Journal*, i (1890), pp. 856–60.
16 Millais acknowledged the assistance of Sherrington, Monkton Copeman and a fellow medical student, A. Dalziel.
17 *British Medical Journal*, ii (1887), p. 320.
18 *British Medical Journal*, i (1889), p. 1479.

Notes to Chapter 17, Mary Tealby

1 C. Pearson, *Dogopolis: How Dogs and Humans Made Modern New York, London and Paris* (Chicago: University of Chicago Press, 2021), p. 25.

Notes

2   G. Jenkins, *A Home of Their Own* (London: Bantam Press, 2010), pp. 11–12.
3   'London dogs', *Leisure Hour*, 23 August 1860, pp. 533–36.
4   G. Costelloe, *The Story of the Battersea Dogs' Home* (London: David and Charles, 1979).
5   P. Howell, *At Home and Astray: The Domestic Dog in Victorian Britain* (London: University of Virginia Press, 2015), pp. 73–101.
6   Jenkins, *A Home of Their Own*, p. 25.
7   Editorial, *The Times*, 18 October 1860, p. 8.
8   'The last freak of the dog', *Belfast Morning News*, 23 October 1860, p. 4; 'The latest absurdity', *Carlisle Journal*, 23 October 1860, p. 2; 'Charity going to the dogs', *Western Daily Press*, 20 October 1860, p. 2; 'Home for lost dogs', *Western Daily Press*, 25 October 1860, p. 4.
9   W. Kidd, 'Home for dogs', *Leisure Hour*, 5 September 1861, p. 565.
10 C. Dickens, 'Two dog shows', *All Year Round*, 2 August 1862, pp. 493–97.
11 Dickens, 'Two dog shows', p. 495.
12 M. Worboys, J-M. Strange and N. Pemberton, *The Invention of the Modern Dog: Breed and Blood in Victorian Britain* (Baltimore: MD: Johns Hopkins University Press, 2018), p. 71.
13 'Temporary Home for Lost and Starving Dogs', *The Times*, 9 May 1863, p. 1.
14 Jenkins, *A Home of Their Own*, p. 45.
15 *Royal Cornwell Gazette*, 21 December 1865, p. 5; *Sheffield Daily Telegraph*, 20 December 1865, p. 4.
16 Pearson, *Dogopolis*, p. 7.
17 'Police sale of stray dogs at Chelsea', *Illustrated London News*, 14 November 1868, p. 478.
18 J. Johnson, 'Home for lost dogs', *Morning Post*, 20 March 1876, p. 3.
19 'The dogs home', *Morning Post*, 1 April 1886, p. 2; 'The Dogs Home, Battersea', *The Times*, 23 December 1886, p. 3.
20 B. Tozer, 'The Dogs' Home, Battersea', *English Illustrated Magazine*, August 1895, pp. 445–49.
21 Jenkins, *A Home of Their Own*, p. 110.

Notes to Chapter 18, Frances Power Cobbe

1   D. Donald, *Women Against Cruelty: Protection of Animals in Nineteenth-Century Britain* (Manchester: Manchester University Press, 2021), pp. 190–236.
2   S. Mitchell, *Frances Power Cobbe: Victorian Feminist, Journalist, Reformer* (London: University of Virginia Press, 2004); L. Williamson, *Power and Protest: Frances Power Cobbe and Victorian Society* (London: Rivers Oram Press, 2005); S. Hamilton, *Frances Power Cobbe and Victorian Feminism* (Basingstoke: Palgrave Macmillan, 2006).

Notes

3 S. J. Peacock, *The Theological and Ethical Writings of Frances Power Cobbe* (New York: Edwin Mellen Press, 2002).

4 Anon., 'Character sketch: Frances Power Cobbe', *Review of Reviews*, 10 (1894), pp. 329–38.

5 J. Verschoyle, 'F. P. Cobbe', *Contemporary Review*, 85 (1904), pp. 829–40.

6 F. P. Cobbe, 'The rights of man and the claims of brutes', *Fraser's* 68 (1863), pp. 586–602.

7 Cobbe, 'The rights of man', p. 601.

8 F. P. Cobbe, 'The consciousness of dogs', *Quarterly Review*, 133 (1872), p. 426. Cobbe translates 'Ubomi' from Zulu as 'carrion', but others suggest 'life' or 'danger'.

9 Cobbe, 'The consciousness of dogs', pp. 428–30.

10 Donald, *Women Against Cruelty*, pp. 129–32; H. Kean, 'The moment of Greyfriars Bobby: the changing cultural position of animals, 1800–1920', in K. Kete, ed., *A Cultural History of Animals: In the Age of Empire* (Oxford: Berg, 2007), vol. 5, pp. 5–46.

11 Cobbe, 'The consciousness of dogs', p. 446.

12 F. P. Cobbe, *The Confessions of a Lost Dog, reported by her mistress F. P. Cobbe* (London: Griffin and Farran, 1867).

13 S. Hamilton, 'Hajjin: photographed from life', *Victorian Review*, 40 (2014), pp. 28–31; F. P. Cobbe, 'Dogs whom I have met', *Cornhill Magazine*, 26 (1872), pp. 62–78.

14 H. Kean, 'The "Smooth cool men of science": the feminist and socialist response to vivisection', *History Workshop Journal*, 40 (1995), pp. 16–38.

15 R. D. French, *Antivivisection and Medical Science in Victorian Society* (Princeton, NJ: Princeton University Press, 1975), pp. 53–56.

16 G. Hoggan, 'Letter', *Morning Post* (1 February 1875), p. 3.

17 F. P. Cobbe, *The Modern Rack* (London: Swan, Sonnerschein, 1889), p. 10.

18 B. Caine, 'Cobbe, Frances Power (1822–1904), writer and campaigner for women's rights', *Oxford Dictionary of National Biography* (Oxford: Oxford University Press, 2004).

19 F. P. Cobbe, 'Professor Horsley and Miss Cobbe', *The Times*, 15 October 1892, p. 12, 17 October 1892, p. 7, 18 October 1892, p. 10, 25 October 1892, p. 7, 20 October 1892, p. 14, 21 October 1892, p. 6, 24 October 1892, p. 11, 25 October 1892, p. 7, 27 October 1892, p. 12.

20 'Vivisection and surgery', *The Times*, 30 December 1884, p. 10, (6 January 1885, p. 10, 31 January 1885, p. 10.

21 'The discussion of vivisection', *The Times*, 9 May 1881, p. 11; 'The charge against David Ferrier', *The Times*, 18 November 1881, p. 10.

22 J. Turner, *Reckoning with the Beast: Animals, Pain, and Humanity in the Victorian Mind* (Baltimore, MD: Johns Hopkins University Press, 1980).

23 N. Pemberton and M. Worboys, *Rabies in Britain, 1830–2000: Dogs, Disease and Culture* (London: Palgrave, 2012).

24 F. P. Cobbe, 'The dog regulations', *The Times* (17 August 1886), p. 7.

25 F. P. Cobbe, 'Muzzling and hydrophobia', *The Times*, 22 October 1889, p. 13.

26 Frances Power Cobbe, *The Life of Frances Power Cobbe, by Herself* (London: Bentley, 1894).

27 'Remarkable will of Miss Cobbe', *The Times*, 10 April 1904, p. 5.

28 'Miss Frances Power Cobbe', *The Times*, 7 April 1904, p. 8.

Notes to Chapter 19, John Cummings Macdona

1 'Sermon by Mr. Macdona', *New York Times*, 14 May 1877, p. 2.

2 'Church Pastoral Aid Society', *Manchester Courier*, 31 January 1863, p. 10; 'Mossley', *Manchester Courier*, 21 March 1863, p. 8.

3 Roger Dawson-Duffield was a count of the Principality of Monaco.

4 'Disgraceful disturbances at a church', *Liverpool Mercury*, 12 April 1865, p. 3; 'The disturbances in Sefton Church', *Liverpool Mercury*, 14 April 1865, p. 6; 'The recent disturbances at Sefton', *Liverpool Mercury*, 21 April 1865, p. 5; 'The disturbances at Sefton Church', *Liverpool Mercury*, 26 April 1865, p. 6.

5 'Testimonial to a clergyman', *Liverpool Mercury*, 31 March 1870, p. 8.

6 C. R. Lane, *Dog Shows and Doggie People* (London: Hutchison and Co., 1902), p. 7 and pp. 150–54.

7 'A celebrated Swiss St. Bernard breeder', *Stock Keeper and Fancier's Chronicle*, 14 August 1892, p. 2.

8 J. C. Macdona, 'St. Bernards as deerstalkers', *The Field*, 6 October 1883, p. 492.

9 E. C. Ash, *This Doggie Business* (London: Hutchinson and Co., 1934), p. 123.

10 E. C. Ash, *The Practical Dog Book* (London: Simpkin Marshall, 1930), p. 78.

11 See the exhibit 'Barry: The Legendary St. Bernard Dog', Natural History Museum Bern. https://www.nmbe.ch/sites/default/files/2021-12/Barry_Broschuere_14_E.pdf (accessed 16 January 2022).

12 J. Watson, *The Dog Book* (New York: Doubleday, 1905), p. 580.

13 J. Watson, 'The St. Bernard myth', *New York Times*, 24 October 1884, p. 4.

14 Watson, *The Dog Book*, p. 58.

15 A. Fernandez, 'Westminster huckster or hero', *Canine Chronicle*, October 2020. http://caninechronicle.com/current-articles/westminster-huckster-or-hero (accessed 31 October 2020).

16 J. C. Macdona, *Diary of a Voyage from Southampton to South America* (Stockport: Steam Printing Works 1886), no pagination.

17 J. Cumming Macdona, 'Liebig's Extract of Meat Saladero at Fray Bentos, S. America', *The Field*, 4 June 1881, p. 771; 'Across the Pampas to the Andes', *The Field*, 4 June 1881, p. 771; 'Across the Andes from east to west: Mendoza to Santa Rosa de Los Andes', *The Field*, 17 September 1881, pp. 424–25.

18 'London', *Harper's Weekly*, 18 March 1899, p. 274.

19 'Dinner to Mr J. Cumming Macdona', *Derby Mercury*, 13 January 1886, p. 3.

20 J. C. Macdona, 'Across the Atlantic', *Derbyshire Times*, 20 March 1886, p. 8.

21 A. Stricklin, *Links, Lore and Legends: The Story of Texas Golf* (Lanham, MD: First Taylor Publishing, 2020), p. 9.

22 'Notes by the way', *Derbyshire Times*, 12 June 1886, p. 5.

23 C. Macdona, *Short History of the Watermen and Lightermen of the Port of London* (London: Waterlow and Sons, 1902).

24 C. Macdona, 'Departmental report on floating derelicts', *The Times*, 5 February 1895, p. 14.

25 'Cumming Macdona', *Wheelwomen and Society Cycling Newsletter*, 24 July 1897, p. 17.

26 'Self-propelled traffic', *The Times*, 11 December 1895, p. 12.

27 'The late Mr. J. Cumming Macdona', *The Field*, 11 May 1907, p. 762; 'Mr. John Cumming Macdona', *The Times*, 9 May 1907, p. 4. Also see T. R. Nicholson, *The Birth of the British Motor Car, 1769–1897, Volume III: The Last Battle* (London: Macmillan, 1982), p. 355.

Notes to Chapter 20, Sewallis Shirley

1 'Coming of age of Mr Sewallis E. Shirley: celebrations as Eatington [*sic*]', *Royal Leamington Spa Courier*, 6 August 1865, p. 8.

2 'The Monaghan election petition', *Freeman's Journal*, 11 March 1874, p. 7.

3 'The Shirley Estate Farming Society', *Belfast Newsletter*, 8 October 1874, p. 3.

4 G.F., 'Mr Shirley's kennels, Newbold, Warwickshire', *Illustrated Sporting and Dramatic News*, 27 March 1886, p. 50.

5 A. Oliver, *From Little Acorns: The History of Birmingham Dog Show Society, Est. 1859* (Birmingham: Birmingham Dog Show Society, 1998).

6 M. Worboys, J-M. Strange and N. Pemberton, *The Invention of the Modern Dog: Breed and Blood in Victorian Britain* (Baltimore, MD: Johns Hopkins University Press, 2018), pp. 107–11.

7 E. Jaquet, *The Kennel Club: A History and Record of Its Work* (London: Kennel Gazette, 1905), pp. 2–7.

8   'The Crystal Palace Dog Show', *The Field*, 25 June 1870, p. 533.

9   'Among the dogs', *The Observer*, 4 June 1871, p. 7.

10 'Kvoy', 'The field trial derby', *The Field*, 16 January 1875, p. 42; J. G. V. Wakeley, 'The National Canine Society', *Bell's Life*, 19 July 1873, p. 11; Our correspondent, 'Country notes', *Bell's Life*, 23 August 1871, p. 6.

11 'The Crystal Palace dog show', *The Field*, 8 June 1972, p. 505.

12 Francis Galton had defined eugenics as 'the science of improving racial stock'.

13 'The Kennel Club and ourselves', *The Field*, 3 October 1874, p. 347.

14 'The Kennel Club', *The Field*, 10 October 1874, p. 382.

15 J. Mills, *The Sportsman's Library* (Philadelphia: Lea and Blanchard, 1846), p. 253.

16 Dinks, Mayhew and Hutchinson, revised by F. Forester, *The Dog* (New York: Geo. E. Woodward, 1878), p. 21.

17 H. Dalziel, *British Dogs: Their Varieties, History, Characteristics, Breeding, Management and Exhibition* (London: 'The Bazaar' Office, 1879), p. 160.

18 Dalziel, *British Dogs*, p. 158.

19 R. Lee, *A History and Description of the Colie or Sheep Dog* (London: Horace Cox, 1890), p. 50.

20 'The Alexandra Palace dog show', *Bell's Life*, 22 December 1877, p. 11.

21 'Canine fancy', *Bell's Life*, 15 December 1877, p. 12, 22 December 1877, p. 12.

22 S. E. Shirley, 'Darlington Show and the Kennel Club', *The Field*, 13 August 1881, p. 231.

23 'The Kennel Club and the Darlington Show', *Stock Keeper and Fancier's Chronicle*, 9 September 1881, pp. 8–9.

24 J. Marlow, *Captain Boycott and the Irish* (London: André Deutsch, 1973).

25 Worboys et al., *Invention of the Modern Dog*, pp. 196–204.

26 'Death of Mr. Shirley', *The Field*, 12 March 1904, pp. 414–15. At probate, his estate was valued at £63,526 (£6.9 million in 2020).

27 J. S. Turner, 'S.E.S.', *Kennel Gazette*, 25 (1904), p. 107.

Notes to Afterword

1   D. McRae, 'A new heart, a new era', *The Guardian*, 26 June 2006. https://www.theguardian.com/society/2006/jun/26/health.southafrica (accessed 26 April 2022).

2   B. Bolman, 'Dogs for life: Beagles, drugs, and capital in the twentieth century', *Journal for the History of Biology* (2021). https://doi.org/10.1007/s10739-021-09649-2 (accessed 12 September 2022).

Notes

3 A. Gardiner, 'The "dangerous" women of animal welfare: how British veterinary medicine went to the dogs', *Social History of Medicine*, 27 (2014), pp. 466–87.

4 L. Morgan et al., 'Human–dog relationships during the COVID-19 pandemic: booming dog adoption during social isolation', *Humanities and Social Sciences Communications*, 70:155 (2020). https://doi.org/10.1057/s41599-020-00649-x (accessed 12 September 2022).

Index

Allingham, Margery 144
Alpine Mastiffs 229, 232
antivivisection 7, 17, 26, 84,
          129–30, 184, 202, 205, 216,
          221–28

Basset Hounds 3, 26, 121, 152–53,
          195–201
Battersea Dogs' Home 3, 6, 26, 207,
          212–22, 248
Beagles 68, 198, 240, 254
Beech, George 4
Birmingham Dog Show Society 4,
          242, 249
Blacker, Carlos 54
Blaine, Delabere 3, 155, 157–59,
          164–66
      books
          Canine Pathology 158, 164–66
          Encyclopædia of Rural Sports 159
Bloodhounds 200–01
Borzois 2, 48, 51–58, 61, 121, 151,
          234
boxing 38–39
Brailsford, Richard 4
British Union for the Abolition of
          Vivisection (BUAV) 130, 227
Brunel, Isambard Kingdom 162
Bull Terriers 240, 245

'Bulldog breed' 35
Bulldogs 8, 28, 31, 33–35, 43, 68,
          76, 123, 124, 168, 176–77,
          243, 257

Canine Castle 2, 15, 28, 31–33,
          35
Chappel Brothers 252
Clumber Park 49–50, 53, 124
Clumber Spaniels 49, 245
Cobbe, Frances Power 3, 7, 130,
          205, 216–28
      books
          Confessions of a Lost Dog (1867)
          219, 221–22
          The Modern Rack (1889) 224,
          226
      on dog consciousness 219–21
      on the medical profession
          224–25, 228
      on rabies 227
      on vivisection 222–27
Collies 61, 85–89, 92–95, 123,
          126–27, 129, 189, 240,
          247–48, 256–57
'Great Collie Ear Trial' 90–91
Cornwell, Alice *see* Mrs Stennard
          Robinson
Cooper, Gary 252

coursing 7, 113–14, 136–39
Waterloo Cup 7, 138
Cruelty to Animals Act, 1835
29
Cruft, Charles 2–3, 11, 49, 52,
109, 145–54, 229, 251, 253,
Plate 6
'British Barnum' 3, 145, 149–50
Cruft's Dog Show 52, 149–53
Emma Cruft 153–54
The First Great Show of All
Kinds of Terriers 11, 75,
150–53

Dachshunds 152, 198
Dalziel, Hugh 12
Dandie Dinmont Terriers 75–76,
234
Dangerfield, Stanley 71
Darwin, Charles 3, 84, 155, 170–84,
203, 218, 221, 225, 256
books
On the Origin of Species (1859)
170, 174–76
The Descent of Man (1871) 170
*The Expression of the Emotions
in Man and Animals* (1872)
180–84
*The Variation of Animals and
Plants Under Domestication*
(1868) 176
on evolution of dogs 175–77
on vivisection 184
Davis, Bette 252
Dicken, Maria 255
Dickens, Charles 28, 79
Two Dog Shows (1862) 210–11
dog breeds *see* individual breeds
breed points 9–10
breed (conformation) standards 3,
9–10, 34, 75, 89, 109, 111,
119–22, 127, 140, 232, 246,
250, 252

see also Dog shows,
conformation standards
dog doctors 3, 155, 157–64
dog shows 1, 3–4, 9, 11, 23–24,
34–35, 44–46, 48–49,
51–52, 55, 57, 68, 75, 76,
82, 88–89, 92–94, 106–08,
109, 118–22, 124–27, 130,
134, 139–40, 175, 185,
188–91, 198, 203, 234–36,
243–50, 251, 255
conformation standards 3, 44,
119–22, 147, 232, 243,
247
Cruft's Dog Show 145–53, 251,
253
Charles Dickens on 210–11
dog stealing 31–33, 41
dogfighting 29, 38, 134, 164, 166
dogs as pets 5, 11, 15, 17, 23–26,
42, 71, 74, 79, 90, 109, 120,
129, 139, 172, 177–82, 190,
207–10, 248, 251
Douglas, John 49
Doyle, Arthur Conan 185
Duchess of Newcastle 2, 15, 48–59,
71, 103, 108, 152
Borzois 51–53, 56–59
Caesar of Notts 26–27
Fox Terriers 56–58
Duke of Newcastle, 7th (Henry
Pelham-Clinton) 48–50

Fancy, The 2, 15, 28, 33, 41–47,
83, 244
field trials 8, 109, 123–25, 140–41,
231, 234, 236, 249, 246
fox hunting 62
Fox Terriers 2, 11, 56–59, 61–62,
68–69, 71, 234
Smooth 56, 58, 245
Wire-Haired 56, 68
French Bulldogs 36, 256

Galton, Francis 195, 199–201
George, Bill 2, 4, 15, 28–37
  Bulldogs 31, 33–36
  Canine Castle 2, 16, 28, 31–32, 35
  'Father of the Fancy' 28
  Mastiffs 22–34
Georgiana, Duchess of Richmond
    65, 75
Gordon, Harry Panmure 2, 61, 85–92
  caravanning 88
  carriage collection 87–88
  eccentric banker 86–87
  'Great Collie Ear Trial' 90–91
  Scottish Kennel Club 88–91
Gordon Setters 234
Grand Duke Nicholas 52
Grand National, The 8, 138
Grant, Cary 252
Great Danes 121, 170
Greyfriars Bobby 5, 27, 220
Greyhound racing 254
Greyhounds 7, 8, 52, 137–40, 168,
    173, 175–76

Harriers 68, 129
Hitchcock, Alfred 252
humane attitudes 1, 5–7, 77, 161
    168–69, 211, 223
  see also Royal Society for the
    Protection of Cruelty to
    Animals (RSPCA)
Huxley, Thomas Henry 176, 218
  'Darwin's Bulldog' 176

Irish Setters 234–35
Irish Wolfhounds 121
Italian Greyhounds 68

Jack Russell Terriers 63, 69, 71–73

Kennel Club 4, 9, 35, 55, 61, 89,
    91 124, 140, 147, 152, 204,
    240, 243

    field trials 246
    founded 1873 121
    Ladies Branch (KCLB) 48, 54–55
    studbook 52, 141

Labradors 247, 257
Ladies Kennel Association (LKA) 2,
    26, 48, 56, 61, 101, 103, 106
  'Dog-Loving Ladies at War' 107
  relations with Kennel Club
    103–05
Landseer, Edwin 2, 5–6, 19–20, 32,
    61, 74–84, 232, Plate 4
  Nelson's Column Lions 83
  on ear-cropping 82
  paintings
    *A Distinguished Member of the
      Humane Society* 77, 84, 223
    *Alexander meeting the philosopher
      Diogenes* 82
    Dignity and Impudence 77, 78
    Fighting Dogs Getting Wind 75
    High Life and Low Life 77
    Stag at Bay 82
    Suspense 80–81
    The Monarch of the Glen 82
    The Old Shepherd's Chief Mourner
      6, 79
    The Sanctuary 82
  Royal Family 5, 19–20
lapdogs 23, 45, 176
Lassie 253
Lloyd, Mary 224, 228
Lloyd Price, Richard 3, 109, 123–33,
    148, 224 Plate 5
  Pointers 124, 128, 130, 133
  Rhiwlas Estate 123–32
  Welsh whisky 132–32

Macdona, John Cumming 4, 205,
    229–39
  clergyman 229–31, 236
  Member of Parliament 237–38

Index

St Bernards 234–45
travels 236
Marples, Theo 4
Mars, Forrest 252–53
Mars, Frank 252–53
Mastiffs 24, 31, 33–34, 152, 168,
176, 191
Mayhew, Henry 1, 43–44
Millais, Everett 3, 155, 195–204
on artificial insemination
199–200
Basset Hounds 197–201
Basset Hound Model 197–98
on distemper 202
opponent of the Kennel Club
203–04
on 'rational breeding' 199–200
Millais, John Everett 79
Morgan, J. P. 2, 61, 86, 88, 92–95,
252
Cragston Kennels 92–94
Sefton Hero 92

Neville-Lytton, Judith 251–52
Newcastle upon Tyne Dog Show
(1859) 4, 117–18, 174
Newfoundlands 75, 168, 176, 189
Landseer Newfoundlands 76–77

Pearce, Rev. Thomas (Idstone) 4
People's Dispensary for Sick
Animals (PDSA) 255
Pointers 8, 31, 75, 113, 117–18,
124, 128, 130, 133, 141, 234
Major 119–20
Pomeranians 17, 23–24, 151, 221
Poodles 11–13
Prince Albert 5, 16, 19–20
Eos 19–20, Plate 1
Prince of Wales 24, 26, 46, 51, 69,
87, 103, 149, 213, 245
funeral when King Edward VII
26–27

President of the Kennel Club 69,
245
Princess Alexandra 26, 152–53
Pugs 21, 23, 96, 102, 170

Queen Elizabeth II 251
Queen Victoria 1–2, 5, 15, 17–27,
44, 74, 83, 89, 151, 213, 225
enters dogs in shows 24
pet dogs
Dash 17–18
Looty 21
Noble 21–23
Sharp 17, 21–22
Turi 17
Queen's Staghounds 20–21

rabies 6, 56, 129–30, 202–03
pet passports 255
ratting 28, 38, 41–42, 44, 46
Retrievers 51, 235, 240, 257
Curly-coated 245–46
Smooth-coated 246
Rin Tin Tin 253
Robinson, Phil 99–101
Royal Society for the Protection of
Cruelty to Animals (RSPCA)
5, 17, 26, 41, 204, 209,
211–15, 222–24
see also Society for the Prevention
of Cruelty to Animals
(SPCA)
Russell, Jack 2, 61, 63–73, Plate 3
'Jorrocks of real life' 66
Parson Jack Russell Terrier Club
71–72
Trump 64

Salter, John Henry 3, 109, 134–44
coursing 136–39
Essex general practitioner 136
field trials 140–41
Scott, Walter 75, 79

Index

Scottish Deerhounds 52, 121
Scottish Kennel Club 85, 88–89,
    91
  Scottish dog breeds 89
Sealyham Terrier 252
Setters 8, 51, 122, 124–5, 234
Shaw, Jemmy 1–2, 15, 28, 38–47,
    Plate 2
  An Early Canine Meeting 42, Plate 2
  Jacko 41
  Member of the Prize Ring (MPR)
    40
  on rats 43–44
  Tiny the Wonder 41
Shaw, Vero 47, 189, 248
Sheepdog trials 3, 125–28
  Alexandra Palace (1876) 126–27
  Bala 125–26, 128
Shirley, Sewallis 205, 240–50,
    Plate 8
  Collies 247–48
  Irish estate 240–43
  Chair of the Kennel Club
    245–49
  foundation of Kennel Club
    244–45
  Member of Parliament 242
  Retrievers 247–48
Skye Terriers 15 1, 75, 89,
    234–35
Society for the Prevention of
    Cruelty to Animals (SPCA)
    161, 207
  see also Royal Society for the
    Protection of Cruelty to
    Animals (RSPCA)
Spaniels 51, 122, 124, 129
Spratt's Patent 144–49
St Bernards 4, 154, 189, 205, 229,
    234–35, 235
  Barry 232–33
Stables, Gordon 155, 185–94
  adventure stories 190

books
  Aileen Aroon 190–91
  Ladies' Dogs, As Companions
    188
  Sable and White 185
  The Practical Kennel Guide
    188–89
  caravanning 191–92
  service at sea 186–87
Stennard-Robinson, Alice 2, 55, 61,
    96–108
  née Alice Cornwell 96
  changes surname from
    Cornwell to Stennard
    Robinson 102
  daughter Myrtle 101–02
  'Lady of the nuggets' 100
  Madam Midas 98–101
Stonehenge *see* Walsh, John
    Henry
Sussex Spaniels 139

Taylor, Elizabeth 252
Tealby, Mary 3, 6, 205, 207–15
  Battersea Dogs' Home 212–13
  Holloway Dogs' Home 207–12
Terriers 11, 38, 161, 168
Tibetan Mastiffs 121
Tsar Alexander 52
Turner, Sidney 141, 250

Untermyer, Samuel 94–95
  'Collie feud' 94

Walsh, John Henry 3–4, 9, 28, 33,
    90, 109, 111–22, 125, 147,
    155, 169, 246–47
  All-England Croquet and Lawn
    Tennis Club 116
  books
    The Dog in Health and Disease
      (1859, 1872, 1879, 1887)
      117

Index

The Dogs of the British Islands
    (1867, 1872, 1878, 1882,
    1886) 9, 63, 117
medical career 111–12
on guns 111, 114
pseudonym Stonehenge 3, 9, 111,
    189
setting breed standards
    119–22
Wilde, Oscar 54

Yorkshire Terrier 151
Youatt, William 3, 11, 117, 155,
    157–69
books
    The Dog (1845) 162, 166–69
    The Obligations of Humanity to
    Brutes (1839) 163–64
London Zoo 162–63
Society for the Protection of
    Animals (SPCA) 161